Kyiv as Regime City

Rochester Studies in East and Central Europe

Series Editor: Timothy Snyder, Yale University

Additional Titles of Interest

The Polish Singers Alliance of America 1888–1998: Choral Patriotism
Stanislaus A. Blejwas

A Clean Sweep?
The Politics of Ethnic Cleansing in Western Poland, 1945–1960
T. David Curp

Nazi Policy on the Eastern Front, 1941: Total War, Genocide, and Radicalization
Edited by Alex J. Kay, Jeff Rutherford, and David Stahel

Critical Thinking in Slovakia after Socialism
Jonathan Larson

Smolensk under the Nazis: Everyday Life in Occupied Russia
Laurie R. Cohen

Polish Cinema in a Transnational Context
Edited by Ewa Mazierska and Michael Goddard

Literary Translation and the Idea of a Minor Romania
Sean Cotter

Coming of Age under Martial Law:
The Initiation Novels of Poland's Last Communist Generation
Svetlana Vassileva-Karagyozova

Revolution and Counterrevolution in Poland, 1980–1989:
Solidarity, Martial Law, and the End of Communism in Europe
Andrzej Paczkowski
Translated by Christina Manetti

The Utopia of Terror: Life and Death in Wartime Croatia
Rory Yeomans

A complete list of titles in the Rochester Studies in East and Central Europe series may be found on our website, www.urpress.com.

Kyiv as Regime City

The Return of Soviet Power after Nazi Occupation

Martin J. Blackwell

UNIVERSITY OF ROCHESTER PRESS

Copyright © 2016 by Martin J. Blackwell

All rights reserved. Except as permitted under current legislation, no part of this work may be photocopied, stored in a retrieval system, published, performed in public, adapted, broadcast, transmitted, recorded, or reproduced in any form or by any means, without the prior permission of the copyright owner.

First published 2016
Reprinted in paperback 2022

University of Rochester Press
668 Mt. Hope Avenue, Rochester, NY 14620, USA
www.urpress.com
and Boydell & Brewer Limited
PO Box 9, Woodbridge, Suffolk IP12 3DF, UK
www.boydellandbrewer.com

ISBN-13: 978-1-58046-558-8 (hardcover)
ISBN-13: 978-1-64825-053-8 (paperback)
ISSN: 1528-4808

Library of Congress Cataloging-in-Publication Data

Names: Blackwell, Martin J., author.
Title: Kyiv as regime city : the return of Soviet power after Nazi occupation / Martin J. Blackwell.
Description: Rochester, NY : University of Rochester Press, 2016. | Series: Rochester studies in East and Central Europe, ISSN 1528-4808 ; v. 16 | Includes bibliographical references and index.
Identifiers: LCCN 2016012476 | ISBN 9781580465588 (hardcover) Subjects: LCSH: Kiev (Ukraine)—Politics and government—20th century. | Kiev (Ukraine)—Social conditions—20th century. | World War, 1939–1945—Social aspects—Ukraine—Kiev. | Land settlement—Ukraine—Kiev—History—20th century. | Communists—Ukraine—Kiev—History—20th century. | Elite (Social sciences)—Ukraine—Kiev—History—20th century. | Power (Social sciences)—Ukraine—Kiev—History—20th century. | Kiev (Ukraine)—Relations—Soviet Union. | Soviet Union—Relations—Ukraine—Kiev. | Ukraine—Politics and government—1945–1991.
Classification: LCC DK508.935 .B57 2016 | DDC 947.7/70842—dc23 LC record available at https://lccn.loc.gov/2016012476

A catalogue record for this title is available from the British Library.

For my parents
John and Susan Blackwell

Contents

List of Illustrations — ix

Acknowledgments — xi

Glossary and Abbreviations — xiii

Note on Transliterations — xv

Introduction — 1

Part One: Resettlement

1. "The Capital Is Being Settled All Over Again": Resettlement from Fall 1943 to Fall 1944 — 19
2. "There Was No Real Battle against Illegal Entry": Resettlement from Fall 1944 to Fall 1946 — 46

Part Two: Reassembly

3. "People Are Going for the Party Who Are Forcing Us to Be Justifiably Careful": The Reassembled Elite — 73
4. "A Textual Implementation of the Law . . . Was Not Carried Out": The Reassembled Masses — 102

Part Three: Relegitimization

5. "The State's Dignity Is Higher Than His Own Dignity": The Relegitimization of Soviet Power — 131
6. "Tashkent Partisans" and "German Bitches": Relationships with Soviet Power — 158

Conclusion — 187

Notes — 193

Bibliography — 213

Index — 223

Illustrations

1.1	The First Ukrainian Front on the Khreshchatyk, November 7, 1943.	21
1.2	"Kyivans Return to Their Hometown," November 7, 1943.	23
1.3	Kyivans sort the ruins of the Khreshchatyk, unknown date.	41
2.1	German POWs are paraded down Sofiivs'ka Street, August 16, 1944.	57
2.2	A burnt-out apartment building on today's Tolstoy Square, 1944.	58
3.1	Korniets, Korotchenko, Khrushchev, Baranovskii, and partisan leader Sydir Kovpak on the Victory Day parade viewing stand, May 9, 1945.	86
3.2	The people of Kyiv pass the parade viewing stand on Victory Day, May, 9, 1945.	86
3.3	Party Leader M. M. Pydtychenko, B. A. Gorban, General V. I. Davydov, General I. I. Iakubovs'kyi, N. S. Khrushchev, F. V. Mokienko, and General A. A. Hrechko at the celebrations of the twenty-eighth anniversary of the October Revolution, November 7, 1945.	96
4.1	"Kyivans Return to Their Hometown," November, 1943.	107
4.2	German POWs cleaning up and "rebuilding" the Khreshchatyk, October 1, 1944.	118
4.3	Soldiers' children listen to the news about the victory with the Allies over Fascist Germany, May, 9, 1945.	124
5.1	Kyivans on the reconstruction of the Khreshchatyk, unknown date.	135
5.2	Bohdan Khmel'nyts'kyi Square in Kyiv on Victory Day, May 9, 1945.	143

5.3	Schoolchildren from Kyiv's Stalin Raion prepare to march in the Victory Day parade, May 9, 1945.	143
5.4	The people of Kyiv parade on Victory Day, May 9, 1945.	144
6.1	N. S. Khrushchev, F. V. Mokienko, General A. A. Hrechko, and P. H. Tychyna (far right) at the celebrations of the twenty-eighth anniversary of the October Revolution, November 7, 1945.	164
6.2	The Ukrainian Soviet Socialist Republic's People's Commissar of Defense, Gerasimenko, reads an *ukaz* from Comrade Stalin to the troops of the Kyiv garrison during the parade of May, 1, 1945. Behind him stand Khrushchev, Korotchenko, and party leader, M. S. Hrechukha.	171

Acknowledgments

I want to thank the following individuals and institutions who helped bring this project to a successful close. First, I wish to thank Hiroaki Kuromiya of Indiana University–Bloomington's Department of History. Without his enthusiasm and patience, this project would have been impossible. Other "Hoosiers"—whether life-long or temporary—whose advice and assistance I have appreciated along the way include James Diehl, Toivo Raun, and Jeffrey Veidlinger, as well as William Fierman, Jerzy Kolodziej, and David Ransel. I also thank the Russian and East European Institute for the Mellon Endowment Travel Grants that first allowed me to present this research at various annual conventions of the Association of Slavic, East European, and Eurasian Studies. Indiana University's Borns Program in Jewish Studies also provided a vital stipend to travel to Moscow for a view of the Kremlin's take on events in Kyiv. The input and guidance of my other colleagues and friends in Bloomington—particularly Heather Perry, Jody Prestia, Margaret Puskar-Pasewicz, and Matt Stanard—also helped me improve this project.

In the region, the support of the Fulbright Ukraine program was essential. Martha Bohavchevsky-Chomiak's enthusiasm and an extension of my Fulbright award made my initial sojourns to the archives a great success. The support and friendship of my Ukrainian "advisor" Stanislav Kul'chyts'kyi and his colleagues Tetiana Bykova and Tetiana Pastushenko at the Ukrainian Academy of Sciences' Institute of Ukrainian History also made my ventures to Kyiv a pleasure. At Ukraine's Main Archival Administration, Konstantyn Novokhats'kyi provided an open ear—both in his offices and at his home in Obolon'—and assistance in gaining access to the archives of Ukraine's Ministry of the Interior. Iryna Komarova and other reading room attendants at Ukraine's Central State Archive of Civic Organizations were helpful and collegial along the way. Friendships with other *inogorodnye* among Kyiv's Meltdown Ultimate Frisbee team made many a late summer evening along the Dnipro among the beaches and shashlyk stands of Hydropark memorable. From the very beginning, the hospitality of the late Anton Strutyns'kyi and his wife Raisa also made Kyiv's left bank seem like home. In Moscow I thank my friend of over two decades, Dmitrii Korotkov, and his wife Anna for their hospitality. In St. Petersburg, support for this idea among the

History Faculty at St. Petersburg State University and cooperation with Liudmila Riabova led to the presentation of my findings to a Russian audience and, later, thanks to Aleksandr Chistakov, to an opportunity to speak at the Russian Academy of Sciences' St. Petersburg Institute of History.

My colleagues on this side of the Atlantic also deserve praise and gratitude. At University of North Georgia, Lee Cheek, Pamela Elfenbein, Chris Jespersen, Ric Kabat, Timothy May, Martha Nesbitt, Jeff Pardue, and Eugene Van Sickle helped with financial support, encouragement, and vital course releases at the end. The library staff at Sewanee: The University of the South, especially Joan Blocher, Cari Reynolds, Heidi Syler, and Courtnay Zeitler, assisted me with obtaining materials and resolving various technical difficulties. Colleagues in the field, including Karel Berkhoff, Richard Bidlack, Ron Bobroff, Chris Burton, David Brandenberger, Kate Brown, Michael David-Fox, Mark Edele, Don Filtzer, Wendy Goldman, Michael Hamm, James Heinzen, Jeffrey Jones, Victoria Khiterer, George Liber, David Marples, Michael Melancon, Matthew Payne, Karl Qualls, William Risch, Myroslav Shkandrij, Joonseo Song, and Serhy Yekelchyk, read versions of my research or provided helpful comments and encouragement. Working with University of Rochester Press, its editorial director, Sonia Kane, and my peer reviewers has also been a great experience that has left *Kyiv as Regime City* much improved. Any mistakes of interpretation, translation, and transliteration in the text are my own.

Finally, without the moral and intellectual support of my wife, Elizabeth Skomp, this project would not have made it to final form. Now we can enjoy the vibrant and vivacious Vivien Alice Blackwell all the more! And to those Russians, Ukrainians, Belorussians, Kazakhs, and others who have opened their homes to me over the past quarter century across the former Soviet Union—a number far too numerous to mention here—I offer deep, deep thanks for the idea of studying what they hold to be the most important events of the twentieth century: the Second World War and its legacy. But it is my parents, of course, who provided me the initial wherewithal to undertake this project. It was their love of travel and discovery that led me to incredible places like Kyiv in the first place, and it is to them that I dedicate this book.

Sewanee, Tennessee
March 31, 2016

Glossary and Abbreviations

This list includes names, acronyms, abbreviations, and translations of foreign words that appear frequently in the text.

All-Union NKGB or Ukrainian NKGB: Narodnyi Komissariat Gosudarstvennoi Bezopasnosti (People's Commissariat of State Security / Union of Soviet Socialist Republics or Ukrainian Soviet Socialist Republic). These People's Commissariats were renamed Ministries (*Ministerstvo*) or All-Union MGB / Ukrainian MGB in March 1946.

All-Union NKVD or Ukrainian NKVD: Narodnyi Komissariat Vnutrennykh Del (People's Commissariat of Internal Affairs / Union of Soviet Socialist Republics or Ukrainian Soviet Socialist Republic). These People's Commissariats were renamed Ministries (*Ministerstvo*) or All-Union MVD / Ukrainian MVD in March 1946.

All-Union TsK: Tsentral'nyi Komitet / Vsesoiuznaia Komunisticheskaia Partiia (Bol'shevikov) (Central Committee / All-Union Communist Party [Bolsheviks])

Gorkom: Gorodskoi Komitet Komunisticheskoi Partii Bol'shevikov Ukrainy (City Committee of the Communist Party [Bolsheviks] of Ukraine)

GKO: Gosudarstvennyi Komitet Oborony (State Committee of Defense)

NKZhGS UkrSSR: Narodnyi Komissariat Zhilishchnogo Grazhdanskogo Stroitel'stova / Ukrainskaia Sovetskaia Sotsialisticheskaia Respublika (People's Commissariat of Housing and Civilian Construction / Ukrainian Soviet Socialist Republic). This People's Commissariat was renamed Ministry (*Ministerstvo*) or MKZhGS UkrSSR in March 1946.

Obkom: Oblastnoi Komitet Komunisticheskoi Partii Bol'shevikov Ukrainy (Oblast Committee of the Communist Party [Bolsheviks] of Ukraine)

Oblast: administrative region within a Soviet republic

Okruzhentsy: Communist Party members who lived on Soviet territory occupied by Germany

Orgnabor: "Organized recruitment" of Soviet citizens for work in the Soviet economy

OSMCh: Osobaia Stroitel'naia Montazhnaia Chast' (a special construction assembly unit composed of Soviet citizens eligible for the draft but not physically fit enough to serve)

Ostarbeitery: "East Workers" (Soviet citizens taken by the Germans to work in Germany and other occupied places)

Partiinost: Party affiliation

Raikom: Raionnyi Komitet Komunisticheskoi Partii Bol'shevikov Ukrainy (District Committee of the Communist Party [Bolsheviks] of Ukraine)

Raion: administrative district within a Soviet oblast or city

RSFSR: Rossiiskaia Sovetskaia Federativnaia Sotsialisticheskaia Respublika (Russian Soviet Federated Socialist Republic)

SNK SSSR and UkrSSR: Sovet Narodnykh Komissarov / Soiuz Sovetskikh Sotsialisticheskikh Respublikov and Ukrainskaia Sovetskaia Sotsialisticheskaia Respublika (Council of People's Commissars / Union of Soviet Socialist Republics / Ukrainian Soviet Socialist Republic. Both of these Councils of People's Commissars were renamed Council of Ministers *(Sovet Ministrov)* or SM SSSR / UkrSSR in March 1946.

Ukrainian TsK: Tsentral'nyi Komitet / Komunisticheskaia Partiia Bol'shevikov Ukrainy (Central Committee / Communist Party of Ukraine [Bolsheviks])

Note on Transliterations

All transliterations of places, institutions, and people in this book use the Library of Congress system with the following rules. Names of places that were located in the Ukrainian Soviet Socialist Republic usually have Ukrainian transliteration, while places that were located in other parts of the Soviet Union are usually given in Russian transliteration. One exception is for those places (cities, towns, districts, villages, streets, etc.) found in direct quotations in the text. These are transliterated from Ukrainian if the document in question was written in Ukrainian or from Russian if the document was written in Russian. A second exception is for those places with names familiar to the western reader such as Lenin Street or Molotov Raion (District). Institutional and personal names mentioned repeatedly are transliterated from Russian because the archival documents employed were most commonly in Russian. Institutional and personal names mentioned only occasionally are transliterated from the language in which their names were found in the archives.

Introduction

On October 28, 1944, a Red Army officer named Kostenko wrote to the leaders of Soviet Ukraine's Communist government, and stated:

> A year has passed since the liberation of the city of Kyiv. About the same amount of time has passed since I started to solicit the return of my family from evacuation in Omsk [Russia] to our hometown of Kyiv. I wrote—and so did the command of my military unit on my behalf—to all organizations for them to help my family return to Kyiv. But what has been done? Nothing! At a time when I have spared neither blood nor my life itself fighting for Kyiv, and for the liberation of Ukrainian land, there are bureaucrats who have saved a few drops of ink rather than write an answer to my requests. . . . And now . . . I am not happy. I am malicious. My hand grips my gun with a burning hatred. I ask myself, what has been done for my family? Where is the payback for my suffering? Just let them know, then, those bureaucrats hiding within the walls of the Kyiv City Soviet, that I damn them. And when I return from the field of battle, I will find them, and I won't mind using a few of my spare bullets on them. I ask that you give them this.[1]

Unfortunately, Kostenko's request had landed on deaf ears. After the Nazi occupation's end on November 6, 1943, the Ukrainian Communists watched helplessly as ordinary people ignored formalities, and returned by any means possible to resettle a depopulated Kyiv, still a "regime city of the first category" according to Joseph Stalin's guardians of state security—the All-Union People's Commissariat of Internal Affairs (NKVD) headquartered in Moscow. As a result of the Ukrainian Communists' management of this reassembling population, Stalin's regime stealthily adjusted its rule to satisfy the anti-Semitic interests of Kyiv's Ukrainian majority—to the detriment of its Jewish minority. And in a situation where scarcity on all fronts ruled, the Ukrainian Communists' best means of relegitimizing Soviet power were by capitalizing on Moscow's public call for ideological vigilance in 1946, and arguing for their own indispensability as the leaders of a damaged—but still popular—state. This book's goal is to examine these clues to better show why the propaganda of the Stalin regime at the beginning of the Cold War emphasized anti-Semitic and statist discourse.

The argument here demonstrates this interpretation of the history of the Soviet Union in the 1940s by studying the archival records of Ukraine and Russia. In particular, this book examines the records of the Ukrainian Communist Party at its local (city and oblast committee) and republic (central committee) levels, the Ukrainian government at its local (city and oblast soviet) and republic (Council of People's Commissars) levels, and their correspondence with each other as well as with the Stalin regime located in Moscow. First, it focuses on the resettlement of a million-strong Soviet city after its emptying by Nazi occupiers during the Second World War. It explores why Kyiv's Communist leaders, as the city's population swelled to 700,000 people by the end of 1946, were unable to purge it of "socially dangerous" people, or prevent the unorganized return of others from evacuation. It also investigates why the Stalin regime's efforts to mobilize labor toward housing reconstruction in Kyiv were unsuccessful even as it guarded the population actually resettling there from such hardships. Second, the work examines the city's reassembled population and explains why the timing of an individual's return was important amid the wartime scarcity of housing. It considers why the local party committees guarded access to their ranks, and why trying to satisfy the interests of the formerly occupied, returnees, conscripted laborers, and demobilized soldiers continually put these leaders in difficult positions. Third, this project studies the Ukrainian authorities' attempt to relegitimize Soviet power as they acquiesced to powerful groups' maneuverings through the postwar order. It explores why the government's argument that they could lead within a partially destroyed but still triumphant state system became its most useful rallying cry, and why those in power allowed anti-Semitic "manifestations," servicemen's crimes, and their own rank and file's dissipate behavior to acquire new legitimacy. In short, this book explains the state-society relationship in Kyiv, Ukraine, after the Nazi occupation to provide context for understanding how the Stalin regime promoted its hegemony, in general, by the end of the 1940s.

Kyiv before the Soviet Liberation of November 6, 1943

Scholarly studies of Kyiv's pre–World War II history provide an introduction to the events discussed here. One portrait of the Tsarist-era city points to its undemocratic politics, which suppressed Ukrainians' social aspirations.[2] Another notes its "imperial atmosphere," which left Kyiv's sizable Jewish minority utterly despondent before the Bolshevik Revolution.[3] The political champions of late Tsarist Kyiv were its Little Russian nationalists who successfully wooed St. Petersburg, as well as the city's masses, by claiming Jewish capitalists and Ukrainian separatists were harming everyone else's interests.[4] Following the Red triumph in the Russian Civil War, the Bolsheviks' promotion of Ukrainian culture during the 1920s, along with their modernization of the Ukrainian Soviet Socialist Republic's economy, spurred both Ukrainian and Jewish hopes for the future. But while relatively urbane Jews benefited from increased career opportunities, Bolshevik leader Mykola Skrypnyk's 1920s "Ukrainization" campaign was less successful, due to the lack of human capital necessary to teach the Ukrainian language.[5] Stalin's suppression of "bourgeois nationalism" followed during the industrialization campaign of 1928–32, and his turn toward Russian culture to guide the building of a socialist society signaled to Kyiv's Ukrainians and Jews that falling in line with Moscow's needs was paramount.

In the decade prior to World War II, Kyiv visibly took part in Stalin's revolution. Newly built and remodeled factories produced equipment for the Soviet Union's shipping, textile, and agricultural machine industries. This expansion of production—the prerevolutionary city had been a center of light industry and food processing—and of the laboring population also increased Kyiv's importance as a transport center. New railway bridges were built across the Dnipro River, and huge depots, freight yards, and repair shops occupied prominent places on the river's banks. After the Stalin regime made Kyiv the Ukrainian capital (replacing Kharkiv) in 1934, the city experienced the arrival of a large number of bureaucrats and scholars, and a set of extensive infrastructure improvements.

Although an ensuing housing shortage remained unsolved, huge new buildings were constructed for the Central Committee of the Ukrainian Communist Party (Ukrainian TsK) as well as the Ukrainian republic's Council of People's Commissars (SNK UkrSSR), and the city's opera house was refurbished. All these projects highlighted Kyiv's new status as an administrative and cultural center. By 1941, the city's population had reached one million, and it became the third-largest city in the Soviet Union. But amid this "proletarianization" of Kyiv there was little mention of Ukrainization, as a gradual Russification had enveloped the city.[6] Nevertheless, such Bolshevization had produced an increasingly urbane group of Ukrainians—now over half the city's population—willing to co-opt Moscow's plans toward success.

Nazi Germany's invasion of the Soviet Union, on June 22, 1941, unleashed a whirlwind of activity in Kyiv. Within a few weeks, 200,000 of its people were drafted into, or volunteered for, the ranks of the Red Army.[7] Some factories were hurriedly converted to war production, and Moscow ordered local party leaders to mobilize Kyivans to build fortification rings on the city's western outskirts. Activity became even more hectic once the Wehrmacht approached Kyiv's outer defense ring in early July, and the Moscow-based State Committee of Defense

(GKO) decided to begin the evacuation of right-bank Ukraine. Within the next two months, some 350,000 Kyivans left their homes for places such as Cheliabinsk and Ufa in the Russian Soviet Federated Socialist Republic (RSFSR), as well as Tashkent, the capital of the Uzbek Soviet Socialist Republic. This group included the city's skilled workers and administrators, its scientific and artistic intelligentsia, and about half of its 37,000-strong party membership and their families. Many of these people were Russians, but Jews were a significant minority as well, for both groups were better educated than the Ukrainians at this point. With them went the full or partial equipment of two hundred of Kyiv's industrial enterprises and as much of the city's artistic and scientific heritage as could be loaded onto the few trains set aside for such purposes.

All of this was done just in time. In mid-September, the Germans encircled those helping the Red Army to defend the city, including a thirty-thousand-strong people's militia, the workers bonded to factories producing war materials, and school teachers instructing the workers' children. These dramatic events occurred after the Wehrmacht diverted its Second Panzer Group south from its advance on Moscow and directed it to join the First Panzer Group now advancing northward along the Dnipro's left bank, after the latter had skirted the city's southern border and crossed the river at Kremenchuk. Although the last fleeing Red Army and NKVD personnel managed to blow up Kyiv's bridges, railroad junctions, and power plants, many soon joined the 665,000 soldiers who became Soviet prisoners of war when Kyiv fell to the Nazis on September 19, 1941.

German rule in Kyiv would last 778 days, a time when the city's population suffered under a regime of constant, barbaric terror. The liquidation of the city's nonevacuated Jews and Communists began immediately after the remaining NKVD personnel blew up the buildings along the Khreshchatyk (Kyiv's main street), killing many of the newly arrived Germans in the process. On September 29, 1941, 33,000 Jews were executed at the Babyn Iar ravine on the city's western outskirts in response to NKVD actions. More than 100,000 Kyivans (50,000 of whom were Jewish) were killed at Babyn Iar during the occupation, many of them by the end of 1941.[8] For those who avoided this fate, the next twenty-two months would be dominated by the possibility of sudden deportation to work in Germany. Another 50,000 Kyivans—anyone over fourteen years of age could have been chosen—became the so-called East Workers (*Ostarbeitery*).[9] Although some managed to escape due to youth or frailty, or by finding fifteen-hour-a-day jobs in the factories eventually reopened by the Germans, life in Kyiv meant tolerating a worthless salary and routine bouts of Nazi looting. Starvation was the intended fate of the city's residents from that point onward.[10] This situation continued up to the Soviet approach toward Kyiv in autumn 1943 and the remaining population's flight from the city to avoid German evacuation orders.

Soviet Power's Prewar Legacy and Chapter Overview

The two chapters in this book's first section cover Kyiv's resettlement after the Nazis. Some background on population control in the prewar Soviet Union will help to introduce this subject. It is a truism that Stalin consolidated power in the 1930s through terror. Recently uncovered evidence shows that his belief in the inevitable invasion of the USSR by the capitalist states partly sparked this murderous "cleansing" process.[11] In an attempt to eliminate threats from within, the NKVD arrested various groups of Soviet people they considered "unreliable elements." These groups included Stalin's former political enemies in the central party leadership who doubted his policy choices and, more importantly, the "bourgeois nationalists" of all ranks in the USSR's outlying republics. Stalin feared that the leadership abilities some of these people had gained during the successful collectivization and industrialization campaigns of the early 1930s might lead to separatism. The NKVD arrested and sent to the Gulag some two million people in this process, while almost 700,000 others were executed.[12] In Kyiv, a mass grave for tens of thousands of Stalin's victims was secretly created at Bykivnia on the city's outskirts.[13]

Included within these larger numbers were other groups Stalin believed to be "socially dangerous" within the supposedly classless and abundant society of "socialism."[14] This highly centralized political dictatorship viewed social disorder as its chief threat before the Second World War.[15] The Stalin regime thus devised the "passportization" campaign of 1933 to rid the Soviet Union's choked urban areas of peasants avoiding the collectivization of agriculture, by requiring an internal passport for employment in the city's economy and receipt of a ration card. In 1937, it ordered the NKVD to implement large-scale "mass operations" (*massoperatsii*) to liquidate the former *kulaks* and recidivist criminals living in the Soviet Union's major cities. In Kyiv's case, however, the city's population growth may have reflected a sense that the country's bright economic future could counter tensions created by such social dislocation. On the eve of the war, in 1940, Stalin's internal police labeled Kyiv a "regime city of the first category" where all the aforementioned transgressors of the social order were forbidden to return; in fact, they were banished to 50 kilometers beyond the city's limits.

Why the Kremlin's wartime focus on defeating Germany led to a resettled Kyiv that the newly arrived Ukrainian Communists found difficult to manage is the focus of chapter 1. As the Stalin regime's need for Red Army reinforcements took precedence over the cleansing of the "socially dangerous," and the city filled up with unorganized returnees, the local Communists realized that Germany's attack now meant a Kyiv unlike that of the prewar era. The chapter then examines why the Stalin regime chose to keep the city open for resettlement long after these authorities voiced their apprehensions about how social dislocation in the rear might create social disorder in a damaged Ukrainian capital. It also looks at what the Kremlin's plans to mobilize rural Ukrainians to assist in Kyiv's housing reconstruction (even as the city filled up with hundreds of thousands of other people) say about its position in the Soviet wartime economy.

Chapter 2 maintains a focus on social dislocation as it chronicles the local authorities' realization of their city's second-rate status as a hyper-centralized wartime economy allocated scarce labor resources. Even the forced arrival of schoolchildren and German POWs to help with the city's reconstruction would not help the city's housing shortage at this point in time. Though the local authorities' protests to their republic-level bosses against continued unorganized return were to no avail, the announcement of the Fourth Five-Year Plan in March 1946 signaled that they could now close off their city to the world. Although this came too late to prevent the arrival of hundreds of thousands of people from the east, these same leaders would, curiously, later issue a citywide "amnesty" as they prepared for the hoped-for arrival of resources. In analyzing these processes, these two chapters on the Ukrainian Communists' management of Kyiv's resettlement provide initial clues to help explain the Stalin regime's efforts to maintain its legitimacy later in the 1940s.

The two chapters in this book's middle section concentrate on how Kyiv's reassembled elites and ordinary people survived amid the scarcity of the postoccupation period. An introduction to how Stalin's Great Breakthrough of the 1930s industrialized the Soviet Union provides essential background. Bolshevik propaganda about "class war" against *kulaks* in the village and "bourgeois specialists" in the factories had powered the First Five-Year Plan to completion.[16] Stalin's industrial revolution also succeeded because it undermined the political coherence of the labor movement in the Soviet Union.[17] But in order to meet their plan quotas and retain their privileged positions, factory managers had to insulate their workers from draconian labor laws. As a result, these managers accepted workers' partial control over plan fulfillment.

Meanwhile, the Bolsheviks created a slave labor force that one day would help them to maintain and defend "socialism." The origins of this labor force dated from 1925, when the Soviet leadership discussed the exploitation of the mineral wealth of Siberia and the Far East through the use of forced labor.[18] But not until the removal of the supposed *kulaks* from the villages of European Russia in 1930–31 did the "special settlers" necessary for realizing such economic dreams start to become available. Some were sentenced to terms in corrective labor camps, which were placed in the hands of the NKVD. But most importantly, the several million victims of the Great Terror sentenced to the Gulag made the Soviet east an economic force by 1940.

In Kyiv, an elite synonymous with the Ukrainian Communist Party led this totalitarian economy. This group had been formed amid Stalin's difficulties implementing collectivization in Ukraine, a process that led to the arrest, trial, and conviction of treasonous "bourgeois nationalists."[19] Over the next five years, Ukrainian party membership dropped 45 percent, from 515,050 members and candidates in 1933 to 285,025 in 1938, at least 100,000 of whom were later shot or exiled.[20] While Stalin purged Ukraine, his ideological henchman Andrei Zhdanov implemented a "party revival" campaign throughout the USSR.[21] Zhdanov believed that good Communists should concentrate on ideological purity—within their ranks and among the masses they governed—instead of micromanaging the fulfillment of the five-year plans.

Instead of recruiting workers, Zhdanov sought to attract the "best people" (a euphemism for highly educated specialists in a given sphere of employment) to membership in order to ensure Stalin's policies would be correctly understood.[22] To help ensure this, the Soviet government allocated party members better housing, consumer goods, and food products through a system of centralized distribution after the official end of rationing in 1935.[23] And while Stalin's Great Terror helped to make people "believers" in the new command economy across the USSR in 1937–38, the Ukrainian Communists required little convincing in light of their experiences earlier that decade. Center-local relations were now based on "new bonds of allegiance and loyalty of a new generation of administrators, supplemented by the fear instilled by police surveillance and terror."[24] The Ukrainian party's ranks rose to prepurge levels (some 564,536 members and candidates) again by June 1941.[25]

The history of ordinary people living in 1930s Kyiv is more difficult to ascertain. Statistics reveal that, while the number of workers doubled during this period, their number relative to the city's population as a whole was still not that significant. The amount of people working in Kyiv's factories climbed from roughly 5 percent of the city's population in the mid-1920s (20,000 people) to 10 percent in the late 1930s (90,000).[26] The majority of working people in Kyiv were involved in light industry, transportation, education, culture, or, from 1934, the bureaucracies of the newly arrived Ukrainian government. But there is no doubt that Stalin's efforts to build "socialism in one country" also brought economic progress to Kyiv. The First Five-Year Plan in Kyiv was marked by a determination of the production profiles and an expansion of the capacities of the city's existing factories in order to meet the needs of Stalin's efforts to overcome "backwardness." Lenin's Forge (*Leninskaia Kuznitsa*) began building ships, Red Excavator (*Krasnyi Ekskavator*) started manufacturing parts for tractors, and the city's main railway junction saw the opening of the Kyiv Steam Engine Repair Factory.[27]

It was the Stalin regime's collectivization of agriculture, meanwhile, that paid for this transformation and was intended to supply cities like Kyiv with abundant food. By 1931, an "institutionalization of supply norms along geographical and social lines" had created a "hierarchy of state distribution" in the USSR where industrial workers' needs were given top priority.²⁸ But in Kyiv, with its small number of industrial workers and terrible transport, sewer, and housing conditions (608,000 people lived on 3.8 million square meters of space in 1932), its longtime denizens may not have felt like "victors" during the Great Breakthrough.²⁹ Many of these people probably welcomed the Stalin regime's 1933 passportization law mentioned above.

The Second Five-Year Plan, however, brought a greater emphasis on investment in light industry, and many Kyivans benefited from this change. From 1933 to 1938, the city witnessed the building of entirely new enterprises such as the Gorky Machine Tool Factory and the Artificial Fibers Factory in left-bank Darnytsa (on the eastern side of the Dnipro River), as well as the introduction of entirely new technologies like the Bol'shevik Factory's retooling to produce machines for the paper industry.³⁰ But when rationing ended in 1935, many ordinary citizens were forced to work harder to earn the money they needed to purchase goods from peasant markets or on the black market.³¹ Although some 445,000 square meters of additional housing were built (mainly to accommodate the arriving party elite), the city's population also increased by 300,000 during these years.³² While many of these new arrivals were fleeing famine and persecution in the countryside, the economic change that characterized Kyiv before the Second World War still suggests that a modicum of hope and optimism existed there at the time.

The Stalin regime tasked the Ukrainian Communist elite with coordinating and expediting Kyiv's reintegration in the Soviet state after the Nazi occupation, and chapter 3 analyzes the political atmosphere amid the great scarcity experienced by the city's reassembling population by studying these party members. While it proved impossible to prepare Kyiv to succeed economically within the Kremlin's planned economy, these Ukrainian men and women would capitalize on the Stalin regime's 1944 decision to curtail the Communist Party's wartime growth. Their decisions about who joined the elite and thus gained access to scarce housing, food, and consumer goods would become examples of sound and sober leadership to Kyiv's ordinary people. Despite this manifest distrust toward the masses—at least concerning the granting of access to the levers of power—surprisingly little trouble ensued for Kyiv's leaders. For those Communists who had lived on occupied territory (the *okruzhentsy*), the men drafted from the formerly occupied territories who served in the Red Army, and others who claimed to have involved themselves in the city's underground resistance, the path into (or back into) Kyiv's circles of power would thus be filled with difficult obstacles.

Chapter 4 then examines the opposite side of the equation by looking at the city's masses. Specifically, it examines four groups: the formerly occupied, unorganized returnees, conscripted laborers, and demobilized servicemen. While an obvious difference between the formerly occupied and unorganized returnees is their date of return to the once empty city, to some extent they are treated together because many were also privileged servicemen's dependents. That connection, however, masks ethnic differences within these groups, which were particularly explosive given the scarcity that the war worsened. By the end of this period, Kyiv's population was again, as it had been before the war, about 60 percent Ukrainian, 20 percent Jewish, and 20 percent Russian.[33] But the fact that the formerly occupied were largely Ukrainians, while many of the unorganized returnees were Jewish, and that much of the empty city's housing was loosely administered by the returning Soviets, is a key point in this story. As the Stalin regime guarded all of these returning Kyivans from mobilization, German prisoners of war became a vital group for the city's reconstruction when the city failed to receive allocations of rural, mobilized labor. Meanwhile, the demands of demobilized soldiers for better housing and jobs would escalate a sense that stalled reconstruction and continued unorganized return might create an untenable situation for the local authorities. These two chapters provide further context for the conclusion that the Kremlin's role in postoccupation Kyiv led to the local decisions that influenced why the Stalin regime employed overtly statist and anti-Semitic discourse by decade's end.

The two chapters in this book's final section explain how the relegitimization of Soviet power occured in postoccupation Kyiv, and how relationships between the rulers and ruled there influenced this process. To this end, some historical background about the workings of earlier Stalinist propaganda is necessary. Sheila Fitzpatrick first argued that ordinary workers' desire to replace "bourgeois specialists" as leaders supported the Great Breakthrough's political and economic intentions.[34] In turn, Stephen Kotkin argued that the Soviet people's acceptance of this path was reinforced by newly nationalistic Soviet propaganda about the need to defend a Russian-led socialist state from defunct Western capitalism.[35] More recently, Jeffrey Brooks added that Stalin's efforts to establish the "otherness" of Soviet society's self-governance—a society no longer governed by the ruthless market, as in capitalism, but by the needs of the state—was the reason those not among the upwardly mobile could be dragged into "socialism."[36] Utterly dependent on those guiding the revolution, such people saw any hopeful or positive developments in their lives as the results of their leaders' smiling down upon them.

But did the Bolsheviks in the Kremlin need to gauge the reactions of the people they ruled over during this revolution? The short answer appears to be no. According to Brooks, the Stalin regime's "alternative reality" meant it could ignore the effects of its revolution on the individuals it governed. But newly empowered workers and factory managers approved of this populist ideology and even practiced "speaking Bolshevik" in order to verbalize their hopes and desires in a safe manner. Still, as one British historian has countered, plenty of information was collected, at least by urban party apparatuses during the 1930s.[37] The Great Terror probably only increased the surviving local Communists' understanding that maintaining a close eye on their city's inhabitants might help them avoid to Stalin's wrath in the future. And while two thirds of the Communists in the Soviet Union in 1945 had joined the party's ranks during the war years, most of the local leaders from the prewar era remained in power at that time.[38]

The attitudes and actions of Kyiv's reassembled population certainly kept these leaders on guard after the German occupation. Anti-Semitism, street crime, and "social dissipation" (some within the party's own ranks) are the subjects on which this section of the book concentrates. During the 1920s, the implementation of a Leninist nationalities policy designed to end "Great Russian chauvinism" helped to curtail anti-Semitism in Soviet society.[39] At the same time, Yiddish culture survived Stalin's effort to destroy "bourgeois nationalism" in the 1930s, in part because the Jews had no Soviet republic of their own.[40] Against the relative improvement of the Jews' position in Kyiv, the NKVD's literal creation of nationalities in the Ukrainian borderlands during the 1920s helped to uncover "bourgeois nationalist" enemies when local authorities needed to find someone guilty of "sabotaging" the Great Breakthrough.[41] Arbitrary terror based on preconceived stereotypes left behind in such places a Ukrainian population that understood barbarism as the definition of the Soviet socialist state.

When Karel Berkhoff examined Ukrainian and Jewish fates through the Nazi occupation, he found the Great Terror and the Second World War left a surviving Ukrainian population (within the pre-1939 borders at least) inclined toward neither nationalism nor Communism.[42] The Nazis' liquidation of the remaining Jews in places like Kyiv in September 1941, Berkhoff argues, was a sudden and terrible shock to a Ukrainian population already traumatized by Stalin's barbarity. He concludes that what Ukrainians in 1943 most desired was the return of the modernizing vision of the Soviet Union without the methods of rule of the Bolsheviks. In other words, they longed for rulers familiar with local circumstances, but who recognized that past "excesses" needed to be curtailed.

The situation surrounding street crime and "social dissipation" before 1941 was framed by Stalin's statement in 1933 that "criminality and a lack of social discipline in the USSR [were] the main threats to socialism."[43] This statement justified the implementation of the passport legislation that year and the NKVD's subsequent enforcement of policies that saw criminality as impossible within a "worker's paradise." By the mid-1930s, the NKVD had come to believe that recidivists and "harmful elements" committed most crimes in the USSR, and only "constant sweeps and expulsions supported by the passport system" could keep these people in line.[44] These events ended only when various quotas were met and the operations considered a success.[45] While a parallel story could be told about efforts to counter abuses of power by "socially dissipated" party members, efforts to combat corruption were rare in the 1930s.[46] Although the popularity of the Stalin regime's propagandized "otherness" made such cleansing possible, the sudden need to exhort the masses to defeat the Nazis would soon leave the Kremlin and its local adjutants without this powerful tool of thought control. "Death to the German invaders" now replaced "building Communism" as the regime's raison d'être as talk of Marxism-Leninism vanished from the newspapers.

The Ukrainian Communists' subsequent struggle to relegitimize the return of Soviet power in a city often ignored by the Kremlin is the focus of chapter 5. It begins by examining why almost all talk about the war years and, most importantly, about what happened to the victims of Nazi rule in Kyiv became taboo soon after the liberation of the city. Then the chapter discusses why ideas for reconstructing and modernizing the Ukrainian capital quickly developed amid the euphoria of victory but faced an uncertain future due to the lack of resources directed toward Kyiv. Recourse to the idea that the city was at least led by competent state representatives would become the way out for local authorities. Such analysis emerges after examining city leaders' efforts to gauge the mood of the Kyivans over whom they ruled. At its core, this meant considering how best to represent their rule to the Ukrainian TsK and to the All-Union Party in Moscow, in order to ready themselves for the Stalin regime's impending moves on reconstruction. The Ukrainian Communists would later seize on Andrei Zhdanov's signals about the Stalin regime's return to "building Communism" (known colloquially as the "time of Zhdanov," or *Zhdanovshchina*) to argue for their own indispensability as leaders of a state organization seen—perhaps by almost everyone involved—as essential to overcoming the war's destruction. The context provided by the previous sections of the book helps to explain why this default to statist discourse made sense to Kyivans and how it might have—under the label of "Soviet Patriotism"—become a focus of the Stalin regime by the end of the 1940s.

Chapter 6 then focuses on the relationships between the rulers and the ruled in a city heavily dependent on the Stalin regime in Moscow. Such dependence would paradoxically legitimize behavior attributed to the "socially dangerous" before the war. The chapter first examines the anti-Semitism surrounding the unorganized return of many evacuated Jews. Local leaders initially cited such returns as the main reason for destabilizing manifestations of anti-Semitism in the city. Later, likely after the Stalin regime privately corresponded with the Communists in Kyiv, such behavior would become politically correct. Then the chapter shifts its focus to incidents of street crime in Kyiv in which many of the most likely perpetrators were men associated with the Red Army. The local Communists' efforts to link the postwar crime wave to unorganized returnees helped give new legitimacy to these servicemen's antisocial behavior. The chapter ends by examining investigations of "social dissipation" among the Kyivan elite during the scarcity of the war era. The *Zhdanovshchina* meant the Ukrainian Communists needed to recognize the extent of moral and fiscal corruption within their ranks in order to remain legitimate leaders in the eyes of the masses. The elite's association with anti-Semitic discourse and criminal behavior now combined with its effort to convince the masses that the Stalinist state could navigate the socioeconomic whirlwind brought on by war to help relegitimize Soviet power in Kyiv. The story told here lays a better foundation for studying the Stalin regime's behavior at the beginning of the Cold War.

The Stalin Regime and the Second World War

Over the last two decades, scholars working in the post-Soviet archives have asked how the Second World War shaped the political life of the Soviet Union. Stalin's fundamental problem at that time was a "paradoxical need to stabilize a regime noticeably strengthened by war."[47] The remedy that was chosen, though, would have sounded paradoxical to Karl Marx. Labeled "Soviet Patriotism," it combined the war-spawned nationalism among ordinary Russians with the "undeniable" argument that the Soviet state was morally correct, to keep the Stalin regime building Communism. As Danilov and Pyzhikov concluded, "This meant that a patriot could only be that person who believed in the same Communist ideals and politics as that of the Soviet state. Any speculation beyond such a framework was considered dangerous searching or something akin to treason or the betraying of one's homeland."[48] One historian later speculated that this statist ideology was the only rhetorical path left open to the regime after wartime bureaucratization in the economic sphere.[49] Another has argued that the supposed disloyalty among Soviet Jews during and after the war was central to "Soviet patriotism's" anti-Semitic campaigns of the late 1940s.[50] Most recently, scholars have suggested that a sense of crisis pervaded this "propaganda state" because of the prewar Stalin cult's disavowal of all other heroisms.[51] But the social history surrounding this war-related overtly statist and anti-Semitic stance by the Stalin regime remains unexplored.[52]

This book studies the wartime social history of the Soviet Union's third city, and capital of its largest minority people, to better determine which processes lay behind the formulation of "Soviet Patriotism," an ideology that animated Moscow throughout the Cold War. Was this ideology appealing to the masses simply because it approvingly compared the Soviet socialist system to a fascistic, capitalist West and its accomplices? Or did ordinary people support its tone for other, more practical reasons? The possible role of the local in shaping such an ideology is also an understudied topic; the one historian to closely analyze center-periphery relations during this period, Donald Filtzer, hypothesizes that the Stalin regime reconsolidated its control over society by restoring the prewar system of production on which that control had been based. But his conclusion that there were still "deep cracks in the political coherence of the Stalinist system" begs further study of what these cracks were and how they originated.[53]

Any search for the roots of Soviet Patriotism's appeal should begin with the idea that a "mosaic of moods" emerged in the Soviet Union during the Second World War. One Russian scholar argues that the Nazis' deep incursion into Soviet lands led to the collapse of the "command system with its bureaucratic nature, supremacy of careerism, and ignorance of the people's interests."[54] But while alleging that a "highly differentiated public atmosphere" had arisen in the USSR by 1943–44, he concludes that the Stalinist system and its people remained "two interconnected but heterogeneous forces." Adding to this broad analysis of popular mood, another Russian argues that the events of 1941 "awoke in each person the ability to think about variants, to critically evaluate a situation, and not take everything as the only given way."[55] But such a spirit of freedom, it was concluded there, could never have changed Soviet existence; the Soviet masses were exhausted and lacked any mechanism for effecting change.

Unfortunately, the geographically diffuse evidence marshaled in such investigations does not allow for a fundamental understanding of how the Soviet Union experienced the war and its aftermath. A comprehensive Western study of postwar reconstruction in Rostov-on-Don points to the bankruptcy of the Bolsheviks' rhetoric about the "socialist democracy" created in the 1930s among the masses.[56] But it does not recognize the Stalin regime's postwar search for a new legitimization politics that would resonate with the people. A study of postwar Sevastopol does highlight such a search as it discusses why local leaders adopted a thoroughly Russian nationalist historical memory to relegitimize efforts to rebuild their city.[57] But why ordinary people's interests might have contributed to this deemphasizing of the ideological imperatives associated with building Communism in favor of simply rebuilding a Russian-led state is not asked.

What is known about postwar Soviet Ukraine also does not clarify how relationships between Stalin's regime and its people may have helped to change the focus of its propaganda. Amir Weiner focused on the republic's Vinnytsa Oblast "within the overarching feature of the Soviet enterprise—the revolutionary transformation of a society from an antagonistically divided entity into a conflict-free harmonious body."[58] With socialism successfully in place, only conflicts along ethnic lines remained to be extinguished in a multiethnic society that had abolished class differences. But this investigation largely ignores the extreme material deprivations associated with the 1940s, which may have been the real reasons, for example, for why Jewish interests could be negated at the Cold War's beginning.

Until Weiner's path-breaking work, however, the best description of the postwar Soviet Jewish predicament argued that Moscow's policy was a complex compromise targeting blatant anti-Semitism and allowing Jews to partake in the life of society, while positions of power were made off-limits and the press hinted that Jews were "a foreign element who possess dual loyalties and are capable of betraying the socialist motherland in times of crisis."[59] After the USSR's collapse, the archives revealed that the wartime efforts of the Jewish Anti-Fascist Committee (JAFC) to promote Jewish interests within the Soviet Union were a possible explanation for the Stalin regime's propaganda focus later that decade.[60] But this only reinforced the Cold War–era idea that the assassination of the JAFC's chairman, the actor Solomon Mikhoels, by the NKVD's postwar successors in 1948 marked the beginnings of the Stalin regime's anti-Semitic turn.

Unfortunately, present-day Ukrainian historians have been unable to expand on reasons for why "Soviet Patriotism" appeared in the late 1940s. Perhaps this is because of these historians' poisonous row over whether the Ukrainian Insurgent Army and the Organization for Ukrainian Nationalists should be considered war heroes.[61] Condemnations of Moscow's role in 1940s Ukraine dominate the textbooks and teaching aids available in independent Ukraine's bookstores, without much analysis of how the Kremlin and its Ukrainian representatives could wield so much power. In telling the story of postoccupation Kyiv, this book concentrates on archival holdings rather than period memoirs since uncensored literature from this period is scant. To have experienced Soviet power's return meant, of course, continuing to live in the isolated Soviet Union of the Cold War.

Equally unfortunate is the fact that none of the Soviet-era sources that treat Kyiv's history in the mid-1940s gives a credible interpretation of the city's life at that time. A two-volume *History of Kyiv*, published in 1964, unsurprisingly stresses the leading role of Nikita Khrushchev's Communist Party of Ukraine during wartime reconstruction and downplays the role of the Kremlin's dictates in that process.[62] The same self-serving emphasis on the local party appears in the edition on Kyiv in the *History of Cities and Villages of the Ukrainian SSR* series published in 1979, in a second multi-volume history on the city that appeared in 1985, and even in the most comprehensive history of the city's reconstruction, Vladimir Smishko's *Kyiv Reborn*, which appeared at the height of perestroika.[63]

Other than the Kremlin's issuance of a "fighting plan"—GKO's August 21, 1943, resolution "On Urgent Measures for the Reconstruction of the Economy in the Regions Liberated from German Occupation"—to guide rebuilding, Moscow's role in Kyiv at this time according to these histories is limited to the periodic allocation of funds, skilled labor, and supplies from the rear for reconstruction. Meanwhile, these works pay little attention to ordinary people; only references to Kyivans' "working heroism" are made to justify their efforts. Nothing is said about Kyivans' critical opinions of those who ruled them or of fellow Kyivans, or, for that matter, about what the authorities thought about those they were now directing.

The major works on Kyiv published in the post-Soviet era assert common tropes of wartime victimhood that have only recently become printable. The tragic fate of the formerly occupied and primarily Ukrainian population, surrounded by a suspicious and newly enlarged Moscow-centered elite, is one such trope accepted without question.⁶⁴ A recent collection of documents, meanwhile, highlights the Soviet state's "insertion into [Ukraine's] collective consciousness of anti-Semitic stereotypes" and focuses on postoccupation Kyiv, although it also acknowledges that Ukraine's story cannot be understood without the context in which it occurred—and warns readers at the outset that this history has yet to be systematically researched.⁶⁵ Still, a recent work on repatriates returning to Kyiv does break down stereotypes as it discusses how the *Ostarbeitery* were in demand after the war because of their penchant for hard work no matter the job.⁶⁶

A comprehensive story of Soviet power's return to post-Nazi Kyiv is an ideal window for determining how the Stalin regime operated at the Cold War's outset. To relegitimize their leadership, the Ukrainian Communists needed to take into account the Kremlin's understanding of Kyiv's wartime role as reflected in the resettling and reassembling of its population. The main problems the Communists faced were the lack of movement on reconstruction coupled with the unorganized return of hundreds of thousands of people to a city, the housing of which had already been redistributed. Could a "regime city" reemerge from this social dislocation to reach a point whereby the masses' interests—and particularly those of the Ukrainian majority vis-à-vis its Jewish minority—might play a key role in reshaping the Stalin regime's future? Could resource scarcity leave the returning Communists' efforts to relegitimize Soviet power so unsuccessful that only the *Zhdanovshchina* allowed them to argue they still possessed the traits necessary to lead a popular but injured state toward recovery? This book answers affirmatively to both questions, as the processes documented here may well have contributed to the formulation of the Stalin regime's anti-Semitic and statist ideological campaigns of the late 1940s, which provided comfort to millions of Soviet citizens and kept the Stalinists in power for decades thereafter.

Part One

Resettlement

CHAPTER ONE

"The Capital Is Being Settled All Over Again"

Resettlement from Fall 1943 to Fall 1944

In the fall of 1943, the Red Army advanced on Kyiv. Ahead of it, Stalin's secret police studied the population about to come under their control. At the end of September, Sergei Savchenko, the head of the Ukrainian People's Commissariat of State Security (NKGB), wrote to his counterpart in the Ukrainian NKVD, Vasilii Riasnoi, about the Nazis' arrests of Soviet citizens in Kyiv as well as their preparations to evacuate ethnic Germans.[1] Two weeks later, Savchenko reported that the evacuation had begun. The Germans were sending whole enterprises and their workers out of Kyiv, and the roads to Zhytomyr and points west were jammed with cars and trucks.[2] Then, a few days later, he reported, "Based on a message from the operative group of the Fourth Directorate of the Ukrainian NKGB 'Eagle' now active in the enemy's rear . . . Kyiv's population is being led away to the west. In the city, only German military units remain."[3]

Later that winter, high-school teacher Viktor Tverskii explained to the Ukrainian Academy of Sciences' "Commission on the History of the Patriotic War in Ukraine" how he had avoided the evacuation:

> In the second half of September 1943, at first far away on the horizon, then closer and closer and more brightly, fires flared up on the left bank of the Dnipro. All of the nearby villages were burning. The retreating Germans had set them on fire. . . . Finally, the left-bank outskirts of Kyiv started to flare up, Darnitsa, Slobodka, and Trukanov Island. . . . One thought then gripped every living being: to last it out until our guys got here, to stay in one piece, to save oneself and to save one's family from death. . . . We decided to go in the direction of Demievka. We lived there until October 21, when another order appeared announcing the whole city was a war zone and obliging everyone to show up at the train station. . . . What should we do? Go to the station where the Germans wanted people to go? No way! That meant penal servitude.[4]

Another person told neither of fleeing from nor evacuating with the Germans. Vladimir M. Artobol'skii, a seventy-year-old zoology professor, spoke of the Germans forcing him to stay behind to look after property belonging to the

Ukrainian Academy of Sciences' Museum of Zoology. After describing his effort to hide during the final days, he made these comments about the end of German power:

> General stealing began. What is more, it was organized stealing. Huge trucks would drive in and be filled up with furniture, tables, tiles, and other things. Along with the furniture, kitchen utensils, too, the most indecent of things . . . all of it was taken away. The Germans are very serious people. Staying in the prohibited zone meant coming under fire or at least getting into big trouble. Walking along the streets at that time was frightening. There was not a soul from the local population. Only Germans, thieves, and patrols, and they moved freely about the streets. . . . In that way Kyiv was given over to plundering.[5]

And the vantage point of his prime Gorky Street apartment in downtown Kyiv left Artobol'skii with these memories of the city's actual liberation after two years of Nazi rule:

> On November 5, I went to the window and noticed unusual movements on the street. People were running around, seemingly quite nervous. They stopped and talked with each other. Were these Germans? No, it was the civilian population. I said to my wife that something was happening in the city. . . . Someone walked in [to our building] and opened the door. I opened my door. It turned out to be our neighbor returning to his apartment. I learned from him that the Germans were leaving Kyiv. We started to save up water. We opened the tap. Water flowed for about twenty-five minutes. It cut out after the Germans had gone. I still did not risk venturing out of my apartment, for the German patrols remained at their posts. The mood that enveloped me at that point is impossible to describe. It was the end of a nightmare. The end![6]

Artobol'skii's relief at the return of Soviet power was understandable. In the immediate aftermath of the Nazi retreat, most Kyivans were probably as frightened and timid as they had been during it.[7] Soviet power, meanwhile, approached the Ukrainian capital cognizant that before the war, the city had been a quiescent place. But as this book's first section argues, the management of the city's resettlement by the Stalin regime provided its local leaders with new challenges as they cemented their rule over Kyiv.

Resettlement and the Formerly Occupied

As the head of the Military Council of the First Ukrainian Front and Chairman of the SNK UkrSSR, Nikita Khrushchev observed on Kyiv's liberation day,

Figure 1.1. The First Ukrainian Front on the Khreshchatyk, November 7, 1943. Reproduced by permission from the H. Pshenychnyi Central State CinePhotoPhono Archives of Ukraine.

November 6, 1943, "There was something eerie about the city. It had been such a noisy, lively, youthful place before the war, and now there was no one around. As we walked down the Khreshchatyk and turned onto Lenin Street, our footsteps echoed along the empty stretch of pavement around us."[8] Two days later, Khrushchev telegraphed Stalin to say he was still establishing order amid evidence of mass killings by the Nazis and an almost complete lack of inhabitants. He ended his telegram, "Kyiv produces the impression of an extinct city."[9] Ivan Mironov, secretary of the Petriv (Podil') Raikom, maintained that the dead bodies of women, children, and the elderly were still visible in the streets at this time.[10]

As Khrushchev's NKVD established order, the Ukrainian NKGB uncovered the magnitude of the atrocities committed by the Nazis. One witness, Vladimir Davydov, volunteered information about the Germans' deeds. Imprisoned in the Nazis' concentration camp at Syrets on the city's western borders, Davydov said he had been forced to burn the human remains of the Babyn Iar massacre before the city was surrendered. He told the Ukrainian NKGB that he helped to burn 70,000 corpses (including those of at least 50,000 Jews) in September 1943. He then added, "[While we were] burning the corpses ... the Germans brought [trucks] of people murdered by gas asphyxiation. ... We were forced to climb into the truck and to throw the corpses of these people into the open. We then laid them out and built a pile of them for burning."[11] While it is unclear how Davydov knew the numbers and ethnicities of the dead, his testimony contributed to the Soviet understanding of the Nazis' genocide in Kyiv.[12] On the eve of the Second World War, some 224,236 Jews (or 26.5 percent of the city's entire population) had lived in the Ukrainian capital.[13] According to these numbers, then, the Nazis had executed a fourth of the city's Jews; most of the rest were either fighting with the Red Army or evacuated to the Soviet rear.

Later, at a March 15, 1944, Kyiv Oblast Party Committee (Obkom) plenum, secretary Zinovii Serdiuk claimed that the Germans had "shot, tortured, and poisoned in 'population destroyers' close to 200,000 people" in Kyiv.[14] He also emphasized that many people from Kyiv were taken to Germany to work during the war.[15] Some 38,000 Kyivans alone were sent to the *Ostarbeitery* program during the first ten months of the occupation, and more recent research puts the total number of Kyivans sent to work in Germany at 50,000.[16] Still, Serdiuk's reference to 200,000 dead marks one of the last times anything like such a number was reported in any forum.[17] Privately, the Ukrainian government noted in October 1944 that 127, 273 civilians and 69,021 Red Army POWs were killed in German-occupied Kyiv.[18] "Over 100,000" dead became the phrase commonly associated with the number of people said to have died in the city under the Nazis, and that is the number recorded on the Babyn Iar memorial itself.[19] Why there was so little interest at this time in precisely how many people died during the occupation is examined in later chapters.

Compared to other major Soviet cities occupied by the Germans, Kyiv's population loss was certainly worse. According to a 1943 All-Union Main Directorate of the Militia NKVD report, Kharkiv lost two-thirds of its population under the Germans, while in Rostov-on-Don (RSFSR), the population fell by about a half.[20] In Kyiv, where 1 million people had once lived, only 220,000 were left in December 1943.[21] But this situation soon changed. And the return of the formerly occupied quickly challenged the arriving Soviet authorities as the city's property was unsecured. For Stalin in Moscow, though, what mattered most was how those resettling the Ukrainian capital might be useful against the Germans.

After Kharkiv's liberation in spring 1943, for example, Ukrainian NKVD troops, white-collar employees, and militia had conducted "mass operations" (*massoperatsii*) designed to clear the rear of spies, saboteurs, enemy soldiers and officers, Red Army draft dodgers, and other "enemy elements."[22] Stalin's internal police had concluded that in a frontline atmosphere, unsystematic *massoperatsii* were the best way to meet the state's security needs.[23] These methods were deemed successful because they uncovered large numbers of "enemy elements." But just who the latter were was revealed by an All-Union NKVD report about its activities in Voronezh Oblast (RSFSR) during the summer of 1943: "During the *massoperatsii*, 6,607 roaming soldiers of the enemy's units were caught . . . as well as

Figure 1.2. "Kyivans Return to Their Hometown," November 7, 1943. Reproduced by permission from the H. Pshenychnyi Central State CinePhotoPhono Archives of Ukraine.

4,347 Russian prisoners of war who had escaped captivity. Besides that, within the limits of the oblast, 4,039 people were uncovered who were either deserters from the Red Army or dodging the draft for mobilization into the Red Army."[24]

The same report also discusses the outcome in neighboring Kursk Oblast (RSFSR): "In the span of three months (March to May) in the city of Kursk and the raions of that oblast, during sixteen mass searches, 670 deserters from the Red Army were uncovered and arrested, [and] 524 servicemen who had left their units and were without documents were captured and sent to the garrison commands or to the military units of Soviet Military Intelligence." Thus, "enemy elements" were mostly people avoiding service in the Red Army, and "uncovering" them had become the NKVD's most important work, as the Stalin regime needed men to defeat Hitler more than anything else.

In Kyiv, the return of Soviet power meant the November 12, 1943, Kyiv Obkom resolution: "On the application of state order to the territory of the cities and regions of Kyiv Oblast liberated from the Nazi occupants."[25] This resolution obliged the organs of the Ukrainian NKVD to register and investigate citizens temporarily living in the oblast as well as those who had arrived during the war. It hints at a draconian attempt to understand who had done what during the years of Nazi occupation. But the first months of Soviet power's return to Kyiv, like elsewhere to the city's east, saw the security organs occupied with other tasks. While they spent most of their time "recruiting" for the army, the Ukrainian NKVD claimed it was also trying to secure "ownerless" property in the city. Kyiv's chief of police at the time, V. M. Komarov, later described these days after liberation as a time when his organization created an apparatus of "destroyer battalions, brigades of assistance, night watchmen, self-defense groups, and court-yard caretakers," but it is unclear how successful these actually were.[26]

The Ukrainian NKGB, meanwhile, was still relying on sympathetic elements within the Kyivan population to voluntarily reveal the enemies of Soviet power.[27] In November 1943, for example, an Ivan Brodskii submitted a declaration about a group of people then hiding in the city who had committed atrocities against Soviet people while imprisoned at the concentration camp in Syrets. During his interrogation, Brodskii accused one V. V. Bystrov: "[He] was one of the active participants in all of these violations of [human] dignity and atrocities committed against the prisoners. He beat people, buried them alive, hanged others, and personally took part in mass shootings."[28] As a result of Brodskii's declaration, the Ukrainian NKVD arrested Bystrov and three other men.

In his own interrogation, Bystrov did not deny these allegations: "While working at the camp, I received an assignment from a Gestapo employee . . . to uncover Communists, Soviet activists, and Jews among the prisoners and to report about them to the Gestapo employees. I agreed to do it."[29] While Bystrov's declaration suggested that he had no choice but to collaborate, the Ukrainian NKVD still dealt with him harshly.[30] He was handed over to a military field court on the basis of an April 19, 1943, All-Union Supreme Soviet decision, which meant certain conviction and a death sentence.[31] But such outcomes appear to have been few and far between, which suggests that the returning Soviet security services remained interested in people like Bystrov only as long as the Nazis remained close by.

Finding men for Red Army service, meanwhile, took precedence over the rapid reregistration of the city's population. After the Kyiv City Party Committee (Gorkom) was reestablished in late 1943, for example, it quickly issued a resolution asserting that the registration of those eligible for the draft was incomplete.[32] Although over six thousand Kyivans had been immediately enrolled in the army, another twelve thousand were given extensions, while others were not included at all as institutional directors "used any sort of pretext imaginable to keep for themselves those who are obliged to join the military."[33] The resolution singled out the director of Kyiv's bread trust, who had petitioned to keep several times more people than he needed. An ever-growing number of "defense-related" industries during the war found that their workers could be reserved and saved from the draft, and tried to use this loophole to their advantage.[34]

As it became clear, though, that those responsible for clearing the destroyed Khreshchatyk and building a new railway bridge over the Dnipro were also hiring people dodging registration, a second resolution on the draft in the city was passed on March 3, 1944. The city's draft boards responded by beginning monthly "reregistration" campaigns. This entailed further *massoperatsii* in the city well into 1944; dragnets and regular checks searching for military registration dodgers, draft dodgers, and deserters from the army occurred on a monthly basis.[35] Once again, the search was now for those avoiding service in the Red Army rather than for the "bourgeois-nationalists" or common criminals of times past. Such a change of focus may have signaled to the formerly occupied population that these Bolsheviks were not the same as the old ones.

For those Kyivans not touched by these processes, the First Ukrainian Front that had liberated the city from the Nazis made the initial decisions concerning mobilization for the Soviet war effort. A resolution passed by SNK SSSR on February 13, 1942, made it possible to mobilize for full-time work all able-bodied men between the ages of sixteen and fifty-five, and women aged sixteen to forty-five living in urban areas who were not already working for state enterprises and institutions.[36] Another SNK SSSR resolution of August 10, 1942, legalized temporary "labor responsibility" for periods of up to two months for urban and rural Soviet citizens in addition to the jobs they had already been bonded to since the war's beginning.[37] Maybe it was to avoid such outcomes that over five thousand working-aged Kyivans eagerly reported to their now destroyed prewar places of employment on November 7, 1943.[38]

For the First Ukrainian Front, however, the priorities were reconstructing the city's railway junctions and building a bridge over the Dnipro. Kyiv Oblast leader Serdiuk's comments at the first meeting of Kyiv's Communists on December 27, 1943, about recruitment for these tasks makes plain the local authorities' conflicted opinions about how to treat the formerly occupied population: "It is not right, that attitude among some of our leaders that I have been told about, that they asked the railroad workers during their first days after our arrival, 'Who are you anyway, you stayed behind. We will take a look at who you are.' Of course, we need to keep an eye out and not allow ourselves to put our finger in their mouths, for it might be bitten off. One need not be absent-minded or an inattentive type [*rotozei*], but to express distrust is also not right."[39] Serdiuk's comments point to why many of Kyiv's formerly occupied remained timid during the first weeks after liberation. But they also show a certain fear among the local authorities themselves, who sensed that too heavy a hand might hinder their efforts to rule the city.

A November 12, 1943, memorandum to Khrushchev from the All-Union People's Commissariat of the River Fleet offers proof of the union-level authorities' intent to bring Kyiv's population into the war effort. This memorandum reported that the "carcasses" of Kyiv's two shipbuilding factories—the Stalin Ship-Building Factory and Leninskaia Kuznitsa—were in one piece, and that 550 workers had been registered at the city's port.[40] Soon these factories became part of the

All-Union People's Commissariat of Ship Building and fulfilled orders for spare parts for the front. Other places that quickly resumed operations included the Kyiv Locomotive Repair Factory (employing two thousand workers by January 1944), the Lepse Tractor Factory, and a factory belonging to the Kyiv Military Region Construction Directorate. Their jobs were to repair machinery needed by the First Ukrainian Front and the surrounding region's agriculture.[41]

But the city's damaged utilities grid—blown up by the Germans on their retreat—presented a major obstacle to the city's return to functionality. Although a SNK UkrSSR and Ukrainian Central Committee (TsK) resolution dated December 8, 1943, temporarily mobilized some three thousand Kyivans to reconstruct the city's energy system, there is little indication that this resolution was ever fulfilled.[42] The Kyiv Obkom, meanwhile, ordered 2,100 Kyivans temporarily mobilized to help the First Ukrainian Front in Kyiv build the new "above-water" railroad bridge over the Dnipro.[43] But after an attack by German aircraft in January 1944, only military servicemen appear on the lists of dead and wounded.[44] Other mobilization orders may have been more successful, but they remained temporary in nature. On December 2, 1943, for example, the Kyiv Obkom also mobilized 2,100 Kyivans into the oblast to clear snowdrifts on the Southwestern Railroad.[45] But no one laboring in the rural regions surrounding Kyiv was supposed to travel to the capital; these people were instead to supply the Red Army with grain.[46]

Hints that Moscow was thinking again about Kyiv's reconstruction came as the Ukrainian leadership resolved on January 20, 1944, to tackle the city's destroyed electrical network. This time it issued a GKO-backed resolution calling on Kyiv's authorities to mobilize 1,500 urban and rural people, and for the Kyiv Military Region and active city enterprises to hand over 2,000 others who were "of limited use militarily."[47] Likewise, a people's commissariat needed the mandate of a GKO resolution to put its prewar factories (or what remained of them) into working order. In early February, such backing meant the SNK UkrSSR could order Kyiv's leaders to mobilize 750 Kyivans to revitalize the local aerospace industry. Factory no. 473 of the All-Union People's Commissariat of the Aviation Industry (the present-day Antonov) was now set to repair airplanes for the needs of the front.[48]

Meanwhile, the new leaderships of the Kyiv Obkom and Gorkom were announced during the first month after the city's liberation. While Khrushchev nominally headed both, Serdiuk was in command at the oblast level while Fedor Mokienko ran matters at the city level.[49] At the first meeting of the city's Communists, Mokienko noted that there were already 1,700 Communists in Kyiv.[50] His speech was followed by one from a "comrade Likholat" from the Ukrainian TsK's Propaganda Group, who asked, "Is the tempo of reconstruction satisfactory? . . . Comrades, there are still many people who, in general, are not working. . . . Kyivans are unsure of themselves because mass-political work is only carried out weakly among them. . . . It is necessary to show the workers a full picture of the German occupants' rule."[51] Finding people for reconstruction within the confines of the Stalin regime's centralized economy would become an almost existential problem for the local Communists. But the idea of talking about Nazi war crimes would ebb and flow as news arrived from the front. In this case, Likholat's bluster resulted from the First Ukrainian Front's drive to the west having just ground to a halt around Zhytomyr.

By winter's end, the number of Communists in the city passed the five thousand mark.[52] While these numbers reveal Kyiv's increased importance in the Kremlin's mind, the arrival of such people almost inevitably meant that attitudes similar to those from the 1930s toward the population might rear their ugly heads. For example, one Kyiv Obkom secretary summarized the problems he saw in the city at that time: "The Party organization needs to pay a lot of attention to the education of workers; to the cleansing . . . of that sore that was inflicted upon them by Goebbels's false propaganda."[53] However, Serdiuk's more forgiving tone, indicating a need to trust the hundreds of thousands of people who had ended up in occupied territory through no fault of their own, eventually carried the day.

But judging by further attempts to ascertain who was living in the capital, it took a while for the Kyiv Oblast leader to win over his comrades. A resolution passed by the Kyiv Gorkom on February 19, 1944, entitled "On the Reregistration of the Population and the Enforcement of the Passport Regime in the City of Kyiv" was the legal basis for these renewed efforts.[54] This dictate echoed the resolution reestablishing state order, which marked the first effort at controlling the city's resettlement. The new resolution sought "the eviction of all persons who fall under passport limitations, as well as those who arrived here during the German occupation, and who are not native residents of the city." Such "limitations" had been last described in the secret protocols of the All-Union NKVD's Passport Statute of 1940. Those key limitations forbade people, based on the law's statutes 38 and 39, from living within a 50-kilometer radius of the Ukrainian capital. People forbidden by statute 38 included those once incarcerated, exiled, or who had arrived as refugees from abroad, as well as those who were without determined citizenship or the right to vote, were children of the "special settlers" (as well as any "special settlers" themselves), or were refugees from the territory of Poland that became Germany in 1939. Those forbidden by statute 39 included those exiled by special tribunals, Koreans resettled from the Far East, and those resettled from the Soviet Union's western oblasts amid the prewar effort to cleanse the border.[55]

At a meeting held on February 27, 1944, two days before the reregistration campaign's beginning, militia chief Komarov outlined his action plan:

> Kyiv is a regime city. . . . It is also well known that for entry into the city before the war one needed either an invitation to work here, or an assignment, or some sort of summons from an organization. [After the Red Army] liberated Kyiv from the German bandits, the situation with the regime in the city has completely changed. . . . At present, there are many people in Kyiv, people who fall under one or another of the passport limitations, people who in wartime conditions appear to be socially dangerous. . . . In order to implement the passport regime in the future and to fix in place the results that we will achieve, it will be necessary to carry out systematic checks of all our house directorates, private dwellings, institutions, and enterprises. . . . We will also uncover Red Army deserters, thieves, those people who have nothing to do with Kyiv, [as well as] those not doing any socially useful work and [occupied by] various types of bad dealings.[56]

The "regime city" moniker Komarov attributed to Kyiv had been used ever since February 1934, when SNK SSSR established a 50-kilometer radius zone around the city and the Ukrainian Communists then purged it of tens of thousands of "unreliable elements."[57]

But, more specifically, Komarov was alluding here to Kyiv's prewar status as a union-level "regime city of the first category." This moniker was pronounced for the first time in the all-union Passport Statute of 1940, which prevented the "unreliable elements," once removed, from ever returning to the city's limits. Kyiv's status thus made it the political equal of Moscow and St. Petersburg as all three cities were now off-limits to all offenders. Such categorization—these people were now labeled *limitchki*—had been in line with the all-union NKVD's prewar tendency to place ever greater restrictions on the movement of individuals and especially ex-convicts.[58] Now, though, Komarov scheduled another group for "banishment": those who had lived in Kyiv before the war but who had had compromising material uncovered about them, those who had been deemed "socially dangerous," and those who were now subject to eviction based on the "laws of wartime." The foundation for this last euphemism had been Stalin's July 3, 1941, speech in which he declared, "All who by their panic-mongering and cowardice hinder the work of defense, no matter who they may be, must be immediately brought before a Military Tribunal."[59] But Komarov's final idea of simply purging those who had "nothing to do with Kyiv" signaled a desire to "cleanse" the city in even more thorough ways than in the 1930s.

When a regime goes to war, the laws it passes to defend itself can result in social and political confusion at home. Komarov's answer to a question regarding the fate of families of people determined to have served as *politzai* (local policemen) under the Germans but then registered, drafted, and conscripted into the Red Army already reveals such confusion. He replied, "We are going to have to proceed in every case separately. There is this law that a family's administrative eviction happens only with a determined category of persons: deserters. We could add *politzai* to that category too if he is not serving in the Red Army right now. But if he was a *politzai* and has since been drafted into the Red Army then his family will be left in Kyiv."[60] Komarov's clarification reflected how the "laws of wartime" actually signaled a relative softening of the Stalin regime's approach.

Despite such qualifications, the new chairman of the Kyiv City Soviet, Luka Lebed', was critical of Komarov's approach to reregistration. "Comrades," Lebed' said, "I believe the answers to these questions seem clear, but when we get down to practical work there will be much that is unclear. . . . We need to check over those who are arriving here right now especially closely. It will be tough for us to figure out the truth and, of course, there will not be many idiots out there saying, 'Yes, I left voluntarily [with the Germans].' In these cases, we will need witnesses."[61]

Reflecting early splits within the local leadership about how best to manage the city's resettlement, Kyiv Gorkom secretary Mokienko still sounded confident: "It is evident that we will have to talk with our agitators. Let them have a talk with the people about these tasks, about creating some order here in the city, and the conscious population of Kyiv must take an active part in solving this problem. A bastard can counterfeit any old document, and counterfeit it in such a way that no commission will be able to figure it out."[62] Concluding that the time had come to "show some anger toward our enemies," Mokienko also urged those doing the reregistration to collect statements from the population about Kyivans' activities under the Nazis. "You surely remember, during the first days, there were those cases when people asked, can we take the 'Germans' [collaborators] prisoner? Can we hack them up? Now we ourselves need to show some anger toward our enemies. All this is totally legal, but there have to be declarations. . . . In this case, Stalin, Kalinin, even Hitler, would have to submit declarations."[63]

Whether or not the formerly occupied were sincere in their desire for revenge against Nazi collaborators, the declarations Mokienko mentioned here were supposed to help find those of operative interest to the Ukrainian NKVD. His hardline tone indicates that at least some members of the local leadership remained determined to maintain a "business as usual" approach despite the extraordinary events swirling around them. A large-scale purge of those deemed "socially dangerous" seemed potentially imminent.

But what followed Mokienko's urge to create a Kyiv even "cleaner" than that of the 1930s was something quite remarkable. While Komarov's organization reregistered 296,107 men, women, and children by the end of March 1944, they found only 552 German "collaborators" and 172 *limitchiki* falling under articles 38 and 39 of the all-union criminal code.[64] These statistics indicate that reregistering the population (the initial step in reestablishing the passport regime) did not in fact result in a large-scale "cleansing" of the "unreliable elements" of the past or the "socially dangerous" of the present. Perhaps the former were not as numerous after all considering the events of the 1930s. As for the latter, maybe these leaders became apprehensive about what these "witnesses'" testimony might mean for the regime's legitimacy, if it allowed for questioning about what had happened in Kyiv following the beginning of the war.

An analysis of the All-Union NKVD's Main Directorate of the Militia yearly report for 1944 covering the reconstruction of the Soviet passport system in areas liberated from the Germans further justifies such questions. This review uncovered 34,325 "collaborators" and 66,105 persons who worked in German institutions and enterprises. Another 18,730 Red Army deserters, 22,756 draft dodgers, and 21,647 violators of the draft law were also unearthed.[65] But these are figures for all of the liberated territories during 1944, when millions in the European part of the Soviet Union were freed from Nazi hegemony. And although the report reflects the relative importance of finding those who associated with the Germans, the focus of the security organs' attention also reflects their lack of interest in wartime social dislocation occurring in the Stalin regime's damaged hinterland. It was the latter phenomenon, however, that now became the most pressing issue for the Ukrainian Communists amid the continued resettlement of their capital.

With registration complete, the next step was passportization itself and a Kyiv Obkom resolution of April 5, 1944, shows it began soon afterward. This step required the Ukrainian NKVD's Directorate of the Militia for Kyiv Oblast "to evict from the 50 kilometer zone around Kyiv all persons who fall under passport limitations, and also persons who arrived in this zone during the German occupation as well as after the liberation who are not native inhabitants except for people who have been summoned here from the eastern oblasts." The language suggests that social dislocation was a growing concern for local leaders. As for those who were allowed to live in the Ukrainian capital, the resolution stipulated that "the issuance of living permits to the population in this 50 kilometer zone will be carried out in accordance with the Passport Statute affirmed by the SNK SSSR on September 10, 1940."[66] But like reregistration, the passportization necessary to recreate a 1930s-era "regime city of the first category" was easier to promulgate than to implement.

A meeting between Kyiv's leaders on May 9, 1944, with the assistant chairman of the SNK UkrSSR, Leonid Korniets, to discuss the "apartment question in the city of Kyiv," illustrates why this was the case. The topic of the causes of Kyiv's housing shortage was quickly pushed aside by the issue of who should or should not be in the city. Komarov opened the discussion by noting that the issuance of living permits had begun and that he had refused "three to four thousand people" such permits, usually because they were in the city without permission. Korniets responded to Komarov by saying that he should "multiply that number tenfold," for such people were "on the move all the time."[67]

The numbers of "socially dangerous" evicted by Komarov's men at the same time appears quite low, however: only seven hundred in total for a city now with hundreds of thousands of inhabitants. And while these people were "basically the Germans' accomplices, prostitutes, courtyard caretakers, house managers and the wives of *politzai*," Komarov's conclusion about how they and their relatives reacted to his militia is quite revealing of the city's atmosphere: "All of them write complaints to the Kyiv City Procurator's Office, the Kyiv City Soviet, and other soviet and party organizations about the decision to exile them from the city. There are facts on hand when the inhabitants of almost an entire apartment building sign off on a recommendation when we have information that says such and such an individual was a direct accomplice to the Germans."[68]

Perhaps Mokienko's drive to uncover what had occurred in Kyiv during the occupation encountered more resistance from those abandoned by Soviet power than expected. Perhaps the local authorities' experiences led the Stalin regime to conclude that such searches might be more trouble than they were worth. An unsigned report of Komarov's found in the archives of the Kyiv Gorkom from late September 1944 reveals that while 5,394 people were "banished" from Kyiv between March and September of that year, only 326 were considered *limitchiki* or Nazi collaborators.[69] Thus, while the *massoperatsii* continued to support the Red Army during the first half of 1944, these banishments amount to the only "mass" evictions from the Ukrainian capital following the principles of the 1930s during the entire period of this study. And although the removal of the "socially dangerous" would have seemed logical to leaders in Kyiv, the Stalin regime's apparent lack of concern over social dislocation continued to cause them worry.

Permission to enter the Ukrainian capital, meanwhile, was governed by a SNK UkrSSR and Ukrainian TsK resolution, "On the Temporary Limitation of Entrance into the City of Kyiv," passed the day Komarov's reregistration effort ended on March 25, 1944.[70] This resolution prohibited return to Kyiv for prewar residents and for those who wished to move to the city from the Soviet rear without permission to do so from a newly created "Temporary Commission for the Regulation of the Entrance of Citizens into the City of Kyiv." A reading of the resolution, however, reveals that this "Temporary Commission" was not the only organization permitting people to return to the city. For example, GKO-based resolutions were also bringing small groups of skilled workers in from the rear. The Soviet armed forces, meanwhile, were to bring in much larger numbers.

The comments made during this meeting reveal a Ukrainian leadership more worried about its lack of control over those "arriving of their own accord" than anything else. At one point, Korniets blurted out, "Here, close your eyes and evict them all," giving an example: "I received a letter from a doctor. He writes that the

People's Commissariat of Health summoned him to Kyiv, but they are only permitting his wife and his daughter to enter. 'That is not enough,' he writes, 'If they do not give permission to all of those about whom I write then I am not traveling to Kyiv.' Then he lists seventeen people including his sister, and his mother-in-law, etc. Furthermore, he writes that before the war they lived in Kazakhstan. And now he is gathering them up from all over and bringing them here."[71]

These leaders also worried about the city's resettled population not helping the war effort as much as it should. The Ukrainian People's Commissar of Communal Services at that time, I. Tabulevich, noted, "We need to press people about working. A person arrives and asks for a living permit. I ask him, 'Where do you work?' He answers, 'Nowhere because I have no living permit. When you give me one, then I will go to work.' We give him the living permit. But he does not go to work at an enterprise. Instead, he goes to the bazaar."[72] This question of why many Kyivans spent their days at the city's markets instead of helping with reconstruction is discussed below.

Tabulevich, though, continued by recounting the beginnings of passportization in Kyiv so as to contextualize the war's influence on the city's resettlement: "In 1933 we had it bad with living space and thus before anything else we said to a person, 'When you have your living permit, and you have living space, then we will take you on for work.' Now we have a different story. We do not have free hiring these days, but mobilization. . . . Why should we not go further in this way? A person arrives. 'How did you get here?' 'By summons.' 'Who summoned you?' 'The Health Ministry.' 'Good. Bring us a memo saying you work for the Health Ministry. Then we will give you a living permit.'" While such a change in the passportization process might have helped to speed reconstruction, it would have definitely meant an even speedier growth in the city's population.

Korniets concluded by declaring his willingness to have the passport law rewritten so that those people coming to the city could quickly join in the task of rebuilding it. He declared, "Without a doubt the law of 1933 is dated and we cannot be guided by it. If we cannot decide ourselves, we can call Moscow, because this is a question of the settlement of a city after the war. This is a new question for all of us and for those who guide us too."[73] The passportization process, though, was never changed, since the Stalin regime's earlier predilections remained intact. But the war's destruction and the economy's continued focus on the front meant a Soviet Union where social dislocation may have been more menacing to local leaders than that brought about by collectivization a decade earlier. The fact that people could continue to enter Kyiv without any occupation and secure living permits without ever finding a job would torment these Ukrainian Communists for a long time to come. Even as some leaders voiced their displeasure with the growing numbers arriving in the city, they would soon need to follow Zinovii Serdiuk's lead to learn how to manage this phenomenon.

Resettlement and Unorganized Returnees

Along with determining who was already in Kyiv, the city's leaders tried to resettle it so that it would soon look and act once again like a Ukrainian capital. On January 8, 1944, SNK UkrSSR and the Ukrainian TsK, for example, decided to move the republic-level government bureaucracy en masse from Kharkiv to Kyiv.[74] Between January 10 and 15, 1944, several thousand bureaucrats arrived along with their personal belongings and equipment. Then, on January 20, 1944, the same organizations allocated ten thousand apartments in Kyiv for the future use of "Republic-level" workers.[75] These included employees of the Ukrainian Academy of Sciences and all of Kyiv's cultural and educational institutions.

This resolution also obliged the Kyiv City Soviet to turn over to the Ukrainian TsK's Directorate of Affairs, the SNK UkrSSR, and the republic's commissariats the apartments that had once belonged to these institutions before the war. Korniets described what happened next during the aforementioned May 9, 1944, "apartment question" meeting: "When we decided the question about the quartering of the central organizations, Nikita Sergeeivich [Khrushchev] said, 'Listen, there are few people right now in Kyiv. Maybe that organization does not need that house. Maybe it is not needed [for them to be] on that particular corner. Still, occupy it. If that organization's representatives are in Kyiv, then let them save it.'"[76]

Korniets further noted that none of these empty buildings would have any "windows, doors, or catches left in them by now" if Khrushchev's ideas had not been enacted that winter. But spring was upon them and, thus, a comrade Zhila from SNK UkrSSR had this idea for the apartments: "Those buildings given over for settlement by the decision of the TsK and SNK, this is no dogma.... Just give us your ideas on the matter: where we should not put anyone; where they have taken apartments and hold them under lock and key; [where they are] not resettling them and not developing them. These are things that can be decided over again."[77] But this republic-level resolution only created new problems for Kyiv's local leaders due to other decisions the Stalin regime was making.

The main matter complicating the Ukrainians' resettlement plans was continued mass return to the city. Initially, these returns likely resembled a story told in 1946 by Dina Pronicheva, a Jewish woman then in her early thirties, to the Commission on the History of the Patriotic War in Ukraine. After being liberated by the troops of the advancing Red Army in the fall of 1943, she returned to her hometown in December to look for her children. After months of searching, she went to see a group of children brought from western Ukraine to the city's Solomenka neighborhood and recognized her daughter, Lydochka Pronicheva. "At first, she hugged me. Then she stopped, for her father had always said to her, 'If you meet your mom on the street, say aunty or else they will shoot us all.' But she hugged me again. And then she stopped and said, 'aunty.' Then when I said, 'Little one, now it is alright to say Mama,' she threw herself at me and, clinging to my neck, cried, 'Mamochka.' What took place next was a touching scene. Everyone around us cried."[78]

Due to new streams of people returning to the city, however, those "organizations necessary for the capital, the Academy of Sciences, the laureates of the Stalin prizes, the people's artists, and, in general, the workers of scholarship" were already having trouble finding housing according to the May 9, 1944, "apartment question" meeting mentioned above. The Kyiv City Soviet Chairman, Lebed', explained there why not all of the latter people could be "banished" in the following manner: "If the family of a serviceman has arrived from the active army we cannot send them anywhere. They go to the Military Procurator and he writes, 'Give them a living permit.'" But a voice called out from among the meeting-goers asking, "What is the soldier's relationship to Kyiv?" Lebed' answered, "It is the fact that he lived here before the war. And there is the ukaz of the all-union Supreme Soviet of August 5, 1941, which says the living space of the families of servicemen is bonded to them."[79] This latter *ukaz*, passed jointly with SNK SSSR on the same day and entitled "On the Preservation of the Housing Fund of Servicemen and the Order for the Payment for Housing Space by Servicemen's Families during Wartime," was to play a huge role in Kyiv's history during the years ahead.

For now, the competing prerogatives of Ukraine's leadership and the Red Army vis-à-vis Kyiv's resettlement created confusion for city- and oblast-level authorities. The military seems to have had the upper hand as its confidence grew with good news from the front. A little later in the meeting, for example, another voice called out, "The city of Kanash, in the Chuvash Autonomous Soviet Socialist Republic (RSFSR), has sent, without any summons, 240 families of servicemen."[80] Further remarks from Chairman Lebed' paint a similar picture: "Red Army men and invalids are writing to the All-Union People's Commissariat of Defense that their families are not given living permits. Then the commissariat gives them permission [to enter the city] as the families of servicemen. They travel here. And we are required to satisfy them. The day before yesterday from the Rokossovskii Front [the Second Belorussian Front], 1,800 families arrived. What kind of people are these? They are all former Kyivans."[81]

Comments here by the Lenin Raikom secretary, Nezhinskii, are particularly revealing about how unprecedented the uncoordinated arrival of servicemen's dependents was during the latter part of the war. After stating that, "In essence, the capital is being settled all over again," the leader of Kyiv's most centrally located raion continued, "I, at my own fear and risk, have conducted such conversations with servicemen: 'Once you are out of the army and sent to Kyiv, then we will give you an apartment. As for now, I wish you good health.' More than from anyone else, we are under siege from servicemen in military units located in the rear."[82]

Raising the stakes further for the local Communists was the rumor that Red Army men by the hundreds had appropriated apartments for themselves in the city after they had liberated it.[83] And Komarov now spoke of the many Kyivans who had once worked for the Germans, then taken better housing during the occupation, and who now presented themselves as the families of servicemen because their men had been drafted. For that reason, it was also hard to evict them in the face of the August 5, 1941, ukaz. Stalin's war of attrition had created a confused totalitarian state.

Korniets concluded his remarks by saying, "A general walked in to see me and said it was easier for him to break through the German defenses than it was to see the chairman of the raion soviet. These are just the buds on the tree, but the berries could be very sour if we do not do something about this matter."[84] Making matters worse was another rumor that arriving party members and soviet workers, who had once occupied single rooms before the war, were now commandeering empty three-room apartments for themselves.[85] How the local Communists relieved the indigestion caused by these "sour berries" is one story this book seeks to tell.

The new leader of the Temporary Commission for the Regulation of Entrance into the City of Kyiv, Tabulevich, concluded with this information: "Some specialists who sell permissions to enter the city have been found in Kyiv. One hairstylist with eleven family members got in for 10,000 rubles.... The wife of a worker petitioned for three months to enter. Near the Kyiv City Soviet, she met one of these 'fixers' [*maklery*] who said to her, 'I feel sorry just looking at you. I would get things done but the leadership takes no less than 10,000 rubles.'"[86] Upon hearing this, the secretary of the Kyiv Gorkom, Mokienko, remained defiantly optimistic about recreating the Kyiv of the 1930s: "We need to remember that this is the capital. Here there was a population of 997,000 and now there is the destruction of the housing fund. We want to make a capital city; there is this decision, ten square meters per person. We need to make a capital city in the fullest sense of that word. Therefore, we need to try and save that space that we have. Those who have come here without permission should not be allowed in. Allow only the organized entrance into Kyiv like there is for Moscow and Leningrad."[87] Mokienko wanted to harden even further the regime's stance toward returnees.

But at meeting's end, when Korniets, the republic-level leader, issued a string of verbal commands laying out a comprehensive strategy for how the Kyivan authorities should regulate access to their regime city, the hardline became less visible. In fact, Korniets's opinion on how to treat such returnees reflected the Ukrainian government's acceptance that they would have to put up with Moscow's line. "People here regard these [returnee] types quite badly," Korniets began. "They look at them as some sort of burden that is strangling us. But remember, these people lived in the city and they are returning here and this is how they are met. I am not for opening the doors for entrance to all, but we need to take a look at whom we need. To whom we should be giving permission and to whom we should not."[88]

A SNK UkrSSR resolution of May 11, 1944, organized a "reevacuation point" in the city of Kharkiv for the greeting and distribution of the Ukrainian Republic's population from the eastern oblasts of the USSR. But in Kyiv's case, GKO-backed groups were still to be allowed into the city. Meanwhile, the resettlement of individual returnees in Kyiv would remain the responsibility of the Temporary Commission.[89] Kyiv's republic-level leadership had kept the city open because of Moscow's need to placate the Red Army, and because of the Stalin regime's apparent lack of concern over social dislocation within its damaged, formerly occupied territories. Neither employment nor a set place to live was yet needed for a permit to enter the Ukrainian capital.

By August 1944, though, further unmandated returns provoked another effort to satisfy Mokienko's desire for vigilance. Such a return was highlighted in a July 17, 1944, Ukrainian NKVD memo to the Ukrainian TsK's Department of Cadres, which stated, "The facts noted about the arrival to the Transport Signal Factory [*Transsignal*] of a group of persons who are not specialists have been completely confirmed. The assistant for cadres, comrade Gornsthein, sent on a trip to Tashkent to dispatch equipment and cadre workers of this factory to Kyiv, used fictitious identification cards to bring back with him the following people who have nothing to do with the factory."[90] The memorandum then listed eleven names and recommended that Gornsthein be fired. With it was a report from the factory's director, who had given an order to have anyone who arrived illegally fired and sent to "the jurisdiction of those organizations from which they arrived or beyond the limits of Kyiv Oblast."[91]

This incident was later mentioned in a new August 5, 1944, SNK UkrSSR and Ukrainian TsK resolution, "On the Measures for the Temporary Limitation of Entrance of Citizens into the City of Kyiv." This decision concentrated on the actions of the Temporary Commission and supplied new orders for how it was to work. With GKO still regulating organized return, the resolution instructed Kyiv's leaders about what to do with everyone else: "[Do not] give permission to enter and to live here to persons arriving in the city in an unorganized manner: without a transfer, agreement, or invitation to work here by an institution, organization, or enterprise. Exceptions to this rule go to invalids of the Patriotic War who previously lived in the city of Kiev, and also to families of servicemen who lived in the city of Kiev at the moment the serviceman was drafted into the Red Army, the Navy, or the troops of the all-union NKVD, if the families are secured with living space in the city."[92] The exceptions mentioned reflected Moscow's desire that those associated with the Soviet military be given preferential treatment. Although servicemen were technically "unorganized," they were still "secured with living space" by the All-Union Supreme Soviet ukaz of August 5, 1941. And while the resolution tried to limit the numbers of servicemen and their families eligible for these exceptions (for tens of thousands of Kyivan men had joined the Red Army voluntarily in the summer of 1941), the August 5, 1941, ukaz was almost universally believed to apply to all who served. This new sense of privilege among those associated with the military meant that, even as housing space in Kyiv remained hotly contested, thousands of servicemen's dependents would take advantage of this porous system and descend on the Ukrainian capital.

The August 5, 1944, resolution did initiate a renewed effort to purge Kyiv of the "socially dangerous" already in the city. But the change in the Stalin regime's focus was now plainly discernible as local authorities learned, step-by-step, why the "laws of wartime" could also limit purging if they so desired. On July 21, 1944, Vasilii Riasnoi, Sergei Savchenko, and the Ukrainian procurator, Roman Rudnenko, wrote a memorandum to the head of the Ukrainian republic's new People's Commissariat of Defense, Gerasimenko (who was also the Kyiv Military Region's commander). In the letter, they listed seven categories of people to be deported from Kyiv in order for it to be considered unsullied by the "socially dangerous."[93] They wanted Gerasimenko to give them the authority to evict beyond a 50-kilometer radius of Kyiv any suspicious types who had settled in the city during the Nazi occupation. The basis for doing so, they contended, was the All-Union Supreme Soviet ukaz that established martial law in localities deemed important for the defense of the homeland on the night the Germans invaded.

The seven categories selected for eviction were subsequently divided into three groups. The first group was those families with a member who had been convicted of anti-Soviet activities, had left voluntarily with the Germans, had formerly served in the Germans' punishment and administrative organs, or had been among the "collaborators, spies, and traitors shot without trial by the advancing units of the Red Army and partisans."[94] In the second group were people and their families arrested but not yet repressed by the Ukrainian NKGB/NKVD for the above activities, as well as women who had lived with German occupiers or collaborators. The third group included people and their families who fell under limitations enacted by the all-union Passport Statute of 1940. This last group consisted mainly of relatives of people who had served time for all manner of crimes (from inciting hatred and strife and speculation to the keeping of brothels and the selling of firearms) and those who had arrived in Kyiv during the occupation itself.

Seven days later, Gerasimenko's Kyiv Military Region issued an order that sought to satisfy the demands.[95] But the Ukrainian NKGB of the Kyiv Oblast quickly protested this in a letter to the Kyiv Military Region procurator, Ryzhkov, who was supposed to inform his comrades in the republic-level leadership about the illegality of the above resolution. The letter's author, a Comrade Nosov, noted the reason for this:

> One cannot indiscriminately evict the families of those convicted of counter-revolutionary crimes. This contradicts the GKO resolution 1926 of June 24, 1942, in accordance with which the families of traitors sentenced to be shot are subject to repression. Families of traitors sentenced to be shot who have in their ranks a serviceman, a partisan, someone who aided the Red Army or the partisans during the occupation, or someone who received an order or medal are not subject to repression. In each concrete case it is necessary to examine the personnel of the family in order not to evict those families who have among them servicemen, partisans, and those who have citations of merit from Soviet power.[96]

Nosov also counseled caution in the evictions of other people mentioned in the decree. For example, the government could not evict the family members of those yet to have been found guilty of committing anti-Soviet activity. In other cases, "incontrovertible proof" of suspicious arrival under the Germans (or of voluntary departure with them) was needed for the evictions of individuals or whole families to take place. Even the eviction of women who lived with Germans could only happen if "incontrovertible proof" of voluntary sex existed.

As a result, the Kyiv Military Region leadership passed a new order on September 6, 1944. Again, based on the All-Union Supreme Soviet ukaz of June 22, 1941, this resolution created six categories of people for eviction beyond the 50-kilometer zone around Kyiv:

> The families of persons convicted of treason and other political crimes, the families of persons who voluntarily left with the German-Fascist occupants, the families of persons shot without trial or investigation by transit units of the Red Army and party brigades for treason and treachery, women who co-habited with the occupants, people who lived in the city or the 50-kilometer zone around the city during the occupation if it could be confirmed that this was because of connections with the Germans or because of suspicious reasons for their arrival, and the families of persons convicted of banditry, battery, thievery, and the stealing of socialist property by the law of August 7, 1932.[97]

But in deference to the Ukrainian NKGB demand, the families of all the aforementioned people were not subject to eviction if it could be proved that they had aided or were aiding Soviet power in some way. The earlier order's stipulation about evicting people before decisions were rendered about their activities was also dropped.

This bureaucratic trail reflects the relative softening of the Stalin regime toward the formerly occupied. Finding bodies for the Red Army was paramount, and the Ukrainian NKGB wanted to make that point clear. As long as able-bodied men joined the war effort, their families could continue to live in the city without trouble. The Stalin regime's needs for survival meant that the Soviet Union was no longer the same place it had been in the 1930s.

A glimpse of the ensuing problems with resettlement was visible at a meeting of the Kyiv Gorkom on September 14, 1944. A Comrade Tepliakov, the assistant head of Kyiv's draft board, commented, "Right now we have several hundred families of military men who do not have apartments. We know why they are in the city. Right now, they are located with their neighbors at the train station or in the corridor. In a month, events will be out of control here, and everyone should draw his own conclusions about what the aftermath of these events will be."[98] The SNK UkrSSR and Ukrainian TsK passed a resolution on September 21 entitled "On the Work of the Kharkiv Reevacuation Point." This resolution declared hopefully that the main mass of the population scheduled to return had already reached Ukraine.[99]

The work of the reevacuation point was to cease on October 15, and from that point on, permission for anyone to proceed to Kyiv could only come from the Southern Railroad's police force. Later that fall, on November 15, GKO passed another resolution prohibiting the reevacuation of people to the Ukrainian capital without its permission until April 1, 1945 (later extended until May 15).[100] The city's Temporary Commission, however, was kept alive, which shows Moscow's desire that Kyiv be kept open for resettlement. The numbers involved were meant to be small, but there remained an opening to the city. Servicemen and their families, as well as the Soviet military itself continued to exploit this opening to return to Kyiv. And as a victorious Soviet army marched west, the result was to be a regime city unlike the one to which the Ukrainian Communists were accustomed.

Resettlement and *Orgnabor* Laborers

What the Ukrainian Communists learned about the labor supply after the Nazi occupation is central to comprehending their management of Kyiv's resettlement. As the city filled up, the Stalin regime ordered the "organized recruitment" (*orgnabor*) of laborers from farflung oblasts to help with reconstruction. The latter were "notionally freely hired" but "subject to labor contracts, which greatly restricted their movement."[101] Kyiv's leaders hoped that these workers would put up with the difficult living conditions on building sites while materials were allotted for housing reconstruction. In most cases, the orders for such mobilizations issued from GKO in Moscow, before they were reaffirmed by republic-level governments.

Local authorities were then obliged to fulfill these resolutions. Union-level industries received priority access to this labor, especially near the war's end, when supplementary resolutions were issued after reported shortfalls. It took a while, however, for the Ukrainian Communists to recognize that their capital's reconstruction was not one of Moscow's priorities.

Initially, of course, there was free labor in Kyiv, and the Stalin regime permitted local authorities leeway to act on this. On December 29, 1943, for example, the Kyiv Obkom mobilized ten thousand young people from the oblast's recently liberated areas to help dismantle ruins on the Khreshchatyk.[102] Kyiv's Committee of Soviet Youth (*Komsomol*) did not take charge at this point of the Khreshchatyk's reconstruction.[103] By February 1944 the resolution was only 35 percent fulfilled and a thousand of the youth who were mobilized subsequently deserted.[104] In an effort to help out, the Kyiv Gorkom temporarily mobilized eight thousand Kyivans from the city's regions on February 18, 1944, for the dismantling.[105]

But as the German Luftwaffe sporadically bombed Kyiv's railway junctions and bridge projects during the winter and spring of 1943–44, this "people's building" (*narodnaia stroika*) campaign on the Khreshchatyk was short-lived.[106] Ukraine's leaders soon placed more hope on the workers of the Special Construction-Assembly Unit (an organization staffed by men of draft age considered unfit for military service) No. 305, belonging to the newly created, and union-level approved, People's Commissariat of Housing and Civilian Construction (NKZhGS) UkrSSR, which would be a dedicated labor supply for projects like the Khreshchatyk.[107] On February 27, 1944, SNK UkrSSR allowed that commissariat to mobilize thirty thousand people from across central Ukraine (although only two thousand were supposed to be from Kyiv) for civilian reconstruction with five thousand of these destined for the Ukrainian capital.[108] It seems doubtful, though, that such numbers were ever mobilized, for there were repeated attempts during 1944 to mobilize thirty thousand workers for NKZhGS UkrSSR following the failures of prior resolutions.

Such resolutions, however, reveal that ordinary Kyivans were rarely mobilized for full-time work restoring their hometown during this period. The few examples include a March 1944 SNK UkrSSR resolution ordering the union-level Stalin Ship-Building Factory restored and nine hundred people mobilized from the city's population to advance this process, and an August 1944 Kyiv Gorkom resolution ordering the mobilization of several thousand unemployed Kyivans for work at the city's two union-level passenger wagon repair factories and an electric company.[109] But temporary mobilizations of Kyivans did occur if they helped to keep citizens somewhat warm and fed. On July 2, 1944, SNK UkrSSR obliged the city's authorities to mobilize six thousand Kyivans from the city's nonworking and working populations for the preparation and delivery of 300,000 stacked cubic meters (*skladometers*) of firewood for the upcoming winter.[110] As for the

"The Capital Is Being Settled All Over Again"   41

Figure 1.3. Kyivans sort the ruins of the Khreshchatyk, unknown date. Reproduced by permission from the H. Pshenychnyi Central State CinePhotoPhono Archives of Ukraine.

harvest, on July 1, 1944, the Kyiv Gorkom (fulfilling an order that had begun at the republic level) ordered another six thousand Kyivans into Kyiv Oblast from the city's nonworking population to help collect the wood.[111]

Such limited mobilization reveals Moscow's desire to shield Kyiv's population amid a stressful time. Unprepared to directly ask large numbers within the Ukrainian capital to sacrifice further for the reconstruction effort, it appears that the Kremlin hoped Kyivans would latch on to employment at enterprises and institutions that the government had already planned for rebuilding. When that reconstruction stalled due to a lack of resources, however, Moscow's shielding of Kyiv's population, combined with its reluctance to prevent unorganized return, created stress for local authorities. Such was the situation in which new ideas to relegitimize Soviet power after the war would gain force.

Mobilization into the army continued. The annual draft recommenced on June 7, 1944, obliging young men born in 1927 to appear at their local raion draft boards within two weeks.[112] Such a step was actually a return to normalcy; when the Kyiv Obkom's Military Department reported on its activities during the first half of 1944, it noted insufficient leadership by the city's draft board had meant draft-dodging, the granting of draft delays, and illegal reservations becoming rife in the city.[113] According to the report, the city's draft board eventually uncovered

2,724 people illegally reserved at enterprises and institutions. Perhaps this report's mention of Ukrainian NKVD *massoperatsii*s unearthing three thousand people in the city said to be avoiding the draft or having deserted the Red Army meant they were essential to finding Kyivans for the front.[114] Whatever the case, the completion of this work to fulfill an All-Union People's Commissariat of Defense resolution would require the work of over fifteen thousand people from across the spectrum of the city's leadership to the undertake "monthly planned round-ups" needed to fulfill it. Such efforts point to the possibility that already, as of 1944, many people resettling in Kyiv were doing little for the cause.

The *orgnabor* of non-Kyivans also failed to provide the city with labor because of the low priority of its projects on the Stalin regime's mobilization totem pole. On June 12, 1944, SNK UkrSSR and the Ukrainian TsK issued another resolution about the securing of thirty thousand workers for NKZhGS UkrSSR by the end of June, as the February resolution had been only 10 percent fulfilled.[115] Unfortunately, this resolution, which obliged mobilization as far west as Ternopil' Oblast for the city's housing reconstruction, was never fulfilled either.[116] What happened later as this commissariat kept trying to mobilize in Ukraine's west, despite the fighting there between the internal troops of the All-Union NKVD and Ukrainian nationalists of various stripes, is covered in the next chapter.[117]

Meanwhile, GKO-backed orders mandating the mobilization of rural Ukrainians for the reconstruction of Kyiv's other destroyed industries were rarely carried out to completion. The Darnytsa Wagon Repair Factory, for example, was supposed to receive five hundred peasants from the right-bank raions of the oblast according to a Kyiv Obkom resolution of March 28, 1944, but by September, only had 252 of the 722 workers it needed.[118] Other GKO-based resolutions that spring were meant to restore the woodworking and building materials industries in Kyiv.[119] But this did not mean that labor was found, as one instructor of the Kyiv Gorkom's Department of Construction testified in September 1944: "For the reconstruction of the [building materials] factory 300 people will be needed including qualified workers/ carpenters, lathe operators, turners, and joiners. At present, the factory has 142 workers—116 of whom are non-specialized women-workers." The instructor then concluded, "The *orgnabor* plan has gone unfulfilled and that influences the fulfillment of the plan for the factory's reconstruction."[120] Together with the Stalin regime's reluctance to mobilize Kyivans, these were signs that the Ukrainian capital's reconstruction would take a very long time.

Despite the thousands of people streaming toward the Ukrainian capital in 1944, the Kremlin still went looking for other sources of labor for the rebuilding work. One idea was the September 11, 1944, SNK UkrSSR and Ukrainian TsK resolution that mobilized eighty thousand urban and rural school-aged children into two-year trade vocational schools (*remeslennoe uchilishche;* RU), railroad vocational schools (*zheleznodorozhnoe uchilishche;* ZhU), and six-month factory training schools (*shkola fabrichno-zavodskogo obucheniia;* FZO) across Ukraine.[121] Through this resolution, the Kyivan authorities learned that five RU/ZhU and nine FZO schools were scheduled to open in their city. Some 1,300 students from within the city and 800 from the oblast were to receive training in these institutions.

The Kyiv Obkom follow-up resolution obliged the local party and soviet organizations "to take first of all those youth who neither work nor study and who live in cities. If the drafted youth who neither work nor study do not complete the fulfillment of this task, it is permissible to draft schoolchildren from the schools of the Ukrainian People's Commissariat of Education and the People's Commissariat of Transportation, especially youth from the eighth, ninth, and tenth classes."[122] It is difficult to imagine that many parents wanted their offspring to head in this direction. Then on September 14, SNK UkrSSR and Ukrainian TsK issued another resolution that called for the opening of eleven factories in Kyiv, six of them with sizable FZOs manned with students from out of town. Here was the revitalization of Kyiv's light industry, at least on paper.[123] In one stroke, Kyiv's three major textile factories—Gorky, Smirnov-Lastochkina, and Roza Luxemburg—were scheduled to reopen, as were its two major shoe factories. But who was intended to work at these places other than a few hundred children is not clear.

Although these moves do hint at the mobilization of sizable numbers of people from rural Ukraine, very few of them were headed toward the Ukrainian capital. Kyiv Oblast's role within the Soviet mobilization effort, in particular, meant even fewer of its workers were available for work in Kyiv. The role of this massive rural area (it included today's Cherkask Oblast as well), with its depleted population (159,000 of its people were sent to Germany during the war), would become to supply agricultural and forestry goods to both the front and the capital city.[124] For example, an April 11, 1944, SNK UkrSSR and Ukrainian TsK resolution ordered Kyiv Oblast's leaders to mobilize six hundred people for timber transport during the "navigation season" along the Dnipro.[125] Only for the most pressing of needs—in this case, supplying the capital city with firewood—did Moscow order its Ukrainian conduits to permanently mobilize people away from Kyiv Oblast's fields. This meant Kyiv's already well-guarded population was now surrounded by an agricultural heartland whose people the Stalin regime was also reluctant to mobilize.

Another example of the lack of mobilization was the May 13, 1944, SNK UkrSSR and Ukrainian TsK resolution ordering the mobilization of thirty thousand people from centrally located oblasts for two months to work on the republic's railroads.[126] With Kyiv Oblast spared, the authorities in Odesa Oblast needed to find seven thousand people by May 25. On the very same day, the Ukrainian authorities issued another resolution that mobilized 16,700 people from right- and left-bank Ukraine to "secure the uninterrupted work of the enterprises of the All-Union People's Commissariat of Ferrous Metallurgy in the second quarter of 1944."[127] With Kyiv Oblast going unmentioned once again, this resolution ordered the mobilization of 7,700 people from Rivne Oblast alone. Two further resolutions issued that summer continued this broad effort to reconstruct the union-level metallurgy industry in Ukraine, but here again Kyiv Oblast was skirted.[128]

Kyiv Oblast, however, was not spared in resolutions to mobilize people for the union-level Donbas coal industry. Here was a mobilization campaign that taught Kyiv's leaders much about *orgnabor*. A May 11, 1944, SNK UkrSSR and Ukrainian TsK resolution included Kyiv Oblast in a permanent mobilization order for 36,300 people from six right-bank oblasts, although the capital's oblast only had to supply 600 of them.[129] But on August 15, 1944, the Ukrainian government asked Kyiv Oblast and the rest of liberated Ukraine—as far west as Ternopil' Oblast—to find 63,800 more workers for the Donbas during the third quarter of 1944. According to the resolution in question, this was because "the achieved level of coal extraction in the Donbas appears already to be completely insufficient in the face of sharply accelerated demand for coal by those industries and railroads undergoing reconstruction in the regions of the south liberated from the Germans as well as in the central industrial regions of the Soviet Union."[130] Kyiv Oblast was responsible for finding 6,300 of these men.

The resolution also expressed why these people needed to be found quickly: "If left unsolved, any further reconstruction of metallurgy, the railroads, and the electrical stations is inconceivable. Therefore, the reconstruction of the coal industry of the Donbas should be carried out first of all, before the other branches of industry."[131] But the last time a resolution included Kyiv Oblast in any permanent mobilization order—even for the Donbas—occurred on November 5, 1944. The SNK UkrSSR and Ukrainian TsK pleaded with the oblast to find an unspecified portion of the 43,000 peasants scheduled to be found for the eastern coal mines. The resolution also bluntly stated that mobilizations for the All-Union People's Commissariat of Coal should take place before any other commissariat. Meanwhile, finding any labor amid the fighting that now embroiled western Ukraine was to become very problematic.

The inclusion of the troubled western Ukrainian oblasts in resolutions that concerned mobilization for the secondary industries of the Donbas like metallurgy now ended completely. On November 6, 1944, for example, a resolution entitled "On the Mobilization of Labor Power in the Fourth Quarter of 1944 for Work in the Enterprises of the People's Commissariat of Ferrous Metallurgy" called for rounding up 18,250 people from only Ukraine's eastern and central oblasts.[132] The absence of the western oblasts is further apparent in a resolution changing the process of mobilization into FZO schools from November 18.[133] The mobilization of youth from Volyn, L'viv, Rivne, and Stanislav Oblasts was no longer considered necessary; the six thousand people needed were to come from the more centrally located Vinnytsa and Kirovohrad Oblasts. The only organization still receiving *orgnabor* from western Ukraine at this point was the All-Union People's Commissariat of Coal.

Such decisions coincided with the scheduled return of millions of repatriated Soviet citizens from Europe to their mostly rural places of residence in Ukraine. This must be why Soviet authorities instilled so much fear in those "displaced persons" previously found beyond the country's borders. The Stalin regime probably expected that such cowed people would need little prodding toward work if they were largely allowed to normally reintegrate into Soviet life. Indeed, the number of resolutions calling for the mobilization of people in Ukraine decreased after the arrival of the repatriated. Kyiv clearly needed such repatriates. While little had been done to reconstruct the capital, the GKO-mandated resolutions reveal that the city's population, and that of its surrounding oblast, largely escaped mobilization—a further example of the Kremlin's wartime leniency with regards to the resettlement of this regime city. The unscheduled arrival of the unorganized returnees from the east, however, was going to complicate matters for Kyiv's authorities at all levels.

Chapter Two

"There Was No Real Battle against Illegal Entry"

Resettlement from Fall 1944 to Fall 1946

From Sverdlovsk Oblast (RSFSR) in the heart of the Ural Mountains, thirteen employees of Kyiv's evacuated Gorky Textile Factory wrote these lines to Nikita Khrushchev in September 1944:

> During the time of our residence in Kizel', the factory collective has lost a number of highly qualified workers due to difficult climatic and material conditions. Some of these people have become invalids; others have been transferred on orders of the People's Commissariat to other factories to save their lives. The rest of the remaining collective, when it comes down to it, has been weakened. Many workers and technicians are sick with tuberculosis and dystrophy. To save the lives of their families, a number of them have sent their children, mothers and fathers, and wives, back to the homeland, to Ukraine, and naturally aspire to return there themselves.[1]

The workers' alarm made sense: the All-Union NKVD's Main Directorate of the Militia had just noted a "significant rise in the death rate" in the Urals compared to the year before.[2] In response, Khrushchev pressed Moscow for the workers' reevacuation just as unorganized return was becoming the rule in the Soviet Union's rear.

On October 21, 1944, however, the All-Union People's Commissariat of Machine Building replied to Khrushchev that such a reevacuation was impossible.[3] According to the commissariat, the workers in Kizel' were now part of a highly successful factory collective. The rebuilding of the Gorky Textile Factory would have to be done "on account of the transfer of a certain number of qualified workers and technicians from other machine-building factories and the mobilization of workers from the local population." Conditions in the Urals, though, were not improving. By 1944's end, the All-Union NKVD noted again a rising death rate there from dystrophy, pellagra, and "exhaustion."[4]

The Ukrainian Communists' understanding of Kyiv's place within the Soviet state improved once they learned that the reevacuation of skilled workers was so difficult. But what did they learn *after* all those mobilized rural Ukrainians discussed in chapter 1 reported to their construction sites? The Stalin regime's choice to settle German POWs in Kyiv certainly did not lead to housing reconstruction there. The local Communists would thus maintain their hardline attitude toward unorganized returnees from the east even as tens (if not hundreds) of thousands of such people now joined with *Ostarbeitery* and demobilized soldiers arriving from the west. The leaders' sudden offer, however, of amnesty to these "illegal immigrants" after the announcement of the Fourth Five-Year Plan in March 1946 reveals their opportunism.

What local Communists needed most of all was an orderly and productive Kyiv prepared for whatever further resources the center granted it. They eagerly responded to the Fourth Five-Year Plan's signal that the focus on defeating the Germans had ended by closing their city to unorganized returnees. However, the atmosphere created by the resettlement and reconstruction they had overseen would need to be accounted for if they were to effectively lead the city. The social dislocation would later impact the state-society relationship in mid-1940s Kyiv. And while the Ukrainian capital remained a "regime city of the first category," the manner of its resettlement would suggest that the meaning behind this term was now shaped by the war more than anything else.

Resettlement and *Orgnabor* Laborers

After the announcements of the mobilization orders discussed in chapter 1, the Ukrainian authorities' task was to fulfill them. An April 7, 1944, telegram to Khrushchev from the director of the Voroshilovgrad Coal Trust, K. Pochenkov, reveals how difficult this was to do—even for those enterprises tied to heavy industries of union-level importance. The telegram noted that of the 38,277 workers the trust had recently mobilized to the Donbas, 10,495 had already deserted. Pochenkov observed, "One of the basic reasons for desertion is the mass recall of mobilized persons from the sides of the raion and village soviets, and directors of the collective farms from which these workers have arrived.... We ask you, Nikita Sergeeivich, to give the necessary directives from your side of things."[5] A December 26, 1941, All-Union Supreme Soviet ukaz had decreed that all deserters from "defense-related industry" should be tried by military tribunals and, if convicted, face up to eight years in All-Union NKVD labor camps.[6]

Information reaching Kyiv later that summer about the labor supply in the Donbas was troubling. An August 1944 report to the Ukrainian TsK from the military tribunal of the Ukrainian NKVD claimed that although 34,376 workers had arrived at Voroshilovgrad Coal during the first six months of 1944, another 38,780 had deserted at the same time. The tribunal's chairman, a Lieutenant Vasiutinskii, commented on this phenomenon: "These deserters are not hiding anywhere. They are quietly working on collective farms, state farms, machine tractor stations, or not working at all but merely living at their homes in the villages. On July 17, 1944, Ukraine's Assistant Procurator laid out the data before us and said an official search would be undertaken for 20,000 deserters. But if most of these people are to be found in Ukraine's agricultural oblasts, is it not possible to ask why so few of them are caught and put before tribunals?"[7] Vasiutinskii's comments reflect the Ukrainian leadership's attempt to fulfill a June 29, 1944, SNK SSSR resolution that had called for an "ending of the insufficiencies" of the December 26, 1941, All-Union Supreme Soviet ukaz just mentioned.[8]

But "ending the insufficiencies" generally did not mean punishing deserters. On August 15, 1944, the Ukrainian procurator, Rudnenko, wrote to Demian Korotchenko (a top Ukrainian TsK secretary who would occupy various posts in the party and government after the war) about renewed efforts to curtail desertion, arguing that they had "brought about, judging by the data we have on hand, an increase in the number of cases of those who left of their own accord from enterprises (primarily collective farm women and teenagers) and returned to those same enterprises." Rudnenko then pointedly asked Korotchenko, "In connection with that, a question emerges: Does it make sense to apply the December 26, 1941, ukaz to these people and to hand them over to military tribunals?"[9] Without waiting for a reply, the Ukrainian procurator answered his own question by suggesting the following: why not prosecute these people for violating the more lenient April 26, 1940, All-Union Supreme Soviet ukaz, "On the Changeover from the Eight-Hour Work Day to the Seven-Day Work Week and on the Prohibition of Truancy by Workers and Employees from Institutions"?

He voiced his justification for this earlier resolution's lighter sentencing (it called for six months in the camps, rather than eight years) this way: "I suggest that an additional reason for putting forth this question might be that the December 26, 1941, ukaz was issued at a time when almost the entire territory of Ukraine was temporarily occupied by the German-Fascist invaders, and thus a significant portion of the population did not hear about its contents."[10] While Moscow refused to support this idea, Korotchenko later wrote to Stalin's henchman in the Kremlin, Georgii Malenkov, to say that only 10,829 desertions were reported to the Ukrainian procuracy in August, compared with 19,436 a month earlier. But instead of pointing to the effort to try these persons in military tribunals, Korotchenko highlighted other reasons for the declining number of desertions: "A significant role in attaching workers to production has been played by the opening of workers' credit for housing and individual building, the distribution of land for gardens, the offering of material aid toward the movement of families, measures to improve catering, and the creation of cultured dormitories."[11]

The Ukrainian TsK leader also questioned the expediency of sending people to the camps. "In a number of cases, the heads of enterprises appealed to the military tribunals for the closure of deserters' cases and for trying them under the law on truancy."¹² But a memorandum written at the same time from the Zaporiz'ka Obkom secretary to the Ukrainian TsK kept to a hard line: "The Obkom and the Executive Committee of the Oblast Soviet condemn the harmful practice of those leaders of village soviets and collective farms who distribute memos to mobilized workers announcing when their work in the Donbas is to end.... The result is that workers abandon work and return to the village on their own accord."¹³ New reasons to keep workers on the job were created in response.

An August 27, 1944, SNK SSSR and Ukrainian TsK resolution that sought to attract labor for reconstruction on a contract basis was one such effort. This resolution ordered Ukraine's oblast leaders to oblige their raion leaders and collective farm directorates "to send from each collective farm for work in the coal industry of the Donbas, one to two farm workers for a period of time lasting from six months to a year with the guarantee of unhindered return to the collective farm following the expiration of that time period, and then to replace those returnees with new workers for the same period of time."¹⁴ Another tactic involved granting new privileges to those mobilized, such as the May 31, 1944, SNK UkrSSR and Ukrainian TsK resolution entitled "On the Patronage [*shevstvo*] of the Oblasts of Ukraine over the Coal Trusts of the Donbas."¹⁵ But although the Communists tried to supply the Donbas with people, food, and materials, there is no evidence that any of these efforts made *orgnabor* more effective.

A reason for this failure can be found in a September 4, 1944, "Report Note" from the Ukrainian NKVD Military Tribunal in Dnipropetrovs'k Oblast, which recounts the "social-biographical data" of those convicted for deserting from "defense-related industry." According to the captain of justice, Zelenskii, "The vast majority of deserters are not full-time workers, but those mobilized for the period of the war from the villages.... A significant number of deserters are housewives and youth who have never before worked anywhere else.... Mass desertions took place in January–March, right after the beginning of the rural population's mobilization for the reconstruction of the metallurgical industry."¹⁶ The reasons for desertions, Zelenskii continued, included the housing shortage, lack of bread, and distance from home. Other mitigating factors included the protection offered to deserters by agricultural and industrial enterprises that took them in, the "general lack of knowledge of the laws of the land these days," and the "feeling that people are going unpunished because of stories heard out of the villages." While the Ukrainian authorities still talked of hunting down and punishing 20,000 deserters in July 1944 (against the backdrop of the larger number of desertions noted above), the number of people arrested for desertion from "defense-related industry" in July and August amounted to only 4,121.¹⁷

This bureaucratic back-and-forth culminated with the December 30, 1944, All-Union Supreme Soviet ruling granting amnesty to all people "falling under the jurisdiction of the December 26, 1941, ukaz who have voluntarily returned to their enterprises."[18] A close reading of this ukaz, however, reveals that if deserters returned before February 15, 1945, they too were to receive amnesty. In a follow-up resolution dated January 10, 1945, the SNK UkrSSR and Ukrainian TsK explained this amnesty process to the authorities in each of Ukraine's oblasts, telling them to explain it to their populations, and to then "carry out in the raions, cities, village soviets, collective farms, and state farms, a total check by summoning forth and questioning all those who have returned (based off of the lists of those once mobilized) to determine the basis for that return."[19] But the resolution also permitted those found in the villages to declare the incorrectness of their mobilization in the first place. If a medical commission could prove a person was unfit, if the composition of his or her family meant the person could be excluded, or if his or her age fell outside the legislation's framework, he or she would be allowed to stay at home.

By the time these rural dwellers voluntarily returned (if they returned at all) to their enterprises, however, the war was about to end and the local labor market was about to change with the arrival of the *Ostarbeitery*. Still, the use of punitive means to enforce mobilization during the war had largely failed.

Despite unpunished desertions, Kyiv's leaders tried to fulfill mobilization orders while they lasted, for it was expected of them and was all they could do to ready themselves should the center and its resources smile on the city once again. It was another unsuccessful effort by NKZhGS UkrSSR to mobilize peasants from western Ukraine for work on the Khreshchatyk that must have confirmed that Kyiv's needs for *orgnabor* labor to reconstruct housing were being ignored.

The NKZhGS UkrSSR effort in question began with an August 16, 1944, SNK UkrSSR and Ukrainian TsK resolution that called on it to mobilize 5,300 western Ukrainians for work in Kyiv.[20] Soon thereafter, one hundred of that commissariat's representatives headed west in hopes of finishing the mobilization by September 10. The reports they sent back testify to how difficult it was to find labor to improve Kyiv's housing situation.

NKZhGS UkrSSR's difficulties with mobilization were documented in a November 1, 1944, report written by V. U. Voiko, the commissariat's plenipotentiary in Ternopil' Oblast, about the effort to secure one thousand people for its Khreshchatyk Construction Trust (*Kreshchatikstroi*). He wrote, "We were supposed to receive, in every raion, upward of 55 to 60 people. . . . After arriving in Ternopil' Oblast, from September 1 to October 24, 1944, we mobilized just 200 people from five out of the seventeen raions we were allotted. At the meeting points, 104 people appeared, while the number that arrived at the place of work (*Kreshchatikstroi*) totals only 44. Labor mobilization is totally unsatisfactory."[21] According to Voiko, one reason for such failure was the "local atmosphere," which he described: "In the raions, the local population conceals itself from mobilization, hides from it, takes off for the forests, or sometimes escapes from the meeting points. . . . In the raions, organized groups of bandits terrorize the population and blow up government buildings. For example, in Vorshchov Raion, the railroad sent three wagons for the mobilized to Vorshchov station. Two wagons were already filled [with the mobilized], but that night a group of bandits attacked and let them out."[22]

Compared to Voiko's tribulations with the Ukrainian resistance, however, the experiences of a Comrade Pirkin, the Department of Cadres leader of the NKZhGS UkrSSR-affiliated Special Construction and Assembly Unit no. 305 (OSMCh no. 305) were even worse. After also finding himself searching for one thousand workers in Ternopil' Oblast, Pirkin and his colleagues returned without mobilizing a single person. He explained, "In the raions . . . the brigade carried out preparatory work such as the distribution of raion executive committee resolutions, and the printing of mobilization papers and summonses. . . . However, despite the fact we handed out these papers and summonses three or four times, those to be mobilized failed to appear. Furthermore, there were occasions when the papers were rejected and even ripped up by such people."[23]

A final report, this time from V. S. Efimenko, the NKZhGS UkrSSR plenipotentiary for the mobilization of labor in western Ukraine's Stanislav (later Ivano-Frankivs'k) and dated November 6, 1944, cataloged the problems of OSMCh no. 305 once again: "The summonses have yielded nothing. This is because people do not appear after receiving them. Instead, they go and hide in the forests. The raion leaderships have done nothing to bring to justice those dodging mobilization. The reason is . . . the operating groups of Banderites who kill representatives of Soviet power once they make an appearance in a village. From the group sent to carry out mobilization, one comrade, Pitomets, Stepan Stepanovich was killed by a group of Banderites on October 10, 1944, at 12:00 PM."[24] Reconstruction-oriented mobilization efforts ended when NKZhGS UkrSSR learned of the Stalin regime's order that the mobilization of Ukrainians for work in the coal enterprises of the Donbas be completed first.

Perhaps it was due to these disappointments with reconstruction that there came a renewed attempt by Ukraine's leaders to stop unorganized return to Kyiv. This effort began by trying again to ascertain just who was settling in the capital city. On December 26, 1944, SNK UkrSSR ordered a census of the nonworking, able-bodied people in the city. On January 24, 1945, the Kyiv City Soviet resolved to fulfill this resolution by employing census takers to interview building and dormitory commandants "without questioning the population."[25] Unorganized return to the city had only continued during the winter of 1944–45. Part of the reason why was the November 15, 1944, GKO resolution that had kept Kyiv's Temporary Commission for resettlement alive while prohibiting resettlement in other liberated territories without its permission.[26]

Fedor Mokienko, the new Kyiv City Soviet Chairman, and Boris Gorban, the new first secretary of the Kyiv Gorkom who took over from Mokienko there in early 1945, wrote in a memorandum to SNK UkrSSR dated April 26, "As of April 1, 1945, 478,000 people live in Kyiv (not counting those in the military), and free housing space in the city is absent. At present the organized reevacuation of workers, office staff, intelligentsia and their families, as well as that of all Kyivan enterprises, has basically finished. Because of that there is no need for the further existence of the 'Temporary Commission.'"[27] Included with this memorandum was a project resolution assigning Mokienko the power to decide who entered Kyiv.

On June 4, 1945, the Ukrainian people's commissar of justice, Babchenko, tersely seconded this idea.[28] Nine days later, the Ukrainian Assistant People's Commissar of Communal Services, Rudin, also gave his approval while clarifying the main problem with the Temporary Commission's work: "In the majority of cases, it was not indicated on the permission slips allowing entrance into Kyiv on what housing space the summoned person was to settle. After arrival, such people began to claim the housing space that they had inhabited before their evacuation. This has led to a large number of court cases."[29] These cases stemmed from one of the most important laws passed in the Soviet Union during the war: the right of servicemen's and -women's families to continue living in the apartments they had occupied before that relative departed for the front.

Rudin continued by noting that on future permission slips, the address of the housing space to be presented to the summoned person should also be stated. This, he argued, would prevent people from trying to appropriate others' living spaces. But he also argued that within the project resolution there lay the seeds for trouble: those demobilized from the army, as well as the evacuated families of servicemen, still did not need permission to enter the city from anyone but the military. Such people did not need to concern themselves with the Temporary Commission, because "those demobilized from the army and arriving in Kyiv with the accordant directive of a military commandant do not have to present memorandums about having housing space in order to receive permission for a living permit. This is because for them, housing space has been set aside by the SNK SSSR resolution of August 5, 1941. It is the same in relation to those evacuated families of servicemen inasmuch as the resolution saves for them their former living space, which they occupied before evacuation."[30] Rudin's note testifies to the powerlessness of Mokienko and Gorban in the face of the Red Army. Reconfirmation of that reality happened two months later, when SNK UkrSSR Assistant Chairman Baranovskii wrote to the Kyiv Gorkom: "SNK UkrSSR deems it necessary to retain the 'Temporary Commission for the Regulation of Entrance into the City of Kyiv' until resettlement here of demobilized Red Army men and commanders and their families who lived here before the Patriotic War."[31]

Complicating matters further for the local authorities was the impending return of the *Ostarbeitery* and demobilized soldiers. At a mid-July 1945 meeting of Kyiv Gorkom, the city's leaders heard the news from Zozulenko, the head of the SNK UkrSSR Department for Repatriation Affairs:

> We are set to return about 2,200,000 people to Ukraine . . . [and] Mironovka is the [Ukrainian NKVD Examination-Filtration Point] for the acceptance of citizens from Kyiv Oblast. But because the railroad is not satisfying requests to supply transport to points east, people are hopping on goods trains and the result is that Mironovka and especially Fastov have become bases where large numbers of people are amassing at once. In Kyiv, Moscow, and Leningrad the registration and entrance of the repatriated is completely prohibited. We do have word that a certain part of this group can be registered in Kyiv.[32]

Local leaders reacted to such confusion by stating their intention to write to the Ukrainian TsK asking that fences be put up around the junctions at Fastiv and Korosten', and that "Examination-Filtration Points" like the one at Myronivka be set up there as well. In reality, only a tiny minority of repatriates were detained at these points after a cursory check at All-Union NKVD "Reception-Distribution Points" along the pre-1939 borders of the Soviet Union.[33]

In Kyiv's case, 11,775 *Ostarbeitery* settled in the city by January 1, 1946.[34] Meanwhile, a February 1946 document shows that Kyiv Oblast was also a popular place to return to. Over 115,000 *Ostarbeitery* had arrived there by that point, compared to the 159,054 taken to Germany during the war.[35] As almost all of these people were doing some sort of "socially useful labor" soon after their return, the fact that a loophole was found for them to inhabit the Ukrainian capital makes sense. Soviet power's drumming up fear among repatriates about return probably had more to do with helping to fix the labor situation at home than has been assumed. Any solution to the labor problem, of course, meant that worries about the arrival of this limited cohort could be pushed to the side.

But the demobilized soldiers now returning to Kyiv did not become as socially useful as the *Ostarbeitery*, and local leaders remained worried. According to a report submitted to the Ukrainian TsK on March 9, 1946, by the Kyiv Obkom Military Department, some 27,000 demobilized soldiers arrived in Kyiv during 1945 and registered for reserve duty with their local draft boards as legally required.[36] But after their arrival, the commissions established to help them transition into civilian life found work for only about twelve thousand of them. The reason for this low number, the department's director, Shamaev, argued, was that some of the city's raions had failed to return to them the housing space they had occupied before mobilization into the Red Army. The former soldiers then lacked the permanent registrations in their passports, issued by the militia, necessary to secure employment.³⁷ The number of unemployed soldiers must have been alarming if one considers that by November 19, 1946, the head of the Political Directorate of the Kyiv Military Region, Savkov, could report to Degtiarev of the Ukranian TSK that there were 16,937 demobilized officers on its registration lists.³⁸ The Kyiv created by the war was no longer the malleable object in the hands of the local elite it had been before the war.

Resettlement, Unorganized Returnees, and German POWs

The Donbas mining sector's needs for *orgnabor* still outranked those of every other industry in Ukraine. To solve the labor shortage, the Stalin regime eventually resorted to the use of All-Union NKVD–managed German POWs to help rebuild the Soviet Union. In Kyiv's case, the Ukrainian authorities hoped that these prisoners would build housing for actual Kyivans as well as for the *orgnabor* laborers who the leaders thought would eventually arrive to restore the city's industrial might. But while they were thankful for the Kremlin's newfound attention, Kyiv's leaders would be disappointed to find that housing in any form—even rudimentary barracks built for factory workers by their people's commissariats—was not a priority for Moscow at this time. The Ukrainians' slow realization of this fact, combined with continued resettlement, led to dramatic efforts to close Kyiv off from the world once the Fourth Five-Year Plan signaled the Stalin regime's return to "building Communism" in March 1946.

The widespread use of POWs in Ukraine may have occurred because of reports like one from a certain Vesennyi, the *orgnabor* plenipotentiary of the union-level Donbas Anthracite Trust (*Donbassantratsit*) in Poltava Oblast, writing to the Ukrainian TsK in summer 1945. Vesennyi's report highlighted the continued difficulties for anyone not "recruiting" labor for the coal mines. Having been in the oblast since March, Vesennyi wrote to Korotchenko on July 7 about his negotiations with its raion leaders to fulfill a January 1945 SNK UkrSSR resolution to supply his organization with 2,225 people: "They declare they have no people, that no one wants to go to the Donbas, that people are running away, that the militia does not want to help, and that the decision of the Ukrainian TsK and SNK UkrSSR is something that cannot be true (*eto nerealno*)."³⁹ Based on Vesennyi's experiences, finding anyone to build housing in Kyiv would have been a near miracle.

Another reason for the recourse to POWs was that Ukrainian authorities found that many demobilized servicemen did not want to join in on reconstruction on anything but their own terms. A summer 1945 telegram from the Ukrainian TsK to each of Ukraine's oblasts, for example, noted that lists of demobilized Red Army servicemen wishing to live and work there were soon to be sent on by those military units located nearby.⁴⁰ The telegram then commanded the oblast leaders to assign these men work based on what they had done in the army, provide them with housing and vegetable gardens, and arrange for the transport of their families from wherever they might be to their new places of residence. Others in the Red Army, who could not wait for this process to be organized, wrote directly to the Ukrainian leadership with lists of men "expressing the desire to stay and work in the people's economy of Ukraine."⁴¹ In one instance, fourteen out of the fifteen expressing a desire to work in Ukraine were not originally from there.⁴² Another document from the Kyiv Garrison shows that forty out of forty-five Red Army men "expressing a desire" to remain in Ukraine had families at that moment living in the RSFSR.⁴³ Whether such people actually settled in Ukraine or Kyiv is not known, but plenty of others did, and it seems doubtful local leaders entirely welcomed them.

It also did not help the Ukrainian authorities that other skilled workers who had been evacuated to the "deep rear," such as those in Kizel' mentioned at the chapter's outset, were in no position to dictate anything to the Stalin regime. On October 16, 1945, twenty-six workers from Kyiv's evacuated Arsenal Factory in Votkinsk, Udmurtia (RSFSR), wrote to Khrushchev: "Now that the war has ended, we ask you, Nikita Sergeeivich, to help us once again to return to our homeland and to reconstruct our factory, to bring our favorite city back to its proper self, to be together with our families (many of us already sent our families back in 1944) and to work in the fashion that is demanded today by our Bolshevik Party and its leader, our beloved Stalin."⁴⁴ Despite the fact that Arsenal's "profile" had long since changed, and that it was now part of another commissariat entirely, another "complaint," dated October 26 and signed by an Ivan I. Zhuzhelytsi on behalf of all of Arsenal's "ordinary workers" living in Votkinsk, was addressed to Soviet President, Mikhail Kalinin: "The war has ended. All the demobilized have gone to their homelands. But we are held here and everyone is talking about being bonded here forever. . . . We have become impoverished, ruined; it cannot be described. We live in terrible conditions and our clothes are worn thin and come what may, we want to go home. Why should we be allowed to die here?"⁴⁵ Such pleas came to naught, however, for an instructor of the Ukrainian TsK's Machine Building Industry Department informed his superiors on April 16, 1946, that the All-Union Ministry of Armaments had decided against reevacuating these men.⁴⁶

Another letter, from a group of seven Kyivan engineers from the city's airplane factory no. 483, once evacuated to Kuibyshev and now merged with another All-Union People's Commissariat of the Aviation Industry factory, appealed to Khrushchev on April 7, 1945: "We believe it is advisable to gather together again this collective that is currently falling apart . . . for the creation of better experimental airplanes, as the workers of the factory have acquired a lot of experience in serial production during the war. . . . The former main constructor of factory no.

81, comrade Iashchenko, V.P., who has a lot of experience and knowledge when it comes to airplane construction, has been recommended as the head of the construction bureau."[47] But over a year later, the response from the Ukrainian TsK's Department of Machine Industry to Korotchenko's assistant, Aleksei Kirichenko, commented, "There is no necessity at the moment to create an experimental construction bureau for airplane construction. The all-union Ministry of Aviation Production and the Ukrainian TsK believe it unadvisable to call back the group of constructors from the former experimental factory no. 483 from the serial airplane production factory. This is because the constructor, comrade Iashchenko, is completely of another profile and cannot be used in the capacity of main constructor."[48] While Kyiv's leaders wanted to start reconstruction and find workers to assist in the task, the very people who could have effectively helped the city were prevented from doing so by what the Stalin regime found paramount: the needs of "defense-related" industries.

Considering the general lack of resources in 1945, it probably made sense to all concerned that reconstruction meant finding a more or less constant labor supply. German POWs were the best option. In Kyiv's case, over ten thousand of them had lived there the previous summer following their dramatic march down the Khreshchatyk in August 1944. In the ensuing months, some of these men worked to clear the main street's ruins, although what they did during the winter of 1944–45, as resources for Kyiv's reconstruction failed to materialize, is less clear.

How important was POW labor in the resettlement and reconstruction of the Ukrainian capital? A close look at a September 14, 1945, Kyiv Gorkom resolution about the rebuilding of some of Kyiv's most important and symbolic factories reveals the answer. According to the resolution, the yearly plans for the reconstruction of the Darnytsa-based textile factory, the Gumo-Generator light factory, and the Bol'shevik electrical factory had been met at only 21.5, 21.5, and 67 percent respectively. The reason why, according to those involved, was that the Kyiv-based All-Union NKVD Directorate of Camp no. 62, which was responsible for managing the use of prisoner laborers across the Ukrainian capital, supplied these factories with only 700 to 800 of the 3,900 POWs they were supposed to be allotted by SNK SSSR on a daily basis.[49]

Placing the blame on the All-Union NKVD was Iuryshev, the assistant head of the Ukrainian Oil Construction (*Ukrneftostroi*), who was assigned to rebuild these factories with POWs as his "main labor power," and whose memorandum to the head of the Ukrainian TsK's Department of Construction, the former Kyiv City Soviet chairman, Lebed', is found together with this resolution. According to Iuryshev, his organization had built a camp in 1944 for 4,000 POWs at the textile factory and another for 1,500 POWs at Bol'shevik, but now the Directorate of Camp no. 62 refused to supply these building sites with prisoner labor.[50] Such a situation, Iuryshev continued, had occurred despite assurances from the assistant

"There Was No Real Battle against Illegal Entry" 57

Figure 2.1. German POWs are paraded down Sofiivs'ka Street, August 16, 1944. Reproduced by permission from the H. Pshenychnyi Central State CinePhotoPhono Archives of Ukraine.

people's commissar of the All-Union NKVD, Chernyshev, that the 3,900 POWs his Kyiv representatives had originally agreed to would be supplied, and no longer parceled off to other construction projects. The result of Iuryshev's letter was another request made by Kyiv Gorkom that the Directorate of Camp no. 62 permanently increase the number of POWs working at these three factories to 3,900.

This bureaucratic back-and-forth suggests that the Stalin regime chose to rely on German POWs to shield the Ukrainian capital's population from sacrifice during times of scarcity and to prevent possible social disorder. The question then became: with what type of reconstruction would German POWs actually involve themselves? Would it be the housing construction so desperately needed, or the city's stalled production lines? Iuryshev's predicament suggests the latter, and other cases, too, show that hopes that these newly settled prisoners would build housing would lose out to the plans of the Stalin regime for rebuilding industry.

At the new "optical mechanisms" version of the Arsenal factory, for example, some 4,000 square meters of living space for the factory's workers remained to be built. According to the circumstances described in the protocols of a Kyiv Obkom resolution dated October 30, 1945, "Despite a sharp deficit of workers for construction, the prisoners of the corrective labor camp are still used for production instead of for what they were intended (the reconstruction of the factory's

Figure 2.2. A burnt-out apartment building on today's Tolstoy Square, 1944. Reproduced by permission from the H. Pshenychnyi Central State CinePhotoPhono Archives of Ukraine.

housing).... The workers who have arrived from Novosibirsk [RSFSR] in August (100 families with children) have been settled in a club that was once a firehouse, premises that are not meant for full-time inhabitation."[51] The prisoners had been meant to rebuild housing for factory workers, and without such housing, little was happening at Arsenal.

In another case, at the Construction and Assembly Directorate no. 26 of the Air Industry Construction Trust on the premises of Kyiv's two aircraft industry factories, 625 of its 1,000 "employees" were POWs as of May 27, 1946.[52] But because POWs were also active there on the production line, instead of building housing for workers, the results, according to a memorandum prepared for a condemnatory Kyiv Gorkom resolution, were that "Construction and Assembly Directorate no. 26 has not fulfilled a SNK SSSR resolution concerning the construction of housing at factories no. 473 and 485 during the first quarter of 1946. This has threatened the chances of factory no. 473 receiving 300 qualified workers."[53] Like those arriving from Novosibirsk discussed above, these were the skilled workers whom Kyiv's leaders desperately needed for the capital's economic success.

Finally, a memorandum from Vasilli Starchenko, the assistant chairman of SNK UkrSSR, to the head of the All-Union NKVD's Directorate of Camp no. 62 on January 22, 1946, about a scheduled tripling of the Lepse Tractor Factory's output in 1946 reveals how Kyiv's industrial production actually began. It reads, "To fulfill that program, the factory needs an extra 420 production workers. The factory's apprentice school will prepare 220. For securing production workers, the SNK UkrSSR asks that, from January 25, 200 POWs be given to the Lepse Factory for a period of six months. They should be housed in camp no. 31 belonging to the Kyiv Directorate of Camp no. 62 located next to the factory's territory."[54] This memorandum indicates again that while skilled workers were still needed in Kyiv, and that an FZO school was also a necessity, it was POWs who were essential to getting production started.

How actual Kyivans contributed to the Soviet economy during 1945–46 remains unclear. The only industry in the capital that had little trouble securing labor was the railways—although even there the numbers did not come from within the city. For example, in accordance with a GKO resolution calling for an increase in repaired passenger and freight wagons at Kyiv's two railway car repair factories, SNK UkrSSR resolved on May 22, 1945, that Kyiv Oblast mobilize 2,500 workers from its urban and rural populations for such work.[55] Perhaps railroad-centered recruitment succeeded because of the wartime privileges of railroad workers, including the prohibition on drafting them into the military.

Some resettled Kyivans were still mobilized into the Red Army, at least until war's end. In March and April 1945, 2,450 were signed up although 7,000 had been requested.[56] Such numbers suggest that while men did exist in the Ukrainian capital, they were not doing much productive work, even at the few factories with attractive opportunities. Still, following Germany's defeat, a Ukrainian TsK memorandum noted, "The Military Commissar of the Kyiv City Draft Board, Lieutenant N. V. Dubovenko, reports [he] has received a verbal command from the Kyiv Military Region to withhold from drafting into the Red Army those men working in the people's economy of Ukraine who are eligible for the draft."[57] Perhaps in the hope that reconstruction of some sort would begin, Kyiv's factories began to hang "help wanted" signs again in their windows.[58]

Maybe it was because Nikita Khrushchev recognized this situation that he addressed Malenkov again about the apparent lack of labor in Kyiv to build housing for workers. In a March 26, 1946, telegram he wrote, "For the fulfillment of the established plan of [housing] reconstruction work, the total need for labor power amounts to 17,000 people. In reality, 9,000 people are working in the organizations reconstructing the housing fund in Kyiv. They are short 8,000 people. Having placed special meaning on the reconstruction of Kyiv's housing fund, SNK UkrSSR asks you to allow the *orgnabor* of 3,000 urban dwellers and 5,000 rural dwellers."[59] There is no record, however, of Moscow's ever allowing this mobilization. Kyiv remained an "island" amid the swirling sea of *orgnabor*, with the lucky formerly occupied and returnee populations already there allowed to ignore the work the local authorities hoped they would begin.

In the end, the settlement in Kyiv of a sizable number of German POWs was the center's main effort to make up for the lack of *orgnabor* labor. By the middle of 1947, dozens of camps with over 28,000 All-Union NKVD prisoners were dotted around the city.[60] Moved around from one construction project to another, the POWs became a central part of Kyiv's permanent workforce. But although industrial production slowly commenced thanks to these POWs, housing reconstruction remained at a virtual standstill.

But what had become of local leaders' plans to purge Kyiv of the "socially dangerous" introduced in chapter 1? Finding an answer begins with the All-Union NKVD Main Directorate of the Militia's 1945 yearly report, which reveals the directorate reregistered over two million passports in thirty-five "temporarily occupied" cities (including Kyiv) that year.[61] The report then notes that only 2,324 people were found and removed from these cities for failing to fall within the limitations of the passportization regime. Perhaps the low number is explained by the militia's workings: "In 1945, the attention of the periphery organs of the militia was addressed at explaining among the population the main obligations of citizens in their observance of the passport law. This was even more necessary than usual, because as the experience of 1944 showed, many citizens, especially in localities liberated from the occupants, did not know or had simply forgotten the existing laws of the passport regime."[62] In Kyiv's case, the real problem for its leaders was not the militia's failure to root out imagined enemies, but the Stalin regime's apparent decision to look the other way on social dislocation.

In January 1946, for example, Gorban and Mokienko sent a memorandum to the SNK UkrSSR and Ukrainian TsK stating that the August 1944 resolution limiting entrance into Kyiv was still not being observed. They then noted that "tens of thousands of citizens have arrived here without permission, are finding work, and are receiving living permits." Receiving the latter implied that a person's passport also contained a stamp saying that he or she was registered in the Ukrainian capital. Exact details of what work these people were doing, though, were nowhere to be found in the police records. Gorban and Mokienko's memorandum also added that there was an "already tense situation with living space" due to the resolution of August 5, 1941, which had bonded soldiers' housing to their families during wartime.[63] This situation, they concluded, had been "significantly worsened" by those arriving from "the eastern oblasts of the USSR."

Kyiv's local leaders called on SNK UkrSSR to prevent entrance for "permanent living" in Kyiv until July 1, 1946. The only people who should be allowed entry, they argued, were those sent for work in central party and soviet organs as well as demobilized servicemen who had lived in Kyiv before the war. They added at the end of their memorandum, "Permit the Executive Committee of the Kyiv City Soviet of Workers' Deputies to send those people now demobilized from the Red Army who lived from the beginning of the war in the city of Kyiv, but whose living space is now either ruined or burned out, and for which an exchange will not be possible, to the cities of Chernovtsy, Izmail, Stanislav, and Drogobich."[64] Kyiv's leaders were trying to stem the tide of unorganized return to Kyiv—even the "politically correct" return of veterans.

The main source of trouble for Gorban and Mokienko was again the August 5, 1941, All-Union Supreme Soviet ukaz dictating that Red Army soldiers and their dependents were legally entitled to the living space they had occupied before the war. As Rebecca Manley has argued, because local procurators enforced this ukaz more often than not, it became a reason for housing evictions in Kyiv.[65] Gorban and Mokienko called on the Ukrainian NKVD to conduct periodic checks of housing units to uncover people without living permits, as the August 1944 resolution had asked for. Their request suggests that the *massoperatsii* that had earlier consumed the NKVD at all levels ended early in 1945 as the Red Army's need for men subsided.

But it was only the March 1946 announcement of the Fourth Five-Year Plan that allowed the Ukrainian leadership to do something about Kyiv's population growth. Perhaps the plan's announcement was the Kremlin's signal that unorganized return could be confronted and the social dislocation of the war years be put to rest. In local terms, this meant stirring the Ukrainian Ministry of State Control—the group legally responsible for enforcing the toothless August 1944 resolution. Soon after the plan's announcement, the Ukrainian Minister of State Control, V. O. Chornovol, reported to the Ukrainian TsK about the resolution's fulfillment.[66]

Here was the first effective effort by Ukraine's leaders to confront the war's legacy amid the system emerging after the war, a system that now seemed destined to stay in place. Chornovol's report documented first how those seeking to live in Kyiv had entered the city and, in most cases, received permits to reside there permanently after the occupation's end. A key moment was the April 16, 1945, decision of the Kyiv City Soviet that placed responsibility for the issuance of permits to live in the city squarely on the shoulders of the Kyiv City Militia, while the task of granting permission to enter the city remained with the Temporary Commission. Mokienko, the new Kyiv City Soviet leader, had recognized that the commission was something he could not get rid of, and thus he tried to make sure the blame for the city's population growth would fall on someone other than himself.

Chornovol's first major revelation explained how people had resettled Kyiv up until then. His report pinpointed the role of N. I. Voronov, the Temporary Commission's secretary, who singlehandedly decided on those declarations it received by mail. According to Chornovol, "[Voronov] examined some 10,523 declarations during 1945 (including 7,340 declarations from servicemen and members of their families). Of these mailed-in declarations, only six were decided positively; the other 10,517 were rejected."⁶⁷ But Chornovol then added, "A significant number of persons who were denied entrance to Kyiv [by the commission] arrived here of their own free will and received living permits issued by the militia. Out of a random sampling of 123 citizens who received a rejection, 45 of them later arrived here and were issued living permits by the organs of the militia." As for the 4,606 permits the Temporary Commission actually handed out in person during 1945—sometimes "to entire families"—many had been received "unjustifiably," Chornovol concluded. It must have quickly become common knowledge in the rear that the only way to overcome this bureaucratic obstacle course was to leave for the city on one's own.

Even so, these statistics do not explain why Kyiv's population had increased so much since the reregistration and passportization campaigns two years before. Such a reality foreshadowed Chornovol's conclusion about the militia's role in the population increase:

> On March 15, 1946, the number of citizens issued living permits for habitation in the city of Kyiv amounts to 598,582. In 1945, the organs of the militia issued living permits to 266,543 people. The Temporary Commission for regulating the entrance of citizens into Kyiv permitted the entrance of no more than 12,000 to 13,000 people during 1945. If one excludes from the grand total of citizens arriving in Kyiv during 1945 those persons who were given permission to enter by the Temporary Commission, those who were demobilized here and assigned here, and persons transferred here for full-time work by order of union- and republic-level people's commissariats, it becomes obvious that the majority of citizens, having arrived [in] Kyiv of their own free will, were issued living permits by the organs of the militia without there being a legal basis for doing so. This data is evidence that there was no real battle against illegal entry into the city of Kyiv.⁶⁸

Chornovol then revealed that the head of the Kyiv City Militia's Passport Department had given orders for the issuance of living permits without keeping any of the documents that would provide the basis for those permits. On paper, these documents included proof of legal entry into the city, proof of legal employment, and proof of legal residence in the city.

While a complete examination of the Kyiv City Militia's workings was impossible without "summoning forth tens of thousands of people," it was nevertheless possible, Chornovol wrote, to show grave mismanagement. One example he gave: "During the examination of the Kyiv City Militia's Passport Department a declaration of the following nature was discovered: 'To: Head of the Passport Table of the City of Kyiv. From: R. E. Mitsman. Declaration, I ask for your permission that I be issued a living permit. Mitsman.'"⁶⁹ According to Chornovol, such a declaration was enough for the captain of the militia, E'lman, to issue a living permit for six months. While this example suggests there were registrations in the city of variable time-lengths, it is plausible, considering the corruption visible here, that Mitsman's first permission to live in the city led to others of more lasting duration in the years ahead.

Another of Chornovol's examples of "population control" in the Ukrainian capital reads, "On October 20, 1945, a citizen Morozov (his name, patronymic, and place of inhabitation are unknown) put forth a declaration to the [Kyiv] City [Militia] Passport Department with the following contents: 'I ask for your issuance of a living permit to my relative V. K. Vartazarova to live at 70 Gorky Street, apartment 6-a. Morozov.' Permission for the issuance of a full-time living permit for Kyiv—based only on this declaration—was given by the Assistant to City Passport department head, comrade El'man."[70] In sum, Chornovol's report documented the issuance of living permits in complete violation of the resolution of August 5, 1944, concerning the temporary limitation of entrance into the city. In just two years, he concluded, some 250,000 people had arrived in Kyiv without permission and, in most cases, had gone on to receive residency permits of one type or another.

Chornovol's main recommendation was to abolish the Temporary Commission. He also recommended additional resolutions be made into law to help to determine who was permitted to live in Kyiv. Indeed, these recommendations were later included in the April 22, 1946, Council of Ministers (SM) UkrSSR and Ukrainian TsK resolution "On Measures of the Limiting of Entrance into the City of Kyiv and for Improving the Work on the Fulfillment of the Laws of the Passport Regime in the City of Kyiv."[71] Unsurprisingly, the resolution placed all power for granting permission to enter the city in the hands of the new chairman of the Kyiv City Soviet, Fedor Chebotarev. The previous holder of that positon, Fedor Mokienko, was removed from his duties at this point and evidently took the blame for the city's chaotic settlement after the Nazis.

This new resolution laid out the types of people allowed to enter the city. Although this list had become clearer over the years, it had never been so complete. Now, war invalids as well as demobilized servicemen (and their families) who arrived in Kyiv would be issued permission to enter if they lived in Kyiv before the war and secured living space *prior* to arrival in the city. Red Army officers and their families, as well as workers summoned to work in Kyiv and their families, would also only be issued permission to enter if they were guaranteed actual living space by the organizations inviting them. Again, all of these people were supposed to give concrete evidence showing that living space had been reserved for them *before* they entered the city. This change was a weighty one. For the first time, there were no loopholes to entrance into postoccupation Kyiv. Even demobilized servicemen would need to show an address before being allowed entrance into the city. And with the city's housing space now already taken—whether legally or not—it seems that, at least on paper, the city was finally closed off to unorganized returnees.

The resolution also obliged Kyiv's militia chief, Komarov, to issue living permits only if a permission slip to enter the city had Chebotarev's signature (or that of his first assistant). This stipulation was hardly a surprise, considering Chornovol's report singled out the militia as particularly guilty in allowing Kyiv's population to balloon. The Ukrainian Ministry of Internal Affairs and Procurator's Office, respectively, were obliged to conduct systematic checks, prompt investigations, and speedy trials to bring to justice all those in violation of the passport laws. Even so, the legacy of the Stalin regime's willful ignorance of social dislocation during the war was something local authorities would have to live with.

The Fourth Five-Year Plan and a Closed City

The SM UkrSSR resolution just outlined would now be followed, because the Fourth Five-Year Plan's announcement suggested that labor and other resources would finally be directed toward the Ukrainian capital. Closing off unorganized return had become crucial if Kyiv's leaders wanted to position themselves as successful managers in the Stalin regime. After the plan's announcement, the city's leaders prepared again for the arrival of *orgnabor* laborers.

A red flag for these leaders was the fate of Kyiv's artificial fibers textile factory in Darnytsa (no. 512), mentioned earlier in this chapter. On April 5, 1946, the Kyiv Gorkom noted that the first-quarter plan for the factory's reconstruction was only 35 percent fulfilled, while its plan for housing construction was only 24 percent fulfilled. Accordingly, a Gorkom resolution seeking to fix matters at the factory noted that "in the first quarter, instead of 2,500 people hired through *orgnabor*, only 400 have been brought on board."[72] The "guilty" party was an organization called Kyiv Industrial Construction (*Kievpromstroi*). According to a memorandum written by the Kyiv Gorkom's Department of Construction and Construction Materials in preparation for the above resolution, Kievpromstroi was at fault because it used building materials allocated to its Special Construction and Assembly Directorate no. 11, and intended for the construction of housing for the latter's workers, on other projects around the city.

The memorandum added that "in accordance with a government resolution, the head of Kievpromstroi was obliged, in the month of March, to reequip the prisoners' camp of factory 512 for use as the living premises for 1,000 construction workers and to build additional new housing for 1,000 people." With the "prisoners' camp" yet to be "reequipped" as of April 1 1946, the memorandum concluded that the new housing remained unfinished because "the leadership of the Special Construction and Assembly Directorate no. 11 cannot decide the question of how to get wood from the water so as to finish this process."[73] While the status of factories was important (the artificial fibers factory was of republic-level importance), and the resource-strapped organizations assigned to rebuild them would always be distracted by other projects, this memorandum is revealing, for it implies that the use of *orgnabor* labor was still the preferred strategy for reinvigorating the Ukrainian capital's industry despite the fact that over 600,000 people lived in Kyiv by 1946.

The Fourth Five-Year Plan's announcement indicated the possible arrival of this hotly sought-after labor, but only if the passport regime was also strictly followed in the city. In the case of *orgnabor* workers, this meant housing would need to be prepared for them at a factory or building site *before* they were given temporary permits to live in Kyiv. In April 1946, for example, the city received word that a new truck repair factory belonging to the All-Union Ministry of Agriculture Purchases would be built in its Kurenivka neighborhood. A Kyiv Gorkom resolution announced such a plan and concluded with this command to the city's militia: "Allow the issuance of living permits in Kyiv on the living space of the auto-repair factory for 250 workers and technicians (with their families) hired by the factory through *orgnabor* or transferred from other factories."[74] Later that year, the assistant chairman of the SM UkrSSR, Ivan Senin, wrote to the Ukrainian MVD's (the successor to the NKVD) Directorate of the Militia to request that it register some 3,755 new *orgnabor* workers in Kyiv and three other cities for the factories of Ministry of Light Industry UkrSSR in accordance with the existing passport regime.[75] As the artificial fibers factory belonged to this ministry, it seems likely that Kievpromstroi did finally finish the barracks mentioned above.

Alongside such signs of progress, Kyiv's leaders now watched over a tightening of access to their city. An April 6, 1946, letter from SNK UkrSSR Assistant Chairman Starchenko to the All-Union MVD assistant minister, Diatlov, reveals this new stringency: "The directorate of the Kyiv Mixing Factory recruited 21 workers—including fourteen repatriates—and then turned to the Kyiv City Passport Bureau petitioning that they be issued Kyiv city living permits. The Kyiv City Passport Bureau rejected the factory directorate's efforts, basing its decision on the fact that they had been in Germany."[76] While it is not known if Starchenko's request for an exception for these workers was granted, a background of having been in Germany suddenly became quite problematic in the Ukrainian capital. By the end of 1946, the number of *Ostarbeitery* permanently settled in the city was a little over sixteen thousand—almost the exact number listed on January 1, 1946.[77] The fact that the *Ostarbeitery* applied themselves right after their return did not help them, given the scarcity of the mid-1940s; they were now politically suspect.

This change occurred despite reports from the Kyiv City Soviet's Department of Repatriation, where its leader, Shutenko, praised the *Ostarbeitery* and their work at over eighty organizations in Kyiv in his yearly report for 1946.⁷⁸ At that point, almost fourteen thousand of them were employed in the city, and almost all of them had been issued living permits as well. But in another report from the same time, addressed to Zozulenko in the Ukrainian Council of Ministers' Department of Repatriation Affairs, Shutenko noted his organization had "determined that the head of the Kyiv Inter-Oblast Office of the Ukrainian Construction Assembly Trust, Maksimenko, and the head of the first construction site of the same trust, Sazonov, have addressed the repatriated in a rude and anti-Soviet manner, calling the latter 'repatriated bastards' and 'compromised people.'"⁷⁹ Things were no different in the heart of Kyiv, where the memorandum continued, "It is also necessary to note the unacceptable attitude of the head of Kyiv's 'Passenger' train station, comrade Grobchak. He rudely and impatiently interacts with the repatriated who ask him questions . . . declaring, 'Get out of here on your own, if you like, I did not send you to Germany.'"⁸⁰ This attitude is why the local Communists could not have expected the formerly occupied, the unorganized returnees, and the demobilized soldiers to passively greet the *Ostarbeitery*, especially considering the deficit of housing in the city.

Meanwhile, the one group the local Communists still wanted more of was German POWs, for they had turned out to be the catalysts for reconstruction of any sort actually beginning. The number of prisoners in the city multiplied, thanks to the Red Army's victories in Eastern Europe. But this did not mean that such labor would necessarily be used in ways desired by Kyiv's leaders. A June 28, 1946, Kyiv Obkom resolution, for example, chided the Ukrainian Ministry of Internal Affairs' Directorate of Camps for not helping to secure Kievpromstroi's reconstruction efforts at the Bol'shevik electrical factory with POWs from the camp located right on the factory's grounds.⁸¹ Instead of the 1,200 POWs needed, only 700 were sent on a daily basis. As a result, deadlines set by the SM UkrSSR and Ukrainian TsK for new electrolysis machine production had not been met.

While the numbers of *orgnabor* and prisoner laborers became more numerous in 1946, the problems preventing such labor from being used for reconstruction remained the same. When it came to rebuilding one of Kyiv's main educational institutions, the Kyiv Technical Institute of the Food Industry (KTIPP), the director of that institute, Gritsiuk, outlined its situation in a letter to the SM UkrSSR of June 26, 1946.⁸² Thanks to its affiliation with the All-Union Ministry of Food Processing, and that organization's contacting the Directorate of Camp no. 62, Gritsiuk's institute was able to acquire materials and the six hundred prisoner laborers of a "special contingent" necessary for such rebuilding. This group of prisoners, though, had been initially assigned to the Ministry of Housing and Civilian Construction (MZhGS) UkrSSR, which lacked the facilities necessary to house them and hoped that using KTIPP's building materials would provide a camp for the prisoners.

Despite subsequent promises by MZhGS UkrSSR's Special Construction and Assembly Unit (OSMCh) no. 305, which had been assigned these laborers, that the housing for them would be built, Gritsiuk's letter concludes, "The building of the camp, along with finishing the building of the student dormitory, was an urgent and first-order task that would determine the success of the work in 1946 and would have provided the institute with the necessary amount of housing for the beginning of the school year. . . . [But] on May 15, 1946, without any warning . . . , [OSMCh no. 305] took all of its labor power from KTIPP and in essence ended its work here."[83] Gritsiuk's problem was that OSMCh no. 305 still controlled how many of its laborers worked on a site at any given time. And according to that organization's director, Novichenko, he was occupied with eighty other projects around Kyiv and had not been given enough labor power, transport, or materials to complete these tasks.[84]

Although *orgnabor* laborers needed housing before they could be assigned anywhere, this was not a new problem. It had always been the case that All-Union NKVD/MVD POWs (or other parts of this "special contingent," such as Soviet or even non-Soviet civilians arrested in formerly German-held territory) needed housing set up somewhere for them before they could be moved from the internal police's camps. Thus, even after the Institute of Food Processing's efforts to secure the necessary materials and labor, the whole effort fell apart because the organization it had contracted with to do the housing construction failed to provide sufficient labor to begin this process.

Here was the crux of the reconstruction problem for the local Communists in 1946—a catch-22 that they needed to overcome. In essence, the reconstruction of the Institute of Food Processing had ground to a halt because another organization lacked the workers to build the barracks necessary to house the workers tasked with doing the institute's actual reconstruction. The only way out for Kyiv's leaders was to control the city's reassembled population long enough to guarantee the social order there necessary to merit sufficient allocations of new labor from Moscow.

Meanwhile, mobilization for less vital union-wide industries, and for the all-important coal industry, had resumed once again in western Ukraine. The situation there is best examined by returning to the travails of the Donbas Anthracite Trust's (*Donbassantratsit*) Comrade Vesennyi, who in the summer of 1946 had moved on to coordinating *orgnabor* in Kamianets'-Podil's'k Oblast. An analysis of Vesennyi's trials also helps to illustrate what it was like for the local Communists amid the stark realization that, at any moment, the Stalin regime's policy shifts could upset their best-laid plans.

To make sense of the situation in postwar Kamianets'-Podil's'k Oblast and its capital, Proskuriv, it bears remembering that despite the social dislocation created by the Stalin regime's wartime priorities, the Soviet Union remained an incredibly centralized place. For example, on June 27, 1946, the Ukrainian acting procurator, Noshchenko, reprimanded the oblast for issuing a resolution authorizing the *orgnabor* of 370 persons to help build the new "House of the Soviets" in Proskuriv. According to Noshchenko, said resolution could not be fulfilled because "The *orgnabor* of labor for work is decided upon by the SM SSSR (resolution number 1781 dated November 5, 1942). On the basis of that decision, the SM SSSR passed a corresponding resolution or order in which it points out who is given the permission to undertake *orgnabor*, in what numbers, for how long, the distribution among oblasts, etc. For carrying out the *orgnabor* of labor power and transport to construct the House of the Soviets in Proskuriv, a corresponding permission from the SM SSSR did not exist."[85]

The main problem for Comrade Vesennyi in Proskuriv was that Moscow had issued him contradictory mobilization orders. Having arrived there in August 1946 with a mandate from SM SSSR to carry out the *orgnabor* of 2,800 workers for *Donbassantratsit*, he was asked in mid-September by the All-Union Ministry of the Coal Industry of the Western Regions to direct his energies toward finding workers for the Rostov Coal (*Rostovugol'*) Trust located in the RSFSR.[86]

But Vesennyi refused to do so, mainly because he had also received around the same time a telegram from the same ministry stating that the new decision did not mean he should curtail his *orgnabor* work in the oblast for *Donbassantratsit*. At that point, according to a letter he wrote to the Ukrainian TsK:

> On September 22, 1946, I was called to the Oblast Executive Committee [*Oblispolkom*], told I was a drunk, and that I was responsible for the failure of *orgnabor* in the oblast. Then [Comrade Shchikula—a visiting representative of the SM UkrSSR's Bureau for the Registration and Distribution of Labor Power] tried to detain me and give me a medical test. . . . I told him that he did not have the right to detain me; that I was no criminal, [and] that he was no procurator. . . . He declared that he could spit on all of the above. What is more, he threatened that he would find a place for me in Siberia, or in the north, and that would finish me off. The workers of the Bureau of Registration and Distribution of Labor Power sent out into the regions prohibited our representatives from collecting people and began to switch over agreements with other coal organizations to Rostovugol'. As a result, *Donbassantratsit* has been confronted with the disruption of its plan for *orgnabor*. . . . I ask that you take measures against Shchikula. . . . His provocative methods do not help, but destroy our work.[87]

According to the other version of these events, one written up by V. I. Porokhova, an inspector with the Executive Committee of the Kamianets'-Podil'sk Oblast Soviet, Vesennyi had agreed to meet and readdress his efforts to the needs of Rostovugol' when the following happened:

At the time we set, Vesennyi did not appear at the Executive Committee.... After an hour and a half, he showed up. He was already drunk and he declared that he was not a boy who runs when he is called by the Executive Committee and that he was busy and not going to the raion.... In connection with the fact Vesennyi showed up drunk, comrade Shchikula called the local sanitation unit of the Ukrainian Ministry of State Security (the doctor on duty) to have Vesennyi checked over. But when the latter heard about this call, he started to leave Kravchuk's office, declaring, "I could spit on that doctor. I am not going to talk to him. And you here are not the ones who give me orders." Despite the efforts of comrade Shchikula to prevent him from leaving before the doctor's arrival, Vesennyi forcefully opened the door, barged out of the office, and disappeared.[88]

Vesennyi had been given contradictory orders by Moscow, and the representatives of SM UkrSSR had made a choice about which resolution to fulfill first. But at the end of 1946, a Ukrainian TsK internal memorandum noted Vesennyi's "drunkenness," and his poor work record in western Ukraine, and concluded, "At the suggestion of the Ukrainian TsK's Department of Coal Industry, the assistant head of *Donbassantratsit*, (comrade Matiushin), has dismissed Vesennyi as plenipotentiary for *orgnabor* in Kamianets-Podil's'k Oblast and called him back to the disposal of that concern. There he has been taken to account, disciplined, and sent to work in the mines."[89]

Some statistics from this time testify to why local Communists likely needed to act carefully to avoid the possibility of social disorder and a similar fate to that of Vesennyi. A Kyiv Gorkom meeting on April 19–20, 1946, noted there were by that date 624,000 people in the city living on an average of 4.25 square meters per person.[90] Of the 6,670 officially homeless families in the city, meanwhile, some 2,000 were the families of the demobilized, while another 2,500 were servicemen's families.

Such statistics emerge from the first systematic efforts to strengthen the passport regime after Chornovol's report. In a June 11, 1946, report to the Ukrainian TsK, an assistant minister at the Ministry of Internal Affairs UkrSSR, Loburenko, noted that the Kyiv City Militia had conducted almost thirty thousand checks in April and May to enforce it.[91] According to an August 5 report of the Kyiv City and Kyiv Oblast Militia chiefs Komarov and Krivoshein, the same number of checks were also carried out "in a planned fashion" in June and July.[92] What is interesting here is that in both of these reports, less than one thousand people were actually "banished" from the city for violation of its "regime city" status. Meanwhile, only thirty-five people were exiled from the city because of criminal actions.

A summer 1946 memorandum written by Gorban and Chebotarev, the new Kyiv City Soviet chairman, to Korotchenko, indicates why such small numbers help best to conclude this study of Kyiv's postwar resettlement: "Because of the inattentiveness of the militia concerning living permit affairs, for quite a while many non-registered people have lived in the city who have used this time to find full-time work and have secured for themselves in the process living space resulting in socially useful labor connected with the city. Thus, it no longer makes sense to refuse them the right to live in Kyiv."[93] In fact, these leaders revealed, of the almost 7,000 people said to be nonregistered found from May 5 to June 20, 1946, 5,628 had already received permanent registrations. The leaders probably issued this amnesty to regulate a population they now understood to have been allowed by the Stalin regime to resettle in Kyiv despite the Second World War's destruction. While it seems doubtful that the people just mentioned had actually been busy accomplishing "socially useful labor" or, in some cases, were even employed, what mattered now was that the Kyivans be ready to help out their damaged city.

Perhaps these men accepted this resettled population because they hoped to maintain social order and lay the groundwork for reconstruction. This meant an amnesty for those already in the city amid the continued reliance on German POWs to begin the dirty work of reconstruction. And Kyiv's population was now growing, thanks to workers recruited through *orgnabor*. Almost seventeen thousand such people arrived in the city during July 1946 alone.[94] If this type of resettlement indicated the Stalin regime's support, then the local Communists had prepared themselves as best they could to take advantage of it. This may have been what they needed to maintain legitimacy amid the social dislocation that continued to influence the postwar Stalin regime.

Part Two

Reassembly

Chapter Three

"People Are Going for the Party Who Are Forcing Us to Be Justifiably Careful"

The Reassembled Elite

Kyiv's reassembled elite found it easier than the masses to access scarce resources following the city's liberation. A letter written by a man named Bitniia-Shliakhta to the Kyiv Obkom in summer 1944 sheds some light on this situation:

> On June 10, 1944, a Kyiv Obkom employee, Beregovenko, burst into our apartment at 19 Engels Street, apartment 7, where my mother and father occupy two rooms. Our big family has lived in that apartment from the time our building was built, or twelve years. From the first days of the war, my brother, who served in the army, went to the front. . . . From the moment he occupied part of my apartment, Beregovenko started to harass my parents and my wife. He started to threaten them and to curse at them. My father sent a declaration to the raion procurator. After a month the raion procurator refused to evict Beregovenko. My father wrote another declaration to the Kyiv City Procurator. After three weeks the Kyiv City Procurator sent that declaration to the raion procurator to be looked over again and the raion procurator then gave this answer, "Forget about your two rooms. They are no longer yours. There are people whom it is impossible to evict."[1]

The outcome of Bitniia-Shliakhta's efforts to recover his family's rooms is unclear. One thing that is clear, however, is that Beregovenko should never have been allowed to occupy them, considering that Bitniia-Shliakhta's brother was in the Red Army. But while procurators usually tried to enforce the laws of the land, the local Communists running the Ukrainian capital often became laws unto themselves during this period.

This chapter examines this reassembled elite, the Communists registered with the Kyiv Gorkom and Obkom. It focuses on full-time party functionaries, for they carried awesome responsibilities and encountered equally great difficulties given Kyiv's position in the war effort. As these elites secured the city's best resources for themselves, or allowed others access to the same, they also risked making enemies among the masses. Thankfully for them, Moscow's move in late 1944 to limit the overall growth of a party, the membership of which had greatly changed during the war, made it easier for these leaders to prevent access to power. Frustrated with the Kremlin's clumsy handling of reconstruction, these Communists had time to investigate those who desired entry into the party. At the same time, party members who had lived on occupied territory, men returning from service in the Red Army, and those non-Communists involved in the city's underground resistance, all made bids to join the elite. Unfortunately for them, almost no one new was going to be given access to the elite's ranks after the war.

As news about the Fourth Five-Year Plan and Andrei Zhdanov's accompanying party-revival campaign arrived in the spring of 1946, it became easier for local Communists to signal to their bosses in the republic- and union-level bureaucracies, as well to as the Kyivan masses, that however impacted they were by the war's events, they were still capable of leading Kyiv into the future. The final section of this book tackles that important moment. This chapter considers how the elite managed the city's economy, made sure that they and others they valued were well provided for, and governed their rank and file to maintain their positions of leadership and ready themselves for actual reconstruction. Who the masses were, and how their postoccupation struggle to survive changed postwar Soviet life, rounds out this section in the next chapter.

The Reassembled Elite and Reconstruction

A Kyiv Gorkom resolution dated July 7, 1944, found 10,000 Communist Party members and candidates in 500 party organizations dotted among the city's enterprises and institutions.[2] This marked a dramatic increase from the 1,700 Communists working in the city at the end of 1943, and had happened due to "the number of Communists sent from other oblasts."[3] Later, a July 13, 1945, resolution of the Kyiv Gorkom noted 1,300 positions of leadership (*nomenklatura*) in the city and revealed what these people occupied themselves with.[4] Half of them were working in the local party, soviet, or security organs. The other half was evenly divided between industry and societal institutions, such as those in education or medicine. Of those cadres involved with party work, only the Kyiv Gorkom's secretaries needed to be confirmed by the All-Union TsK before taking office. The city's leaders, however, found many workers in industry and higher education also occupied their jobs only after confirmation by the TsK in Moscow.

The equal importance of these jobs in the *nomenklatura* testifies to the equal importance of these cadres in Moscow's eyes. And given the centralization of the Soviet economy, the directors of Kyiv's many union-level factories—like Beregovenko, discussed above—became laws unto themselves. Kyiv's local Communist leaders, though, held the tougher jobs, for the Stalin regime tasked them with coordinating and expediting everything within the city and the surrounding oblast to meet its goals. The local party bureaucracy needed to make sure that the center's orders were fulfilled just as much as they worked to maintain social order in the capital through their own various resolutions. Although they were powerless in the face of Moscow's reconstruction priorities, local leaders were in competition with factory managers within their own city, as both tried to fulfill the center's orders.

By October 1946, the total number of members and candidates belonging to the Kyiv Gorkom had grown to over 32,000 people active in 1,220 party organizations across the city.[5] The arrival of almost 17,000 Red Army officers was a main reason for this tripling in size.[6] Inexperience was probably the notable characteristic of these new Communist arrivals.[7] In the Kyiv Obkom's organization at that time, for example, over 45,000 of its 70,000 Communists had only become members since 1942.[8]

After the Red Army retook Kyiv, these local Communists' task was to draw the city's resources into the war effort. But at the beginning, they could only offer the First Ukrainian Front labor to repair the city's transportation links and to fulfill military orders using the few materials left behind by the Nazis. Such military orders included repairing machinery and producing rudimentary necessities like wooden bolts for pontoon bridges.[9] To complete the new above-water bridge over the Dnipro, for example, the SNK UkrSSR and Ukrainian TsK were forced to pass a resolution on January 20, 1944, calling on factories in Dnipropetrovs'k and Kharkiv to provide the iron beams and bolts for its construction.[10]

But Kyiv's economy was not entirely dead. On January 3, 1944, the head of the right-bank Darnytsa Raikom wrote to his supervisors in the Kyiv Gorkom that a commission from the All-Union People's Commissariat of Light Industry had examined the Kyiv Regenerated Resin Factory to see whether it could be recommended to their superiors in Moscow for reconstruction.[11] Such a check apparently had already been done at one of the city's aviation factories belonging to the All-Union People's Commissariat of the Aviation Industry.[12] By March 1944, many representatives from union-level people's commissariats in Moscow had visited Kyiv to identify the factory carcasses to be rebuilt for future use.

For a factory to receive a decision from the centrally located GKO authorizing it to reestablish operations was of primary importance. In practice, however, a people's commissariat could take control of a factory, and even have some production orders assigned to it, before GKO gave the authorization for a significant investment of resources. For example, a document from late 1944 signed by Aleksei Davydov, a second secretary in the Kyiv Gorkom, contains the following title: "On the conditions of the enterprises in the city of Kyiv subordinated to union-level people's commissariats that in the opinion of the Kyiv Gorkom it is necessary to reconstruct."[13] But a look at affairs during 1944 at the giant Arsenal factory in Kyiv's central Pechersk Raion, high above the Dnipro, makes it clear that Moscow really dictated how the city was reconstructed.

A July 1, 1944, letter from a Kyiv-based plenipotentiary at a factory in Sverdlovsk belonging to the All-Union People's Commissariat of Armaments to the SNK SSSR Chairman describes what happened after GKO resolution transferred to that commissariat "all of [Arsenal's] production buildings and structures, apartment houses, and social and cultural service institutions" in order to facilitate the opening of a new "optical-mechanics" factory on its premises. The letter announced, "To execute this decision, the All-Union People's Commissariat of Armaments began reconstruction and the organization of production. From base factory no. 217, in Sverdlovsk, 'worker-builders' and production equipment have already left. In September 1944, based on the plan [of the commissariat], the output of product, the main production of the factory, should begin. But the deadlines for the reconstruction of the factory have not been met due to the location on its territory of the Armored Tank Repair Factory no. 7 belonging to the All-Union People's Commissariat of Defense."[14]

This letter shows the fluid nature of Kyiv's industry in the mid-1940s, and how major decisions impacting the city's future were discussed almost entirely in Moscow. Indeed, these two union-level-based commissariats fought over this prestigious site again later that year, with the defense commissariat's tank repair factory losing out and departing for the city's right-bank region of Darnytsa. On April 7, 1945, the SNK UkrSSR and Ukrainian TsK finally announced the renaming of Arsenal as no. 784 of the All-Union People's Commissariat of Armaments and scheduled it to begin producing optical-mechanical tools for the Soviet armed forces.[15] Although in-fighting in Moscow had slowed this factory's reconstruction, at least there was a resolution.

With the exception of such defense-related heavy industry, however, the reconstruction of Kyiv's heavy industries continued slowly. At a meeting of the Kyiv Gorkom in March 1946, Davydov summed up the overall work done in the heavy industry sector: "In the past two and a half years, we have achieved only 24.1 percent of prewar production levels. That is not a large percentage and without a doubt it cannot satisfy us."[16] Speaking a little later, during that same March 1946 meeting, Zaliznychnyi Raikom Secretary Zheliak summed up matters: "The real battle for the reconstruction of the people's economy is only now beginning."[17]

Davydov concluded the discussion by explaining the city's economic future: "The directors of enterprises and other managers should, when all is said and done, understand that the widening of productive possibilities is connected to an increase in the amount of labor power working there. The question of attracting new laborers and keeping those already there at the factory depends most of all on how much our managers provide our workers with normal living conditions."[18] Despite Davydov's emphasis on workers' housing conditions as being essential for the city's economic future, little could be done to correct this problem, for the local Communists were ultimately dependent on Moscow and its all-union ministries for resources. And while ensuring productive heavy industry was their ticket to success within the Stalin regime, their other main task was securing the population's everyday living conditions.

But supplying the city's population with consumer goods was next to impossible. The Nazis had destroyed showpieces of Kyiv's 1930s-era light industry boom such as the Gorky Textile Factory in Protiasiv Iar, the meat processing plant in left-bank Darnytsa, and the Bol'shevik chemical-production equipment factory in the heavily industrialized Zhovtnevyi Raion on the city's right-bank outskirts. In an example of the measures undertaken in the wake of the Nazi occupation, the Kyiv Gorkom ordered the city's local industrial trusts on March 31, 1944, to increase the assortment of consumer goods available by using "mainly local materials such as horns, bones, pottery, ceramics, and wood."[19] The same resolution obliged the directors of those factory carcasses to make "more full usage of the byproducts from local materials" to meet locally established plans for consumer goods production. Within the Stalin regime's economy, local leaders enjoyed little agency as they tried to create growth.

Meanwhile, on August 11, 1944, SNK SSSR resolved to begin reconstruction of the destroyed light industry sector in Ukraine.[20] On September 26, 1944, SNK UkrSSR and the Ukrainian TsK similarly pointed out the growth in industrial production cooperatives in Kyiv, but added, "We have also noticed the extremely inadequate production of high-quality consumer goods, and the limited assortment of products made here by our enterprises. Even now there is unsatisfactorily organized the daily servicing of the population."[21] The text of an accompanying resolution called on the Kyiv Gorkom to organize the production of consumer goods at thirty enterprises of union- and republic-level subordination, to set up over 150 points of "everyday servicing" including eleven *amerikanki* (quick-service snack bars) and to "uncover masters of individual production of artistic goods and attract them to production."[22]

It is hard to tell whether the above resolution was successfully implemented. However, on June 1, 1945, the Kyiv Gorkom again resolved to increase the production of consumer goods at factories of union- and republic-level subordination. From what materials these goods were to be produced becomes clear from the fourth point in the resolution, entrusting a "city planning commission" to "register the remains of all byproducts of production" at such enterprises.[23] The appendix of this resolution then listed the goods these factories were supposed to be producing, from a few pairs of wooden teeth to 200,000 metal Red Army stars.

Three consumer goods factories of union-level subordination—the textile factory (no. 512) of the People's Commissariat of Textiles, the Regenerated Resin Factory of the People's Commissariat of Light Industry, and Bol'shevik of the

People's Commissariat of the Electrical Industry—also received orders from GKO to begin rebuilding at this time.[24] But as outlined in chapter 2, the OSMCh of the Ukrainian Oil Construction (*Ukrneftostroi*) Trust assigned to rebuild these factories was distracted by other projects.[25] And the situation does not seem to have changed much as that winter approached. An excerpt from a Darnytsa Raikom meeting protocol dated December 26, 1945, shows that another OSMCh (no. 11 of the All-Union People's Commissariat of Construction) also failed that fall in its effort to get production started at the textile factory there.[26] Most likely a lack of building materials meant that housing for the workers necessary to begin production had yet to be built.

Correcting the problems of union-level light industry was beyond the local Communists' abilities. But the output of smaller enterprises under the jurisdiction of local organizations such as the city's own "Industrial Council" (*Mis'kpromrada*) was something they could at least try to control. A Kyiv Gorkom protocol of March 22, 1946, concerning a November 23, 1945, resolution about consumer goods production clarifies, however, what was happening: "A large number of enterprises and cooperatives of local production still have a rather slovenly appearance. The production processes there are badly organized. . . . The byproducts of union- and republic-level industry (as well as their scrap) are used insufficiently by local and cooperative industry."[27]

The situation with Kyiv's consumer goods production was similar to that of its heavy industry: bad. A March 29, 1946, Kyiv Gorkom resolution summarized matters: "Despite the fulfillment of the [1945] yearly plan for consumer goods production by light, local, and cooperative industry at 112.7 percent, that amount is only eleven percent of prewar levels, something that by no means provides for the needs of the population."[28] A Kyiv Gorkom resolution from May 10 also noted that Bol'shevik and Arsenal's directors (among others) were also not on board, concluding, "This has upset the plan for the issuance of consumer goods during the first quarter. The director of Bol'shevik refused to lay out an agreement with Kyiv Consumer Goods Trade (*Kievpromtorg*) claiming that his ministry had prevented him from doing so."[29] This document blamed the local Communists' rivals within Kyiv's elite, the union-level factory directors, for the failure to provide articles of everyday consumption. After all, if the local population became disorderly as result of the lack of consumer goods, these union-level "barons of industry" might not receive the resources necessary to rebuild their factories and then everyone's jobs could be on the line.

On housing, meanwhile, the Ukrainian Communists focused on restoring the Khreshchatyk and its surroundings. Earlier chapters touched on the March 1944 SNK UkrSSR and Ukrainian TsK resolution that formed NKZhGS UkrSSR to rebuild the city's destroyed center.[30] This new ministry replaced the unsuccessful *narodnaia stroika* campaign, but it failed to recruit the labor necessary to move forward during 1944. It was not until March 1945 that republic-level Communists focused again on rebuilding housing in Kyiv. After listening to Kyiv's raikom secretaries about housing, Nikita Khrushchev responded, "If we are going to talk about the tasks at hand, we have got to talk first about building. We have passed the resolution on NKZhGS UkrSSR. And now we are passing resolutions on the building of cities, including Kyiv. Thus, I want to suggest that the city soviet, raion soviets, and the leaders of the city and raion committees note those enterprises where building supplies can already be produced. We do not have much labor or time."[31]

He then added, "Your task is made up of not only giving orders, but also of picking out examples (of potentially producible supplies), approving those examples, and with those examples, forcing factories to produce such things." As with the situation of consumer goods, Khrushchev wanted union-level factories involved in producing building materials, for that was the only way out of the housing crisis enveloping the city. In his concluding remarks, he weighed in once again on the labor situation: "Take into account the chance of getting prisoners. . . . Summer is upon us. It is possible to make a pretty nice camp for the Germans. To put up some tents here, to place a few kitchens there, and to let them live."[32]

But in a June 1, 1945, memorandum to SNK UkrSSR, the head of the Construction Directorate of the Kyiv City Soviet, N. Proskuriakov, reported that civilian construction orders had been fulfilled at only 9 percent of the yearly plan. A major reason why, he continued, was that "the number of workers in the trusts is not going up. Actually, it is going down. For example, during the first five months of this year . . . from OSMCh no. 305, 500 workers left. The use of POWs as labor power up until now has been very ineffective. Taking into account the fact that the plan has not nearly been fulfilled, the need for additional labor power for reconstruction amounts to at least 15,000 people."[33] Such a plea must be seen in light of the fact that Kyiv's population was on its way toward 600,000. Although asking the capital's shielded population to sacrifice might have damaged the Stalin regime's standing, POWs could have only worked for NKZhGS UkrSSR if that organization had access to building materials.

It was after the meeting with Khrushchev that the Kyiv Gorkom passed an April 20, 1945, resolution pressing Kyiv's union-level enterprises to produce some of those materials. The introduction to an August 17 Kyiv Gorkom resolution makes it clear, however, that those enterprises were not actually helping: "The directors of the Dzerzhinsky Factory, no. 473 (Dudnik), no. 485 (Vlasov), Tsepy Hallia (Zhuyko), and the Stalin Ship-Building Factory (Miudushevs'kyi), have, even now, not started manufacturing the building supplies determined by the above resolution."[34] By the end of that summer, SNK UkrSSR and the Ukrainian TsK believed that they had found a remedy. To rationalize the use of building materials and technical resources in the city, they assigned NKZhGS UkrSSR monopoly control over many of Kyiv's building organizations in a newly named Main Directorate for Construction of the City of Kyiv.[35] As for labor, NKZhGS UkrSSR now awaited an infusion of 4,500 POWs to begin building a "workers' settlement" for 5,000 people, and to complete the reconstruction of ruined buildings for the housing of incoming technicians and workers.

In early 1946, though, SNK UkrSSR and the Ukrainian TsK announced that almost 1,700,000 square meters of living space in the Ukrainian capital (over a third of the total amount potentially inhabitable) still awaited reconstruction.[36] It is doubtful that POWs ever worked much for NKZhGS UkrSSR during this period, since the organization lacked the support from the Stalin regime necessary to get building underway. By April 15, 1946, a Kyiv City Soviet Executive Committee memorandum foresaw around 170,000 square meters of such reconstructed housing "put into exploitation" by three distinct groups: those of union- and republic-level "ministerial" subordination, the Kyiv City Soviet, and NKZhGS UkrSSR, now renamed the Ministry of Housing and Civilian Construction (MZhGS) UkrSSR. Of course, such "ministerial" housing meant that some buildings that had once housed those in evacuation or returning in unorganized fashion now ended up in the hands of others, which probably only exacerbated tensions in the city.

As for new housing, all Secretary Gorban could note at a Kyiv Gorkom meeting of April 19–20, 1946, was that a paltry 1,713 square meters of such housing had been built in the capital during the first quarter of 1946.[37] In a city with over 600,000 people, the average Kyivan now lived on 4.25 square meters of space—well below the prewar average of 6 square meters. The new chairman of the Kyiv City Soviet, Fedor Chebotarev, acknowledged this pitiful situation in a report to Khrushchev in April 1946.[38] There he warned that enterprises that had not completed the reconstruction of apartment houses assigned to them by SNK UkrSSR in winter 1943–44 would have them taken away. Factories such as Bol'shevik, he added, had already been warned to begin reconstruction with the "significant material-technical resources" they possessed. But a resolution of the Kyiv Gorkom dated June 7 indicates that only 18 percent of the yearly plan for new housing construction was completed by the end of May 1946.[39] As with heavy and light industry, the local Communists found their housing campaigns hampered by union-level enterprises belonging to powerful Moscow-based ministries with other priorities.

The Reassembled Elite and Living Conditions

Upon their return to Kyiv, some Soviet authorities picked up where the Nazi looters left off. A 1944 declaration by a Ukrainian NKVD employee named

Georgii Leont'ev written to the Kyiv Obkom while on trial for theft sheds light on this subject: "After arriving in Kyiv on November 6, 1943, and being named temporary head of the Ukrainian NKVD in Kyiv Rural Raion (neighboring Kyiv proper), I witnessed how, under the guise of trophies, property, apartments, and similar things were taken away from the population. Due to the fact that no one from the Ukrainian NKGB's leadership for Kyiv Oblast warned us about how to behave on liberated territory and seeing that leadership personnel were themselves collecting trophies, many of our workers also busied themselves with such affairs."[40]

It is clear that a portion of the elite used their positions to legalize a process whereby some of the city's unoccupied housing was divvied up by returning Kyivans. To understand this process, it is important to remember the two union-level resolutions that played a major role in regulating Kyiv's housing at this time. First was the August 5, 1941, resolution, which guaranteed that all those serving in the armed forces—for however long they were on active duty—would be allowed to keep that housing space they had resided in before going to war. According to Soviet-era histories of Kyiv, some 200,000 people from the city were either drafted by or volunteered for the military in the summer of 1941.[41] And this August 5 ukaz was almost universally understood to apply to all serving in the military and to those who resided with them. Such a situation meant that a large chunk of Kyiv's housing was still legally bonded to its prior inhabitants, whether or not they were actually in the city. Because such housing would now be taken by others, a second resolution of October 17, 1937, grew in importance. It stated that any evictions from or "compressions" (the division of separate apartments into multi-family living space) within the housing fund would need to be decided in the courts.

This rearrangement of status through housing happened primarily because the returning Communists failed to enforce the August 5 resolution. The ensuing events may be the most important reason why there were efforts to prevent unorganized return during 1944 and 1945. On December 1, 1943, SNK UkrSSR's plenipotentiary in Kyiv, V. Chornovol, had given the Kyiv City Soviet temporary power to allocate "unsupervised property" in the Ukrainian capital.[42] Many fine apartments were unoccupied because half a million Kyivans had either fled the city or been killed by the Nazis during the occupation.

But evidence of Chornovol's move only came later, when Kyiv City Procurator Krizhanovskii wrote to the Kyiv Gorkom's Fedor Mokienko on May 30, 1944: "In connection with use of the 'Temporary Situation on the Rules for Settling the Living Space of Kyiv' dated December 1, 1943, and confirmed by SNK UkrSSR, a textual implementation of the law of August 5, 1941, was not fully carried out because living space that once belonged to soldiers and their families was now subordinated to no one."[43] What provoked Krizhanovskii to write these lines, and what ultimately reveals the Ukrainian Communists' divvying up of space and property in the city before the mass return of people in 1944, was the aftermath of trying to enforce the October 17, 1937, ukaz.

Because of that ukaz, Krizhanovskii's memorandum continued, "In the majority of cases, for apartments of military men, there were given out two to three orders by the raion [soviet] housing departments. That brought about the arguments that were ultimately resolved through the courts."[44] At this early point after Kyiv's liberation, Krizhanovskii reported that 2,364 complaints had landed in his office demanding the evictions of people said to be illegally occupying apartments, some 784 of which were from servicemen. By that point, however, he and his office colleagues had succeeded in examining only 188 of these declarations, a process that had resulted in 155 evictions. These numbers suggest that many people were never evicted from the apartments they occupied.

"Compressions" were occurring, but not, it seems, of illegally occupied apartments. Krizhanovskii's memorandum elaborated on the work of the special commissions set up in March 1944 to begin registering the capital's housing space: "On the basis of [their] conclusions, raion soviets repeatedly hurried to 'compress' and resettle people who were legally occupying housing space. This contradicts the law of October 17, 1937, about the solution of questions relating to the confiscation of housing space only happening in the courts. 104 appeals for administrative compression have been rejected in the offices of the Procurator."[45] And, as noted above, procurators tried to follow the ukaz of August 5, 1941, which usually produced decisions that favored servicemen and their families, and evicted those occupying their apartments. But that was only where local procurators actually acted on the declarations. In Kyiv, the number of declarations concerning housing that went unaddressed only rose over time.

Nothing much changed with this scenario after the Kyiv City Soviet took over housing allocation in the city in fall 1944.[46] On March 30, 1945, the Kyiv Gorkom passed a resolution that stated emphatically, "Even now there is no proper registration of the housing fund in the city as a whole, of that which is freed from 'compression,' of that which has been illegally settled, as well as where there are excesses of space."[47] Mokienko, now the chairman of the Kyiv City Soviet, did not escape the resolution's criticism about his organization's handling of complaints about housing in city. "They have not established control," the resolution continued, "as a result they have not examined a significant number of these documents. Some of them have disappeared. 40,500 declarations and complaints that arrived from November 1943 to November 1944 were not examined at all and were taken to the cellar of an archive."[48]

That some forty thousand declarations concerning housing problems went completely unacted upon suggests a mass exchange of coveted apartments during the mid-1940s. And the October 15, 1945, passage of the SNK UkrSSR resolution "On the Organization of a Group to Account for and Distribute the Housing Fund in the City of Kyiv" indicates that the local Communists made little progress toward improving the housing situation.[49] Perhaps the local authorities hoped to avoid the fireworks that meddling might cause, or their repeated failure to take any responsibility for the city's housing problems might paradoxically have given them legitimacy among those who had succeeded in taking space intended for others. Whatever the case, insufficient housing is one reason that so much ink was spilled advocating that the city be closed off from unorganized returnees soon after the occupation ended.

Those in the elite, meanwhile, benefited from housing laws that circumvented the resolutions just mentioned. One example is when the party-member artists of the Lesi Ukrainky State Russian Drama Theatre ran into problems in the fall of 1945. One "People's Artist of Ukraine" wrote to Boris Gorban in the Kyiv Gorkom and to Mokienko in the Kyiv City Soviet about the evictions of his colleagues as a result of the August 5 resolution, as well as about the "nervous mood" surrounding the fact that the theater's director—the people's artist of the former Chechen-Ingush Autonomous Soviet Socialist Republic, V. A. Nelli—now faced the same fate. He then asked the city's leaders to "give an instruction about applying the union-level resolution dated June 24, 1945, 'on the non-application of the resolution of the SNK SSSR of August 5, 1941, with regard to eminent figures of art and science' to the leading creative workers of the Lesi Ukrainky Theatre."[50]

Some laws contained preferential treatment for elites. One example is a SNK UkrSSR and Ukrainian TsK resolution of August 29, 1944, which established a "wartime living norm" of 6 square meters per person in the cities of Kyiv and Kharkiv.[51] At the same time, it noted, "Academics and others in science and art and the directors of enterprises, as well as those who have the right to more living space, have the right to additional living space."[52] While Moscow's arbitrary leadership made housing allocation a political minefield for Kyiv's Communists, such policies also probably did little to help the intelligentsia's standing among the masses.

The allocation of food was no less hierarchical. In November 1943, SNK UkrSSR and Ukrainian TsK passed a resolution hinting at a return to the prewar "organization of supply" that had existed in the Ukrainian capital in the 1930s.[53] This resolution sought to open thirty cafeterias (with one each set aside for scholarly and artistic workers), thirty food shops, and two restaurants to sell meals at market prices by December 15, 1943. Such planning seems wildly optimistic considering the food needs of the advancing soldiers of the Red Army during the winter of 1943–44. An unusual SNK UkrSSR resolution dated March 27, 1944, entitled "On the Delivery of Grain for the Supplying of Stalin and Voroshilovgrad Oblasts, and the City of Kyiv" hints at the status Kyiv needed to receive any food at all as the Red Army marched westward.[54]

The local Communists thus implemented the Stalin regime's plan to have food available at state commercial prices in state-owned commercial food stores. Such prices were somewhere between those of rationed goods and the market prices seen at the city's bazaars. On May 17, 1944, in accordance with a resolution of the union-level government, SNK UkrSSR and the Ukrainian TsK resolved to organize more of these so-called commercial state stores and restaurants in Kyiv. This was done under the auspices of the Main Directorate of Special Trade (*Glavosobtorg*), a part of the All-Union People's Commissariat of Trade.[55] Three grocery stores and two restaurants were planned for Kyiv including Food Store (*Gastronom*) no. 1, located at the corner of the Khreshchatyk and Lenin Street at the city's heart, as well as the restaurants Dnipro and Teatral'nyi.[56]

A month later, Ukraine's leaders passed a resolution entitled "On the Opening of the Commercial Shops and Restaurants of Glavosobtorg in the City of Kyiv." This resolution specified how these commercial stores might benefit the city's elite. Four groups totaling fifty thousand people were to be given discounts from the state commercial prices set in these shops and restaurants:

> [This contingent is to] include: a) scholarly workers, technical workers, and literary and artistic workers in agreement with the list presented here (6,000 people) b) the officer staff (from junior lieutenants) of the Red Army, the Navy, and the troops of the Ukrainian NKVD and NKGB who are located in Kyiv (17,000 people) c) workers and technicians who are occupied in production at enterprises in state industry and in transport (who have worked there for not less than three years in a row) (20,000 people) and d) office workers of state enterprises and institutions who have worked at those enterprises and institutions for not less than six years (7,000 people).[57]

While the Kyivan elite was quite a bit smaller than these numbers indicate, most party members would have at least tried to shop using this discounted pricing. This is evident from an August 23, 1944, letter signed by the "Chairman of the Organization Bureau of the Central Committee of the Union of Workers of Higher Education and Research Institutions in Kyiv Oblast" and addressed to the All-Union People's Commissariat of Trade located in Moscow: "The shop allocated for the servicing of scholarly and artistic workers, Gastronom no. 1, systematically overflows (with people) on account of it having been assigned contingents from other categories. The shop is not physically large enough to hold the lines that form because of the above and because of infrequent sales of quality food products in insufficient qualities."[58]

The chairman's letter likewise mentions the type of foods distributed: "Instead of a number of 'norm' food products . . . there are given out replacements that are of obviously bad quality and are not needed by consumers. Instead of meat and fish, [for example], raw and sour milk, dried goby and common roach [fish] not fit for human consumption, are [also] handed out.... It should be recognized that the provisioning of the large collective of scholars in Kyiv (more than 1,500 people) is unsatisfactory.... All of this results in just censure from scholars and for its regulation demands immediate directives to the organizations in question."[59] While scholars may still have suffered, a July 10, 1944, resolution covering the second half of that year declared that almost 10,000 workers from the "people's commissariats and central organizations of Ukraine" were to receive additional food rations during that period, while some 6,500 of them were to receive a second hot meal daily because of their work in the evenings. That resolution also included "leaders and leading workers of the party organizations of Ukraine," but their exact numbers are not mentioned.[60]

Alongside these discounts at state stores and supplemental rations, the Ukrainian Communists kept expanding the options for purchasing food at market prices in the city. This might partly have been to pad their incomes through bribery, as alluded to by the Ukrainian People's Commissar of Communal Services, Tabulevich, mentioned earlier. Those places ranged from the first amerikanki, which set up shop in September 1944, to the city's "Cocktail-Hall," which opened in early 1946.[61] By the summer of that year, another fifty shops had been "organized for the servicing of special contingents" in the city, including twenty specifically for party and soviet workers and six set aside for scholarly workers, although what the prices were is not clear.[62] Meanwhile, with drought apparent that August, the eight hundred other food stores in Kyiv serving those outside these "special contingents" seem to have had on hand only potatoes, albeit at rationing prices.

Those who were part of the Kyiv Gorkom or Obkom enjoyed greater chances at securing scarce resources, since they were intimately involved in the city's distribution networks. Joining this elite, especially because of its access to housing, became more important with each delay of the reconstruction process. Thousands of Communists who had spent at least part of the war on Nazi-occupied territory were now waiting to have their cases for readmission considered. And they were only one group among many who hoped to join the party's ranks. While Moscow worked to slow the party's wartime renewal in 1944–45, those who experienced the living conditions in the Ukrainian capital probably saw the admissions process as something determined foremost by how many people deserved access to scarce resources.

The Reassembled Elite and Access to Its Ranks

The power and privilege accorded Kyiv's Communists made access to their ranks a charged question. While they were caught in difficult circumstances due to stalled

Figure 3.1. Korniets, Korotchenko, Khrushchev, Baranovskii, and partisan leader Sydir Kovpak on the Victory Day parade viewing stand, May 9, 1945. Reproduced by permission from the H. Pshenychnyi Central State CinePhotoPhono Archives of Ukraine.

Figure 3.2. The people of Kyiv pass the parade viewing stand on Victory Day, May 9, 1945. Reproduced by permission from the H. Pshenychnyi Central State CinePhotoPhono Archives of Ukraine.

reconstruction and unorganized return, they were still the stewards of the city's resources and had already seen some of the formerly occupied take advantage in terms of housing. That most of these leaders arrived from the rear occurred because accepting or reaccepting almost anyone who had spent time under the Nazis was now impossible after the suffering the formerly occupied had endured. But it was the Kremlin's simultaneous decision to limit the party's growth due to its wartime renewal by newly joining servicemen that greatly helped Kyiv's authorities enact this unwritten policy. As the apparently sober managers of their own ranks—something that occupied a lot of their time, for there was often little they could actually control—they could appear as able leaders to the Kyivan masses despite the conditions in the city.

Such a restrictive policy though did not exist as Soviet power returned to Ukraine in the spring of 1943. After the military successes that followed the Red Army's victory at Stalingrad, the Ukrainian party had to deal with over 66,000 *okruzhentsy*, that is, Communists who had lived in Nazi-occupied Ukraine after the Wehrmacht surrounded them.[63] This was about a third of the union-wide total of Communists found to have spent time in territories occupied by the Germans.[64] But with most of their ranks either in the military or in evacuation, the first party bureaucrats to return desperately needed qualified help as they assumed responsibility for the Ukrainian republic.

This search for assistance led to a March 16, 1943, letter to the Ukrainian TsK's temporary headquarters in Kharkiv from an instructor with its Organization-Instruction Department warning against the party reestablishing itself too quickly in Ukraine. This instructor criticized the Voroshilovgrad Obkom:

> I find exceptionally shocking the fact that the secretary of Voroshilovgrad Obkom for cadres, comrade Orlov, sends *okruzhentsy* to work in the raions without checking over what they were up to under German occupation, [and] where there documents are, etc. . . . For example, the assistant head of the political department of the Horse Processing Plant [*Konezavod*] no. 64, Evstigneev, found himself surrounded during evacuation, and then returned to the factory, where he lived openly. He took part in binge drinking sessions with the Italian commandant and Hitler's bureaucrats. During one session (as champagne flutes were raised to the victory of Hitler and Mussolini) the commandant said to Evstigneev, "Mr. Evstigneev, you sold out Stalin for three rubles, [and] we have liberated you. Join us in drinking to the victory of Hitler." And the latter drank. All the employees of the Konezavod know about this. Following the liberation of the raion, Evstigneev once again occupied his prior post. As he gave a speech to a meeting of women on March 8, 1943, and said there were still people out there who had sold out to the Germans and were awaiting their return, there was general laughter in the hall directed at him as someone who had sold out to an Italian commandant for a glass of vodka.[65]

To prevent further embarrassment, the Ukrainian TsK issued a resolution on November 1, 1943, entitled "On the Creation of Party Organizations in the Regions of Ukraine Liberated from German Occupation and Improving Their Leadership."[66] It was designed to help the Stalin regime put its best foot forward as its representatives reentered lands traumatized by war.

The resolution stated that *okruzhentsy* could not to be readmitted as members and given "responsible work" until the question of their level of commitment to the party, or their "partyness" (*partiinost*), was resolved. It also made clear that the raion-level party organizations where these Communists had been registered before the war were the ones where the process of resolving such "partyness" would occur. Such raions, it was argued, were usually closest to where *okruzhentsy* lived during the occupation, making it easier to find witnesses of the activities in question. In Kyiv Oblast, 6,905 Communists declared they had stayed behind on occupied territory; of these, 6,170 applied for readmittance.[67] Within that latter number is an unknown number of Communists who had been members of the capital's own party organization. To gain readmittance, all *okruzhentsy* were supposed go through a series of background checks: one each at the raikom and obkom levels, or one each at the raikom, gorkom, and obkom levels if the person had lived in a place like Kyiv where there was a city committee.

In the vast majority of cases, if an *okruzhenets* was readmitted at the raion level, then he or she was also readmitted at the higher level or levels. But according to a Ukrainian TsK memorandum of March 22, 1946, only 1,840 of Kyiv Oblast's Communists had progressed through all of those steps by that date.[68] According to A. Zlenko from the TsK's Department of Cadres, it took anywhere from ten days to two months to investigate one personal case at the raion level. The Ukrainian TsK did resolve to quicken the examinations of the *partiinost* question on April 19, 1946.[69] But the early rush to recreate the party presence witnessed with Evstigneev had obviously been replaced by foot-dragging. Few, it seems, wanted to talk about what had happened after September 19, 1941, in Kyiv. After all, discussing the war's events also meant opening up possibilities for challenging matters like the postoccupation redistribution of property and housing.

An examination of correspondence between the local Communists and a typical *okruzhenets* shows how much of the recent past needed to be rehashed to conduct an investigation. In response to a declaration from G. M. Ivanov, an *okruzhenets* then serving in the Red Army, Kyiv Oblast's Tal'kovskii Raikom required him to send the following documents in 1945 for an examination of his partyness: "1) Send a declaration to the Tal'kovskii Raikom. 2) Send a note that confirms that you really did surrender your party card to the raikom with an explanation of why you surrendered it. 3) Send an explanatory note about the circumstances behind why you stayed behind on occupied territory with confirmation of this by that raikom on whose territory you were located during the occupation."[70]

While Ivanov's presence was "absolutely necessary" at the committee meeting that decided on his partyness, the Kyiv Gorkom conducted its investigations by first sending memoranda like one to Kyiv Oblast's Kaniv Raikom dated October 29, 1945. It concerned an Abram Mahaziner who had fled the city during the occupation: "[We] ask that you inform us about the type of work Mahaziner carried out in the village of Syniavtsi in the battle against the German-Fascist occupants. In his own words, and in confirmations by a citizen in the village of Syniavtsi, Klaudia Ivanovna (and four others), he conducted anti-Fascist propaganda while working as a loader near the mills and organized the stealing of bread (and other things)."[71] Five peasants then needed to be questioned about the activities of one local Communist hiding in their village during the war. No matter how slow, examinations of partyness occupied an important place in Kyiv's life during this period, for there was little else the local Communists could directly control. It was a process that involved thousands of declarations and recommendations and witness interviews.

The following are some typical cases of *okruzhentsy* whose partyness was investigated after the occupation. While some of the formerly occupied had already benefited from the returning Communists' decisions, others may have recognized the lengthy hurdles for reacceptance as signs their leaders correctly comprehended the city's difficult place within the Stalin regime. Resources were scarce and the number of people with special access to them needed to be limited. Nevertheless, the reacceptance of some *okruzhentsy* after the occupation makes it hard to argue that Evstigneev's example compromised the future of every Communist who ended up behind enemy lines.

Two Communists who escaped the city in September 1941 to work in the rear before returning to occupy important positions are examples of successful returns to Kyiv's elite. One was Fedor Chebotarev, a forty-seven-year-old Russian with a high school education who became a party member in 1921 and worked in Kyiv before the war. A February 3, 1944, Ukrainian-language Kyiv Obkom resolution states,

[Chebotar'ov] having left the city of Kyiv on September 19, 1941, organized a brigade of those Red Army men lagging behind their own units. After handing that brigade over to a Lieutenant Kapleev, Chebotar'ov entered the partisan detachment of Osechkin. On September 26, 1941, the German occupants defeated this detachment and Chebotar'ov departed for Berezan' Raion to escape encirclement. There he was captured and sent to the Iahotyns'kyi concentration camp. On the road to Iahotyna, he destroyed his party card. Chebotar'ov spent until October 2, 1941, in that camp before he escaped. On December 22, 1941, he crossed over the frontline near the village of Vovhanov'ka in Kharkiv Oblast.[72]

Once behind Soviet lines, Chebotarev departed for Saratov with the Ukrainian TsK's permission and was sent to Tashkent to join his family where he worked until

November 1943 as plant director for Tashkent City Industry (*Tashkentmisk'prom*). On January 17, 1944, the Kyiv Gorkom reaccepted Chebotarev, and he would become chairman of the Kyiv City Soviet in 1946. The need for skilled leaders trumped any political misgivings at this early point after the occupation.

A similar case is that of fifty-four-year-old D. A. Hoikhberh-Tul'chins'kyi, a Jew and party member since 1930 who had worked in Kyiv before the war as an assistant editor of a newspaper belonging to the Southwestern Railroad. By September 28, 1944, he had returned and was working again at that paper when the Kyiv Gorkom offered this decision: "[Hoikhberh-Tul'chins'kyi] in September 1941 evacuated from Kyiv with the Southwest Railroad's leadership. Near the village of Berezan', the enemy surrounded him and he buried his party card. On September 28, 1941, the Germans sent him and other captured railroad workers in the direction of the Pereiaslav and Darnytsa camps for prisoners of war. On October 5, 1941, as a railroad worker, the Germans freed him and commandeered him for reconstruction work in Kyiv. After his return to the city, he hid for close to a month, and then left by foot for the east."[73] On November 30, 1941, Hoikhberh-Tul'chins'kyi crossed over the frontlines where he was soon freed of military responsibilities and sent to Cheliabinsk to work as the head of cadres at a building site. After the Zaliznychnyi Raikom decided on December 25, 1943, to reaccept him, the Kyiv Gorkom seconded this decision and asked the Kyiv Obkom to confirm this resolution.

Chebotarev's and Hoikhberh-Tul'chins'kyi's cases demonstrate both the need for skilled leaders in the early days after the occupation and the limited ideological litmus test for those who had been behind enemy lines. Rather than any active resistance, simple escape from the Germans seems to have been enough. But as the reconstruction process stalled, the proportion of *okruzhentsy* readmitted would become a distinct minority.

Typical of those reaccepted was Keli V. Shvartsman, whose case was decided in August 1945. While she no longer lived in Kyiv, she had been registered with the Kyiv Gorkom before September 19, 1941. At the time of her partyness decision, she was working as a "record keeper in the Directorate of Military Construction no. 167" in the city of Simferopol' (RSFSR). The Kyiv Obkom's investigation into her case after she evacuated with a Lenin Raion "destruction battalion" in the summer of 1941 reads as follows: "Near the village of Boryspil' in Kyiv Oblast, the enemy surrounded her. On September 25, 1941, Shvartsman went to the Donbas. On January 18, 1942, she arrived in the village of Shkarlupyno in Stalin Oblast where on January 23, 1942, the Red Army liberated her. From then until to April 15, 1942, the All-Union NKVD investigated Shvartsman in Novorossiisk [RSFSR]. From May 1, 1942, Shvartsman worked as an instructor in the Union of Prison Medicine and Sanitation Workers [*Medsanturma*] in Alma-Ata [Kazakh SSR]."[74] After spending until September 29, 1944, working as a controller in an

"Oblast Card Bureau" (*Oblkartbiuro*) in Kyzl' Orda [Kazakh SSR], Shvartsman was sent to work in Simferopol' where she continued to receive positive recommendations. On July 23, 1945, the Kyiv Gorkom agreed to reaccept her.

There are three reasons why Shvartsman's case is typical. First, there is no mention of resistance to the Nazis, only that she made an effort to escape. Second, *okruzhentsy* liberated by the Red Army often passed through All-Union NKVD filtration before they were sent to the rear. Third, the reacceptance of someone not in the city had few repercussions for the Communists involved. By that point, amid the scarcity that now enveloped Kyiv, any sign that someone was being favored was something they wanted to avoid. Here was one policy that made everyone in Kyiv who had lived through the war—no matter where—feel better about him- or herself. If few people could join the party, maybe it was not such a bad thing to be left out after all.

The *okruzhentsy* who were most politically feasible to reaccept were Red Army veterans. The experience of Hnat I. Alekseenko was described in the April 8, 1946, protocols of a Kyiv Gorkom meeting:

> An investigation has established that on September 18, 1941, Alekseenko together with the employees of Kievpromtorg evacuated Kyiv. Near Boryspil' the enemy surrounded him and he remained on occupied territory. In his own words, he destroyed his party card. Until October 18, 1941, he lived in Kyiv. On October 15, 1941, the police arrested him. In his own words, this was because he had no living permit. He was released a day later. After that, he went to live in the villages ... of Zhytomyr Oblast (where he was born) until February 1943. He did not work anywhere and hid from the police who searched for him. From February until October 1943, he worked as a repairman at Kozhanka railroad station.[75]

With the Red Army's arrival, Alekseenko was drafted into the military and awarded medals "For Courage" and "For Victory over Germany in the Great Patriotic War, 1941–1945" before he was wounded in battle and, ultimately, demobilized in September 1945. After the centrally located Lenin Raikom resolved on October 31, 1945, to restore him to the party's ranks, the Kyiv Gorkom confirmed this resolution. Although Alekseienko's experience of occupation was suspect and placed him in the same category as anyone who had been out of the Stalin regime's control during this period, his battlefield valor was irrefutable. If one succeeded at the front, then there was a chance to restore one's status.

A similar situation happened to a certain Odinokov, a prewar Podil' Raikom second secretary who lived in Kyiv at the time of the Kyiv Gorkom resolution about his case in 1946. It had taken the city-level committee nearly three years to decide on Odinokov following his initial reacceptance into the party by the Podil' Raikom on November 23, 1943. The Kyiv Gorkom resolution reads, "[Odinokov] left Kyiv on September 18, 1941. Together with units of the Red Army, in the raion of Boryspil', he was surrounded by the enemy. As he made his way to the east, Odinokov reached the city of Poltava where he remained on occupied territory. In Poltava, Odinokov became a metal worker at a fabric factory where he worked until the arrival of the Red Army on May 15, 1943. From that date he worked as a metal worker on the reconstruction of a milk factory."[76]

After Kyiv's liberation, Odinokov worked as an assistant to the head of the Podil' Raion Draft Board before joining the Red Army in February 1944 and earning the order of the "Red Star" and the medals "For the Capture of Konigsburg" and "For Victory over Germany" as a battalion head before demobilization in 1946. The resolution's final lines, about Odinokov's statement that he failed to partake in any underground organizations or with any partisan detachments during the occupation because he was sick, were probably the reason for the delay in his reacceptance, though military valor seems to have overcome any objections.

These stories show that active resistance to the Nazis was not essential for reacceptance. One's position in the returning bureaucratic structures or the army, as well as sheer luck or possibly the fact that one was no longer in Kyiv to begin with, helped. A study of the Kyiv Gorkom's meeting protocols from February 1, 1944, to mid-1946 reveals that of the 1,291 personal cases of *okruzhentsy* partyness decided during that time, 450 (or 35 percent) of the resolutions resulted in reacceptance. But rejection was still by far the most common occurrence; in many parts of Ukraine, it occurred in nine out of every ten cases.[77]

A good illustration of why rejection was so widespread is the example of Andrii H. Mekhed, whose case was decided by the Kyiv Gorkom on December 10, 1943. Mekhed must have been among those *okruzhentsy* near the Ukrainian capital in November 1943, for it had not taken him long to put in the paperwork needed to make a decision on his partyness. The Kyiv Gorkom concluded its investigation about his activity on occupied territory with this information:

> Despite the fact that in the village of Rozhky, where he was hiding, there existed partisan detachments, he did not join them. In this way, he manifested his indecisiveness and cowardice by placing his own interests higher than the interests of the party.... After a check of the materials handed in by Mekhed in the village of Rozhky, Kyiv Oblast, comrade Dvoinoe, Dmytro Danylovych (a member of the party since 1932) has characterized him negatively. Mekhed, Andrii Hnatovych, as someone who does not justify the party's trust, and for having shown himself to be a coward who put his own interests above those of the party's, is excluded from the party.[78]

The wording of this resolution is rare in that it mentions what likely made up a part of each investigation: the testimony of witnesses. But judging by the way rumors spread in Kyiv, the fact the local Communists had applied the moniker "coward" to anyone who failed to resist the Nazis also helped to smooth their way back into power in the city. As further examples show, there was little resistance in Nazi-occupied Kyiv during the war.

Such an approach probably galvanized support for the Communists among the city's burgeoning population. At least no one was going to get ahead unfairly and be given a chance to upset the status quo. Consider the February 7, 1944, exclusion by the Kyiv Obkom of Semen L. Rapoport for failing to "carry out any work directed toward the battle with the German invaders." This decision read in part,

> An investigation has determined that Rapoport in 1941 did not evacuate from the city of Kyiv because of illness. On September 24, 1941, the police stopped him on the street and took him to a police station where they took his passport and then released him. On September 25, 1941, he was arrested for being a Jew and a Communist, put in a prison, and accused of setting fire to the Khreshchatyk. That very day, Rapoport was taken first to a concentration camp for Jews, and then to the Gestapo. On January 24, 1942, he escaped from the Gestapo and then hid at his friends' place in Solomyntsi [a Kyivan neighborhood on the city's southern outskirts].[79]

At the time of his exclusion, Rapoport worked as the head of the ration card bureau in Pechersk Raion. That his wartime past suddenly made him "untrustworthy" may have had more to do with envy among the formerly occupied population than anything he had done during the occupation. Perhaps the local Communists hoped their city's inhabitants would see such a tough policy toward the *okruzhentsy* as just. In no way could someone who had suffered under the Nazis be publicly seen to be getting ahead when everyone else had suffered too, especially after some of the formerly occupied had been able to secure better housing for themselves during the first year following the occupation.

The fate of the *okruzhentsy* in Kyiv demonstrates Soviet power's ability to judiciously rule the city. Emotions were kept under control because many of the Communists excluded from the party were already absent from Kyiv by the time the decisions about them were made. As the local Communists soon found out, a much graver problem was the many people applying for party membership for the first time. Here, again, the leaders needed to prove to the city's population that they were critical of all attempts to join the party, in order to help reestablish the legitimacy of Soviet power in Kyiv.

Those with the best chance for acceptance as new party members were those active in the Soviet military. Even as Moscow worked to slow new acceptances, a Red Army political officer named Leonid Brezhnev wrote a January 21, 1945, letter to the Kyiv Obkom about a group of Red Army men who "by their blood" had earned the right to join the party: "The 159th Fortified Region [has] sent a number of inquiries to Kyiv Oblast's raikoms about sending recommendations concerning persons who earlier lived on its territory during the German occupation.... At present, the above-named comrades are in active units of the Red Army and express a desire to join the ranks of the party. We ask for your influence over this matter."[80] In response to Brezhnev's request, the Kyiv Obkom passed a resolution entitled "On the Irresponsible Position Taken by Some Raion and City Committees toward Fulfilling the Requests for Information by the Political Organs of the Red Army."[81] This resolution's text mentioned Kyiv's Stalin Raion with twelve unanswered inquiries and Darnytsa Raion with twenty-one as typical of the "mechanical" approach of party secretaries toward the Red Army's needs.

An example of a response to this resolution comes from Kyiv Oblast's Bila Tserkva Gorkom dated April 28, 1945. A portion of their report reveals the work involved in keeping up with these ambitious Red Army men who had once been on occupied territory. The note reads, in part, "Thirty-one inquiries asking for references about servicemen serving in the Red Army arrived here at the Gorkom. To all of them an answer has been given. Concerning the absence of the needed investigations as mentioned in the decision of the Kyiv Obkom of April 24 [*sic*], 1945, the Bila Tserkva Gorkom reports that the investigations are literally done in the localities."[82] It had been the responsibility of the raikoms to first look into the soldiers' pasts in their home neighborhoods and places of work. But the need for a peaceful population had trumped prompt investigations into what happened during the occupation. A culture of silence developed as locals recognized that their leaders also wanted as little as possible to do with that moment when the Soviet state had let its people down. Publicly talking about what happened during the occupation soon became politically incorrect.

But what about those people who wanted to become party members in Kyiv who had nothing to do with the Red Army? A look at the March 6, 1945, Kyiv Gorkom plenum that discussed a question entitled "On the Growth of the Party Organization and Work with Young Communists" finds leaders from Kyiv's raion and factory party organizations talking about the need to increase the number of Communists in the city. The main idea emanating from these discussions, though, was that party members should now be on guard to defend their ranks from the unworthy. A comrade Pavlovich from the Pechersk Raikom struck the correct tone when he said, "We should take into account the atmosphere that we are working in. Now is not the time when the Germans were outside Moscow and Leningrad and we were sure that self-seeking elements would not go for party membership. But now that our party is near Berlin, things could be different. People are going for the party who are forcing us to be justifiably careful."[83] Considering the scarcity in the city and, as chapter 5 reveals, the lack of Marxist-Leninist rhetoric in Kyiv during the war years, the idea that people might be "going for the party" due to selfish reasons rather than idealistic ones makes sense.

A representative from the Gorky Machine-Tool Factory then spoke about the factory known locally as simply the *Stankozavod*: "Through reevacuation there returned to us somewhere around sixty people, forty of whom are Communists. . . . The rest of our collective, that is up to 1,000 people, is a new contingent, the majority of whom stayed behind on occupied territory. We of course should not separate out those who are reevacuees from those who stayed behind. However, we need to be on the watch for the particularity of our party work with a collective where the vast majority of comrades stayed behind on occupied territory."[84] At OSMCh no. 305, meanwhile, three thousand workers had probably suffered a similar fate, for not a single one of them had been accepted into the party's ranks. The same situation could be found at the Kreshchatikstroi building trust, where not a single one of that trust's two thousand workers had become a Communist during 1944–45. That some of the formerly occupied had done well following Soviet power's return meant this approach likely soothed those still fighting their way back into Kyiv's life.

But the reason given for such blanket "distrust" according to Kyiv Gorkom Secretary Gorban in his conclusion to the meeting was that "There is more responsibility with [the formerly occupied]. Without a doubt, there needs to be significantly more educational work done with them than with comrades we have been educating all the time."[85] By emphasizing again the need for "education" of workers, Gorban returned for a moment to the old crutch that the formerly occupied population was somehow "poisoned by Goebbels's propaganda" and thus politically unreliable. Such a ruse conveniently created an escape valve for the local party when the sensitive question of party growth was raised. But the unspoken issue remained that local authorities had enough problems relegitimizing Soviet power without battling for scarce resources with even more colleagues.

Who, then, from among the civilian population was accepted into the party? The March 6, 1945, Kyiv Gorkom plenum, as well another dated June 8–9, 1945, provide some clues. At the beginning of the former plenum, Secretary M. Khmel' of the Zhovtnevyi Raikom noted, "We have grown because of the acceptance of technicians. In no way, though, can it be said that an engineer and a bureaucrat are one and the same, the former are the main figures at the factory."[86] Next, a Secretary Neliubin from Molotov Raion added, "Among those [we have] accepted are the main constructor of the Ukrainian Cable [*Ukrkabel*] Factory, comrade Levskovskii, comrade Chernyshev (an engineer-chemist), comrade Belik (the main engineer of the spirits industry), Fetisov, and others (doctors and surgeons). . . . We see that all of these comrades are the best progressive part of their enterprises, mills, and factories."[87] Thereafter, a Comrade Kostiuk from the centrally located

Figure 3.3. Party leader M. M. Pydtychenko, B. A. Gorban, General V. I. Davydov, General I. I. Iakubovs'kyi, N. S. Khrushchev, F. V. Mokienko, and General A. A. Hrechko at the celebrations of the twenty-eighth anniversary of the October Revolution, November 7, 1945. Reproduced by permission from the H. Pshenychnyi Central State CinePhotoPhono Archives of Ukraine.

Lenin Raion, which accepted 487 people (compared to the industrial Molotov and Zhovtnevyi Raions, which admitted just 65 and 32 people respectively) during 1944 and the first part of 1945, began his comments by saying, "We have accepted the best people of our raion: fighters and the Soviet intelligentsia."[88] Keeping the numbers down, though, was easy because the vast majority of Kyiv's people did not fall into such groups.

Three months later, at their June 1945 plenum, the Kyiv Gorkom elaborated on this tendency by discussing again the question "On the Growth of the Kyiv City Party Organization from the Period March to May 1945." Secretary Aleksei Davydov summarized matters: "The growth of the party during the period of March, April, and May . . . is characterized by the active additions to her ranks of the best people. [These are people] who battled for our motherland and proved their loyalty with their heroic work and courage in those severe, threatening days of the battle with the German-Fascist occupiers."[89] The "best people" idea was a leftover from the party membership drives of 1937–41. It now replaced the mass enrollments of Red Army men that had marked recruitment from December 1941 to October 1944, and then "set the tone for party recruitment policies for the remainder of the Stalin period."⁹⁰ While 357 candidates for membership in the Kyiv Gorkom had become full members during that time, 317 of these people were "office workers" while only 40 were workers. For ordinary Kyivans and especially any late-arriving returnees, such a restrictive policy on party membership probably provided comfort, considering the city's lack of resources.

But an office-worker-oriented approach could never be admitted to be the party's sole policy on admittance in a "worker's state." So Davydov again noted as "a serious insufficiency" the fact that his organization was still not accepting workers. "For example," he remarked, "in Stalin Raion, out of 56 people accepted as candidates for party membership, only five of them were workers. In Molotov Raion, out of eighteen people accepted, only three were workers and there is an analogous situation in other raions."⁹¹ But Davydov concluded with the example of the union-level Stalin Ship-Building Factory where the right conditions for the acceptance of workers did exist: "That factory has a large number of workers, those who work immediately with machine tools. Furthermore, these are workers who have been reevacuated from the east."⁹²

Davydov's mentioning of workers who had "reevacuated from the east" shows again that the formerly occupied population needed to be marginalized somewhat following its successes during the early months after the occupation. At that point, a representative from Kaganovich Raion contributed the news that at the Karl Marx Confectionery Factory, with its thousand workers and a large party organization, not a single one had been accepted into the party during 1945.⁹³ No one new, except for a few army men and members of the intelligentsia, was being accepted, and that meant the status quo would be maintained in Kyiv, at least for a while.

By the end of this period, the Ukrainian TsK's Organization-Instruction Department would note the following about Kyiv Oblast: "Of [1,620 people] accepted as candidates for membership during 1946, workers made up ten percent of the total, collective farm workers were 6.9 percent, while office workers and students made up the other 82.7 percent."⁹⁴ The return of the "best people" idea might even have been seen by ordinary Kyivans as a soothing continuity with the prewar era.

Was there anyone else, though, who could have hoped to join the party at this time? Members of unofficial Soviet partisan formations and unofficial underground party committees did make efforts to gain recognition of their activities under the Nazis as potential justification for entrance into the party. This process was prominent in Kyiv because there had been no officially recognized resistance in the city by the time the Nazi occupation ended. But if these unofficial groups could secure recognition, their chances of joining the Communist elite were better than anyone else among the formerly occupied population. But Kyiv's Communists took their time in recognizing that any unofficial organized resistance had existed in and around their city. Here, especially, vigilance on party membership added to these leaders' legitimacy in the eyes of the masses.

Only on July 2, 1945, did the Kyiv Gorkom confirm the existence of an unofficial resistance group in the city during the occupation. In this case, it was the underground Zaliznychnyi Raikom that had functioned throughout the occupation, but over which the evacuated party had been unable to maintain surveillance. Left behind in Kyiv, the leader of this committee, Pirohivs'kyi, and his men conducted this work:

> On September 18–21, 1941, there were blown up main railroad shops, the Andreev depot, the post office at the train station, and the Solomia'ns'kyi and Kadets'kyi highway bridges. During the length of September 1941 until November 1943 . . . by the raion there was carried out great work to create underground organizations and groups on the railroad and in the enterprises of the raion. . . . Besides that, the underground Zaliznychnyi Raikom organized and led the underground work of groups of certain other raions in Kyiv (Zhovtnevyi, Pechersk, and Stalin raions) and systematically helped them with the organization of the battle with the enemy. In this way, the underground Zaliznychnyi Raikom under the leadership of comrade Pirohivs'kyi, O.S. recruited 41 Communists, nineteen Komsomols, and 73 non-party members and brought them into active battle with the German-Fascist invaders. . . . In desperate and frantic battles with the enemy, there died courageous and self-sacrificing Bolsheviks, members of the Biuro of the underground Zaliznychnyi Raikom and party leadership, and also during the last days before the liberation of Kyiv from the Germans, that true son of the party and the fatherland, the popular Bolshevik, the organizer of the battle with the enemy, and the secretary of the underground Zaliznychnyi Raikom, comrade Pirohivs'kyi, Oleksandr Sydorovych.[95]

Before it went on to confirm the existence of Pirohivs'kyi's work and the number of participants in the organization at 133 people, however, the Kyiv Gorkom also noted that a committee member had "not sufficiently subordinated himself to the needs of conspiracy, credulously relating to those types whom he recruited into underground work," the results of which were that "random and questionable types" had penetrated into the organization.[96]

One month later, the work of an unofficial "underground Bolshevik organization" in Kyiv's Pechersk Raion was also confirmed as having taken place. That resolution highlighted again the role of Pirohivs'kyi's underground Zaliznychnyi Raikom in this organization's success:

> The Kyiv Gorkom states that in Pechersk Raion during the German occupation of Kyiv, from June 1942 to October 1943, there was active an underground Bolshevik organization headed by a comrade Sherbakov, Pavel Il'ych, a party

member since 1931. . . . In June 1942, this underground organization established contact and worked with the leadership of the underground Zaliznychnyi Raikom and its secretary Pirohivs'kyi O. M. [*sic*]. Becoming models of heroism, steadfastness, and courage in the battle with the enemy, the underground groups of Pechersk Raion committed acts of diversion at enterprises and on water transport, frustrated the removal of Soviet people to Germany (for slave labor), equipment and food, carried out a large amount of agitation and mass work among the population, and gave help in the form of arms, medicine, and people to partisan detachments. The underground Bolshevik organization of Pechersk united thirty-eight people among whom there were ten members and candidates of the party, four Komsomols and twenty-four "non-party" persons. . . . The Pechersk Raikom in Kyiv on July 27, 1945, affirmed this Bolshevik underground raion organization's report.[97]

The extensive role of Pirohivs'kyi in the unofficial resistance during the German occupation uncovered during the summer of 1945, and judged to have really taken place, may testify to the limited nature of the unofficial resistance as a whole in the city. By August 17, the Kyiv Gorkom had moved on to underground Bolshevik organizations at the Kyiv-Moscow Railroad Depot with thirty-one "active participants in the underground anti-Fascist battle," and another underground group led by a Comrade Synehubov that numbered forty-four people and had been active in Podil' Raion. Most important are the small numbers concerned here, which show that access to the elite was closely guarded. Very few people were recognized as parts of these unofficial resistance groups, considering that the overall population of Kyiv in the summer before liberation numbered around 200,000 people.

A final Kyiv Gorkom document casts more doubt on whether there was any citywide resistance. Entitled "On Looking over the Report of the Activity of the Underground Kyiv Gorkom Led by Comrade Petrushko, B.I. during the Period from August to November 1943," it suggests that an underground Kyiv Gorkom was organized by Pirohivs'kyi's underground Zaliznychnyi Raikom on orders from the official Khrushchev partisan formation in July 1943. The group's task was to create new underground raikoms in Kyiv, to unite them, and to carry out an armed uprising.

Pirohivs'kyi selected Petrushko from among his own ranks to be this underground committee's secretary. The latter's leadership group consisted of two Communists, A. D. Iahyn and M. U. Malevynchuk, and a nonparty man by the name of Smyhyn. A report described the effort of these men to unite and direct the activity of "all underground Bolshevik organizations and groups in the city of Kyiv":

> During the examination and study of the activity of the underground organizations and groups that existed during the German occupation of Kyiv, it has

been established that the underground Kyiv Gorkom incorrectly oriented itself in terms of people, organizations, and groups. This committee did not check, and did not become convinced of, the latter's political direction and practical activities. As a result, unchecked, unstable and even enemy elements and groups penetrated into the underground raion committees of the party that the underground city committee had oriented its own work around (with the exception of those created in 1941, 1942, and 1943, which had their activities directed by the underground Zaliznychnyi Raikom.) The overwhelming majority [of these raion committees] did not carry out any sort of anti-Fascist battle at all. Those underground raion committees in Stalin, Molotov, Lenin, Zhovtnevyi, and Petriv [Podil'] raions that were confirmed by the underground Kyiv Gorkom before the liberation of Kyiv by the Red Army did not get their work underway and their respective raikoms and the Kyiv Gorkom have not recognized their activities as actually having taken place.[98]

Such a finding obviously did not bode well for the investigation of whether this unofficial, underground Kyiv Gorkom resisted the occupying Nazis during their last months in Kyiv. Kyiv's elite concluded,

Orienting themselves toward an armed uprising in Kyiv, the underground Kyiv Gorkom, at the beginning of September 1943 created a staff office and placed before it these tasks: 1) The organization of an armed uprising in the city at the moment of the approach of units of the Red Army, and 2) The safeguarding of industrial and military objects from being taken away to Germany. . . . The task of organizing an armed uprising in the city was not realistic because [the staff office] and the underground Kyiv Gorkom did not establish, and did not have any contact or communication with, the frontline units of the Red Army. Because of the absence of active and multi-sided preparation for the uprising, a sufficient number of people and armaments did not take part in it. While centering its attention on this unrealistic task, the underground Kyiv Gorkom let go by the wayside the other main task during this period: the effort to save enterprises and equipment from ruin or from being taken to Germany. The fighting groups that were created did not carry out a single armed operation and did not manifest any activity against the German occupants who—amid the pressure from the attacking Red Army—were leaving the city and without a doubt causing ruin to various important objects. On October 28, 1943, the Germans arrested the secretary of the underground Kyiv Gorkom, comrade Petrushko B. I., and from that point the underground committee stopped its activities.[99]

On January 22, 1946, the Kyiv Gorkom finally refused to accept Petrushko's group as official. This decision was based on the above investigation's conclusion:

that the underground Kyiv Gorkom "did not develop its work and was unable to cope with those tasks that were placed before it."[100] This decision about the most important of the unofficial resistance groups in Kyiv under the Nazis indicates that this route into the Kyivan elite was rarely traveled right after war. Considering the success of the Red Army men in joining the party during the war, and the continuation of the "best people" policy from the prewar era, however, it is quite likely that many people still tried to use this route to gain entrance into the elite later in the 1940s.

Ultimately, the refusal of union-level bureaucrats in Moscow and union-level factory managers in Kyiv to allocate resources made it impossible for local Communists to begin the city's reconstruction. But because they enjoyed a say over some of other resources existing in the city, these leaders' status was coveted. It must have been clear to most Kyivans that those in the party—like Comrade Beregovenko—could circumvent laws they did not like, or even write new ones. But Moscow's move to slow the party's growth in late 1944 probably helped these leaders maintain social stability in the city, because they could now approach almost all applications to join their ranks with equal distrust. By refraining from touching too often on what had happened under the Nazis, the local Communists helped their efforts at being seen as fair and balanced leaders among the masses. Openly talking about what had gone on under the Germans likely ran the risk of delegitimizing Soviet power, since the Soviets, of course, had failed to prevent the death and destruction from happening in the first place.

There were obvious problems resulting from the Stalin regime's ignoring Kyiv's reconstruction needs, due to the collision of the Great Breakthrough's economy with the Second World War. And there were other processes playing out in the Ukrainian capital: the reassembly of its privileged groups now shielded from mobilization and struggling to survive, the long search to find a message from above relegitimizing the Soviets' abilities to lead, and the inevitable challenges to such leaders from below brought about by the misery of the war years. How these processes influenced decisions made by the Ukrainian Communists in the mid-1940s is the story this book now seeks to tell.

Chapter Four

"A Textual Implementation of the Law . . . Was Not Carried Out"

The Reassembled Masses

In May 1945, the family of a Red Army major, the Ostromogil'skiis, faced a court-ordered eviction from the apartment they had inhabited since Kyiv's liberation. Soon thereafter, an instructor, Dirin, from the Kyiv Obkom's Organization-Instruction Department arranged to meet with the new Kyiv City procurator, Langunovskii, about his decision to allow a man by the name of Vaisberg to inhabit the Ostromogil'skiis' apartment. Their encounter led Dirin to write to the Ukrainian TsK:

> I arrived at the Kyiv City Procurator Office. . . . However, Langunovskii declared his day to receive people would be on Sunday, June 2, and that, therefore, he would not converse with me. I presented Langunovskii with my documents . . . but he declared his actions could only be controlled by the Ukrainian Procurator and thus he was not going to show me anything and that I should leave his office. Then he became rude and brusque with me. . . . To my point that we were not talking about someone who knows someone better in the Ukrainian TsK than someone else, but about the fate of a serviceman's family with small children, Langunovskii answered, "Why are you agitating me?" and emphatically turned away not wanting to talk with me anymore about anything. It was only after the Ukrainian Procurator's office called him that Langunovskii agreed to issue the order of June 5, 1945, stopping the execution of this decision.[1]

Such an episode suggests that, as returnees like Vaisberg inundated the Ukrainian capital to take advantage of the privileges they had earned during the war, they battled the formerly occupied over scarce resources. While the Ostromogil'skiis managed to stay in their apartment, the local Communists had been unable to prevent this battle from taking place. Dealing with stalled reconstruction and an increasing city population, local Communists spent much of their time trying to meet demands for better living conditions from an ever-growing number of people.

This chapter examines Kyiv's reassembling masses by looking at four groups: the formerly occupied, returnees, mobilized laborers (ranging from youth mobilized through *orgnabor* to German POWs), and demobilized servicemen. While the difference between the first two is the date when they first called the city home, they are treated together because many, if not most, were also privileged servicemen's dependents. The laborers are also differentiated in that some were free while others were not, though the Germans were not necessarily the worse off of the two. Finally, the returning victors' expectations—and their accompanying demands—made them a particularly difficult group to satisfy. The war gave many of these people, in fact, new opportunities to assert their interests in a society once chastened by the Great Terror.

In the face of the failures surrounding "unorganized return" and reconstruction, to what extent and how did these local leaders take sides in order to maintain control over their city? The ways in which they relegitimized Soviet power in the face of these groups' competing agendas, as well as the latter's relationships to such policies, are subjects examined in coming chapters. Chronicling why a new "regime city of the first category" emerged and why that provides clues as to how the Stalin regime ruled the Soviet Union after the war is the goal of the second half of this book.

The Reassembled Masses: The Formerly Occupied and Returnees

For the formerly occupied, the period just after liberation presented a paradox. Food and quality employment were almost nonexistent, but the city was empty and its contents ready to be seized. One thing was clear: deference to the returning Soviets needed to be paid. In November 1943, a Ukrainian TsK Organization and Instruction Department instructor, Khrapunov, described the postoccupation city to his boss, A. N. Zlenko: "After liberation and the decisions of the Ukrainian TsK and SNK UkrSSR on measures for the reconstruction of Kyiv passed in the first half of November, the situation is getting better on a daily basis. . . . The population of the city is growing. . . . Kyivans want to work. At the Executive Committee of the Kyiv City Soviet, hundreds of people show up every day looking to be directed somewhere to work."[2] While both sides wanted to start reconstruction, there was little to be done after the Nazi retreat. At first, many simply congregated at their destroyed places of work in hopes of finding something to do, and of avoiding conscription into the Red Army.

There were, however, temporary mobilizations of labor to meet the military's reconstruction needs. As mentioned earlier, GKO had legalized temporary mobilizations for up to two months in August 1942.[3] Kyiv's railroad junctions and bridges were the main beneficiaries of this mobilization. Such work was backbreaking and dangerous, and without any real reward save a ration of food. In the early days, this might have been enough. But temporary mobilizations were few and far between, and the formerly occupied soon became disenchanted with such *narodnaia stroika*.

A Kyiv Gorkom resolution of September 27, 1944, for example, noted what happened after many of its raion committees became less inclined to send people to work on the city's main street: "This has resulted in the non-fulfillment (within the time limits set) of work plans on the Khreshchatyk. . . . On the "collector" [the giant trench for sewers], only 295 meters out of 1,110 have been completed."[4] In the end, it was up to the Ukrainian NKVD's Local Anti-air Defenses to finish digging the sewer.[5] It took a year, however, before that organization's leader, Riasnoi, could report to Khrushchev that it had completed the 1,100-meter-long trench "dedicated toward the most modern communal services the Soviet Union can provide."[6]

The first temporary mobilization of labor out of the city occurred with a SNK UkrSSR and Ukrainian TsK resolution dated July 1, 1944, ordering 300,000 stacked cubic meters (*skladometers*) of firewood to be collected and brought in from rural areas to Kyiv by September's end.[7] Altogether, some six thousand Kyivans were mobilized for this campaign. But a follow-up resolution dated October 10 from the same two organizations reveals this task had yet to be completed.[8] The wood had been collected, but only 6 percent of it had been brought to Kyiv for distribution. The result was further temporary mobilizations of labor to complete this task, which continued into the winter. All of this occurred alongside the mobilization of other Kyivans into the fields to help with the harvest. Even these temporary mobilizations ended by 1945 as the Stalin regime apparently sought to protect the Ukrainian capital's population from having to sacrifice too much.

The first full-time jobs were also small in number compared to the 300,000 people residing in the city by March 1944. Evidence for this can be found in a series of resolutions that winter designed to restore the city's energy network. On January 20, 1944, SNK UkrSSR and the Ukrainian TsK obliged the director of Kyiv's electrical company (*Kievenergo*) to begin restoring the city's electrical power stations and substations.[9] This resolution also required Kyiv's oblast and raion leaders, as well as the commander of the Kyiv Military Region, to find 1,500 people from the "non-working city and rural populations," 500 "qualified workers" from active enterprises, and another 1,500 people obligated to serve in the Red Army but listed as of "limited use" to complete this work.[10]

The resolution also demanded that housing for those mobilized be organized. It ordered the Kyiv City Soviet to allocate to Kievenergo from the enterprises of the Southern Energy Construction Trust (*Iuzhenergostroi*) living premises for 2,800 people, plus the apartment buildings that had belonged to it before the war, while also evicting all those living in the Construction Trust's premises who did not work for its parent organization, the All-Union People's Commissariat of

Electrical Stations. Such demands, however, could no longer be made once the city's housing was occupied.

The fate of the Lepse Tractor Factory belonging to the All-Union People's Commissariat of the Machine Tool Building is another example of what opportunities were available in Kyiv. A memorandum written by its director to the Kyiv Gorkom's Industrial Department in the middle of 1944 declared, "The factory is to be restored without reevacuation, which means it needs to find new workers and new equipment."[11] On September 23, the Kyiv Gorkom obliged three Kyivan raions to mobilize three hundred people for work at the factory. But this was never fulfilled.[12] More time elapsed before SNK UkrSSR and the Ukrainian TsK passed another resolution with measures to help the Lepse Factory maintain the local tractor fleet with spare parts as quickly as possible.[13] To keep the three hundred people still scheduled to be mobilized, the factory now received a dormitory for a future school, a food store and cafeteria on its premises, a right to rent two houses on the prestigious Reitars'ka Street in the city's center, and a prohibition on the temporary mobilizations (for firewood and harvest collection) of its skilled workers.

Another clue as to who was employed and what they were doing after the occupation can be found in a September 27, 1944, Kyiv Gorkom resolution describing the problems that stymied building materials production at the Construction Details Factory (*Buddetal'*). Despite an order from its Moscow-based ministry saying it should begin work by May 1, 1944, production had been at a standstill due to "the inadequate organization of labor, the untimely delivery of building materials and reception of earlier evacuated equipment, the insufficient enlistment of qualified labor power (only five such people have been hired in the last nine months), [and] the absence of the preparation of such workers from those already employed at the factory."[14] Part of the problem might have been that not a single one of the 116 women hired by the factory during 1944 had been educated for a building trade specialty.[15]

The situation over at the shell of the former Dzerzhinsky Tram Factory (now a part of the All-Union People's Commissariat of Mortar Defenses) demonstrates the fate of the many unskilled women in Kyiv at this time. Perhaps they were attracted to this factory because its new importance in a "defense-related industry" elevated its status, and thus made food easier to come by. But a December 18, 1944, memorandum from the Kyiv Gorkom about the failure of the factory's director, Platonov, to fulfill a February GKO resolution reveals that the factory failed to supply these workers with food because it lacked the wherewithal to teach them the skills necessary to secure long-term employment. The situation was similar to that at Buddetal': "During the whole time that the factory has been working, by brigade and individual training, there have been prepared all of eleven people. According to the plan of the [Commissariat's] directorate, the factory was supposed to prepare 258 people just in the fourth quarter."[16] Both of these resolutions suggest that factory directors were loath to train unskilled women until their enterprises received the resources necessary to actually begin production.

A May 18, 1945, SNK UkrSSR resolution entitled "On the Reconstruction of Locomotive Repair, Wagon Repair, and Engine-Building Factories Belonging to the [All-Union] People's Commissariat of Railways on the Territory of Ukraine" ordered the mobilization of 2,500 workers from the city into these factories, while also prohibiting the Red Army from drafting them.[17] Such a qualification indicates that male workers were probably among those mobilized into these three major factories. This order also appeared before the general demobilization announced on June 24, 1945, which suggests that many of the people involved were men who had been waiting for more "sensible" employment. After all, Kyiv's railways belonged to an all-union commissariat, and some no doubt hoped that such an organization might provide better housing opportunities.

In sum, by war's end, many in Kyiv were either underemployed or simply remained unemployed until resources were directed toward the city. Although the Stalin regime wanted them to help with reconstruction, few Kyivans wanted to become involved. Work in the city's factories did, however, pick up a little after war's end. In June 1945, the Kyiv Obkom ordered a GKO-initiated resolution mandating the production of spare parts for automobiles and tractors at many of Kyiv's major factories be begun in addition to the "defense-related" production already assigned. Another resolution was entitled "On Accelerating Loading and Unloading Work and Shortening the Stay on the Railroad Delivery Lines of Industrial Enterprises."[18] It prohibited some of these factories from mobilizing "loaders and other workers of transport shops and departments of enterprises for any work not tied immediately to the loading and unloading of wagons." Still, as chapter 3 showed, the city's economy largely remained at a standstill during the mid-1940s.

How, then, did Kyiv's citizens survive? Early on, of course, there was a better chance at securing a separate apartment, for the war had destroyed only a quarter of the city's housing stock according to the Kyiv City Soviet. In the opinion of that organization's chairman, Luka Lebed', 1 million square meters of living space could not be repaired as of February 23, 1944. According to Lebed', there was room for 670,000 people in the Ukrainian capital, although the likelihood of their having to occupy less than the prewar norm of 6.6 square meters per person could hardly have been welcomed.[19]

And the more "entrepreneurial" Kyivans certainly partook in the looting and claiming of unsupervised property after the occupation. Evidence can be found in a November 17, 1943, SNK UkrSSR resolution "On the Registration of the Use of Housing Space and the Order of Securing the Unsupervised Property of the Population and Enterprises of Kyiv." This resolution obliged SNK UkrSSR's local

"A Textual Implementation of the Law . . . Was Not Carried Out" 107

Figure 4.1. "Kyivans Return to Their Hometown," November 1943. Reproduced by permission from the H. Pshenychnyi Central State CinePhotoPhono Archives of Ukraine.

plenipotentiary in Kyiv at the time, V. Chornovol, "to check the correctness of the distribution of orders for the occupation of housing space," and "to nullify those orders handed out with exaggerations of existing norms and violations of valid rules."[20] For those "free agents," meanwhile, who had acted on their own, the resolution was much harsher: "Those individuals guilty of willfully arrogating or concealing unsupervised property from the census, as well as willfully occupying housing space, will be brought to justice based on the laws of wartime."[21] Such cases were supposed to be decided on by Kyiv's courts and investigative organs within forty-eight hours. But although the registration of the city's "unsupervised" property began in December 1943 in accordance with the instructions of the All-Union People's Commissariat of Finance, and proceeds from the sale of non-housing-related items later went to the Executive Committee of the Kyiv City Soviet, many if not most of the evictions from those "willfully arrogated" apartments never actually happened.

Evidence for this comes from a May 20, 1944, memorandum by Kyiv City Procurator Krizhanovskii to Kyiv City Soviet Chairman Fedor Mokienko after the former received over two thousand petitions from returnees or those planning to return asking to receive their apartments back. His main point was, "In connection with use of the 'Temporary Situation on the Rules of Settling the Living Space of the city of Kyiv,' of December 1, 1943, as confirmed by SNK UkrSSR, a textual implementation of the law of August 5, 1941, was not carried out in Kyiv because living space that once belonged to servicemen and their families was 'unassociated with any individual' (*obezlichen*) and the argument about the right to occupy that old living space was to be decided in the courts."[22] Although this "Temporary Situation" is hardly mentioned in the archival record, it adds up to the seedbed of new social and political capital for a formerly occupied population that was by and large Ukrainian.

As Krizhanovskii noted, by that point in 1944, less than a tenth of the two thousand petitions had generated actual court cases. That number should be added together with the forty thousand declarations that were sent to the managers of the city's housing in the Kyiv City Soviet—including most likely that of Kostenko, whose story began this book—and later found stashed, unanswered, somewhere in the "cellar of an archive."[23] To such numbers could also be added over nine thousand written complaints that arrived at various Kyiv government offices during the first five months of 1944, according to another memorandum that Krizhanovskii wrote to Mokienko at this time. That memorandum noted, in part, "In connection with a check conducted by the organs of the Kyiv City Procurator of the practice of looking over the complaints of workers, there have been established a whole number of violations of the resolution of the All-Union TsK dated January 22, 1943, about measures to improve the work of the Soviet organs' helping the families of those serving in the military."[24] Most such complaints would have also involved housing in some way, due to legal difficulties in the application of the ukaz of August 5, 1941, to these people's predicaments.

That a "textual implementation" of this ukaz was not enacted means that one of the most important wartime laws was not enforced during the months after Kyiv's liberation. The formerly occupied Ukrainians had taken advantage of the fact that 350,000 Kyivans were still in evacuation while at least 100,000 others (including 50,000 Jews) had been murdered by the Nazis. And an inventory of who was living on what space in the Ukrainian capital was not fully conducted for some eighteen months after liberation.[25] As later chapters argue, local Communists were forced to take this change in the formerly occupied's status into account amid their efforts to relegitimize Soviet power.

There was another resolution passed by the republic-level Communists that also helped shape who had access to some of Kyiv's best housing. Many of the damaged but repairable apartment buildings that had been ignored by the people's commissariats Khrushchev had initially assigned to rebuild them were parceled out to factories and institutions given the green light to resume operations.[26] Some two hundred "factory collectives" participated in this action, orchestrated by SNK UkrSSR and the Ukrainian TsK. The publicly declared reason these groups were given the chance to repair and occupy these damaged apartment buildings was as a "reward" for work done on the Khreshchatyk during 1944.

In Soviet-era historiography, this effort to rebuild Kyiv is portrayed as a "spontaneous" initiative by a brigade of workers from the Ukrainian Special Communications (*Ukrspetssviaz*) enterprise led by a V. S. Kolos. Thanks to this initiative to rebuild apartment buildings (ones assigned to the factory by Kyiv Gorkom and Kyiv City Soviet because no people's commissariat had bothered to repair them), Kolos and his workers were given the right to inhabit 49 Chervonoarmiis'ka Street, a prestigious address in the heart of the Ukrainian capital. This "right" was then repeated through the republic-level resolution entitled "On the Initiative of Brigade of V. S. Kolos from the Collective of Ukrspetssviaz."[27] But most, if not all, of these buildings were still by law to be inhabited by those prewar inhabitants who survived the war against the Nazis.

Resolutions like this must have considerably solidified support for local leaders as they made the city's housing problem look as if it were being addressed. But they also sowed the seeds for further social disorder when unorganized returnees started arriving in the city to reclaim their housing based on new wartime legislation. Given the timing, most of the rebuilders would have been formerly occupied men of Ukrainian nationality. A positive outcome for the unorganized returnees' efforts to claim their housing, especially considering the number of unanswered declarations already noted, also seems doubtful. Perhaps they made little progress because many of these "squatters" were the families of workers or servicemen mentioned above?

Tensions mounted as the formerly occupied and returnee populations clashed. Such frustrations were noted in the letters leaving Kyiv by the Military Censor of the Ukrainian NKGB's Kyiv Oblast branch. A June 19, 1944, report from that organization's assistant head, G. B. Progrebniuk, to Kyiv Obkom Secretary Serdiuk revealed 412 letters with complaints from families of servicemen about the "heartless-bureaucratic attitude of certain leaders of local Soviet organizations toward their needs" as they sought what was entitled to them by government resolutions.[28]

An inventory of housing did begin amid the city's built-up areas during the summer of 1944. As this happened, SNK UkrSSR required the republic's big cities to implement the all-union resolution of October 17, 1937, "On the Preservation of the Housing Fund and the Improvement of the Housing Fund Economy in the Cities."[29] This resolution was infamous because it sanctioned the "compression" of housing by city soviets if an apartment was considered to have too much space (in Kyiv's case, 6 square meters per person) relative to the number of inhabitants registered there. But in each case, such "compressions" were to be based on the consent of the procurator of the raion where the housing was located.

On November 10, 1944, SNK UkrSSR revisited this situation in a resolution entitled "On Ordering the Usage of the State's Housing and Non-housing Space and the Land It Is Situated On." When deciding who should live where, this resolution obliged Kyiv's raion soviets to follow the all-union October 1937 compressions resolution and that of August 5, 1941, "On the Preservation of the Housing Fund of Servicemen."[30] This November 10, 1944, resolution was bound to be explosive. But given their unjust treatment of newly empowered returnees in the resolutions just mentioned, Ukraine's authorities probably thought they had little choice but to issue it if they wanted to maintain the good graces of the Kremlin.

The efforts of the returnees, meanwhile, produced scenes such as the one recorded in a police officer's report included with an October 7, 1944, memorandum from the republic's lead procurator, Roman Rudnenko, to the Ukrainian TsK about a party member named Kinkalo:

> I, Zontov, as a beat cop from the first militia station, on this date [September 29, 1944], have drawn up this document, in the presence of citizens Alekseeva, M. Kh. and Spokoinyi, K. S. It is about the fact that, in accordance with a resolution of the Ukrainian Procurator dated September 26, 1944, I arrived at 5 Darwin Street, Apartment 23, where citizen Kinkalo lives [and] I suggested to him that he fulfill the order of the Procurator. That being that he should free up one room for the settlement of Alekseeva, M. Kh. But in his answer to my request, comrade Kinkalo manifested hooligan actions. He ran from the kitchen into the living room, where he took up arms (a Browning) and began by force of arms to drive me out of the apartment with the threat that he would shoot everyone. At that point, his mother grabbed the weapon away from him. After that, he grabbed me around my upper torso and threw me out of the kitchen into the [internal] hallway and against the outside door. Kinkalo also threw Spokoinyi into this internal corridor. As for Alekseeva, he grabbed her bag away from her (tearing it to pieces in the process) and threw it into the corridor, too. At that point, he started swearing, and calling everyone bastards.[31]

In this case, party member Kinkalo was offered a new apartment. Alekseeva's fate is unknown, although she likely gained access to the apartment if she was a serviceman's dependent and had resided in it before. As Rebecca Manley has posited, procurators generally tried to implement the all-union housing resolutions mentioned above.[32] But the outcome probably depended on who was to be evicted, if the case ever came before the courts.

Even after securing housing, daily survival was still extraordinarily difficult. Very few Kyivans enjoyed running water and electricity, while firewood was the only heating source for the vast majority. In her survey of the availability of food and consumer goods in Ukraine's cities after the Nazi occupation, Tamara Vrons'ka concluded, "It started out awful and remained that way."[33] But in the capital's case, the Ukrainian TsK and SNK UkrSSR did pass the resolution "On

Immediate Measures toward the Organization of Supplies for the Population of Kyiv" right after liberation.

This resolution declared that cafeterias sufficient to supply thirty thousand people should be opened by December 5, 1943.[34] A December 21, 1943, decision from these two organizations also reveals that ration cards, including those for consumer goods, were to be printed beginning on January 1, 1944.[35] But these hopeful-sounding words contrast with a resolution of the SNK UkrSSR and Ukrainian TsK from two weeks earlier that set concrete goals for allocation of grain to the Red Army by farms in the left-bank areas of Kyiv Oblast liberated from the Germans.[36]

The result was that people went hungry. An April 1944 SNK UkrSSR and Ukrainian TsK resolution summed up the food situation in Kyiv during the spring of 1944: "In March and April, there were incidents of interruptions in the supply of bread to the population. On some days, the decrease in the output of bread in the trade network approached 50 percent of average daily output."[37] A letter intercepted by the Military Censor of the Ukrainian NKVD for Kyiv Oblast and presented to Kyiv Obkom Secretary Serdiuk on June 19, 1944, indicates as much. Written by the wife of an active-duty soldier named Konik to her husband, she wrote,

> I could not write to you. . . . I thought I would be giving my soul to God considering the conditions I found myself in. I received your note (*spravka*) but it helped me like a mirror helps a blind man. . . . I took it with me so they would help me, but they would not do anything for me. That is how people pay attention to you around here. They gave me some bread ration cards but they do not give any bread out. It has been just today, the twenty-fifth day of the month, when I have received my first bread: 300 grams a person and they count it out as they are supposed to. We get 900 grams of bread for the three of us every day. If we got it every day then we could somehow get by but the way things are patience is wearing thin. The children will soon torment me to death. They get up in the morning and demand something to eat.[38]

The note was likely a document that proved that this woman and her children were the dependents of a Red Army soldier and deserved ration cards. While a majority in Kyiv employed such cards, others must have been judged more deserving of food than Mrs. Konik's family.

The existence of effective rationing except for those few working in the city's heavy industries is difficult to prove. Judging by her letter, it is doubtful that Mrs. Konik frequented the private markets dotted around Kyiv. If she ventured out to the markets, she would have found conditions as described in a SNK UkrSSR and Ukrainian TsK resolution of August 2, 1944: "The sale of agricultural products, due to a deficit of tables, takes place on the ground, while those stalls and booths that are on hand are not used and are falling apart. The unregulated trade of clothes, etc. takes place right alongside the sale of food. . . . The central covered market lies in a state of neglect. It has gone to the dogs."[39] Because most Kyivans survived through the trade of goods at such markets, everyday survival must have seemed quite disconnected from the state. Working for the government only made sense if one was lucky to find a job at a well-supported factory that might also be able to supply its workers with suitable housing or food from the Kyiv Oblast-based collective farms with which it directly associated.

The effort to improve food availability began with collecting the 1944 harvest. On July 27, the Ukrainian TsK and SNK UkrSSR trumpeted the seriousness of this issue through the wording of a resolution for rural localities: "Do not allow the late departure of collective farm workers for work or for their leaving from work early before the sun goes down. During the forced stoppages of the harvest machines due to technical malfunctions and bad weather, the chairmen of the collective farms and the directors of state farms are obliged to use collective farm workers and the workers of state farms servicing these machines, for the harvesting of grains by hand, by scythe, and by sickle."[40] Thanks to such measures, a subsequent SNK UkrSSR and Ukrainian TsK resolution of September 6 hailed the food supply's stabilization in the Ukrainian capital.

But this resolution also reveals that the state's role in supplying ordinary people with other support was quite marginal. It noted, "A check has determined a number of occasions of irresponsibility from the side of raion departments of state security toward the examination of complaints and declarations of families and servicemen about the issuance of subsidies and pensions. In Kyiv Oblast, Babak raion—1,758 declarations, in Boryspil' raion—5,243 declarations of servicemen's families lay unexamined for over two months."[41] This phenomenon, of unexamined declarations regarding "subsidies and pensions" going unfulfilled, mirrors the situation with housing. Even so, a lack of food is not mentioned again in the archives related to Kyiv's history until the famine of the fall of 1946. But food—other than bread—remained quite expensive for it was sold at state commercial prices in state commercial stores or on the free market, which operated outside of rationing. Only when more consumer goods were available for rural dwellers to purchase would the amount of food brought into the city increase and prices come down.

There were, of course, very few consumer goods in Kyiv because local Communists remained unable to compel the union- and republic-level factories located there to produce them. At the outset, there must have been some hope, as when the Ukrainian TsK and SNK UkrSSR passed a resolution on September 26, 1944, affirming a Kyiv City Soviet and Kyiv Gorkom plan for the organization of 151 "points" (*punkty*) to service the needs of the population by the end of 1944.[42] Such *punkty* were supposed to include forty-seven booths for the repair of clothes and shoes, eleven for the repair of knitted fabrics, sixteen *amerikanki* serving various snack foods, twenty-four metal-working shops for the repair of such things as sewing machines and watches, four furniture repair shops, and fourteen places for dry cleaning. But although these places provided employment, they hardly speak to the production of new goods.

What could ordinary Kyivans do, then, to survive the food scarcity of the war years? One option was to apply for an individual garden to grow a personal food supply. According to a report dated April 5, 1945, from Gorban and Mokienko to Korotchenko in the Ukrainian TsK, support for this idea was widespread: "As of April 1, 1945, the number of families declaring that they want an individual garden has gone over the 100,000 mark. In order to provide for those families we have a one-time need for seven to eight thousand hectares of lands for gardens. . . . To meet this need for space, the Kyiv City Soviet and the Kyiv Gorkom ask that they be allowed to use the lands of the Syrets firing range [on Kyiv's western edges] for these individual gardens."[43] But the Kyivan leaders' request was turned down; the Ukrainian People's Commissariat of Defense declared it still needed the firing range. If land was set aside for individual gardens, it must have been even further from the city center, necessitating a lengthy journey. This situation only adds to the overall sense of a Kyiv at this time made up of "speculators" negotiating with peasant traders or their fellow urbanites for needed items.

Many Kyivans relied almost exclusively on themselves for day-to-day survival, including food or consumer goods that could not be obtained via an employer. But when it came to housing, those who arrived earlier had a clear advantage. Occupying someone else's housing, or rebuilding a destroyed building, gave chances for greater social and political capital to the largely Ukrainian formerly occupied population. While the laws passed during wartime may have come back to haunt some of these people as returnees arrived from points east, here was real change for Kyiv, as ethnic Ukrainians not only made up the largest single group in the city (at almost 60 percent of the entire population by May 1947), but had considerable social and political prestige as well.[44] And because eviction was uncommon (some were relatives of Red Army servicemen, after all), they were likely able to stay on in these new quarters for many years.

As for the late-arriving returnees, many of whom were Jews composing almost 20 percent of the population (according to the same Kyiv Military Commissariat document), the wartime legislation did not help as much with garnering social and political capital.[45] The fact that ethnic Ukrainians were the majority was a point the local authorities could not have missed. Caught between Moscow's *diktat* and these competing populations, local leaders weighed the interests of both sides as they worked to relegitimize themselves as the leaders of the Ukrainian capital. The subsequent arrival of German POWs and demobilized servicemen was not going to make this task any easier.

The Reassembled Masses: The *Orgnabor* and POW Laborers

While the formerly occupied and returnees took advantage of the empty city or worried about their entitlements, *orgnabor* became the Stalin regime's first remedy for the capital's labor troubles. Children were the easiest to mobilize, and some wound up in Kyiv despite the relative unimportance of the city's reconstruction to union-level planners. These youth were mobilized into the so-called factory apprenticeship schools (*shkoly fabrichno-zavodskogo obuchenia*, FZO) or trade schools (*remelesnnye uchilshchi*, RU) located on the premises of many of the enterprises mentioned already.

SNK UkrSSR and the Ukrainian TsK announced the planned opening of these schools in Kyiv on September 11, 1944.[46] Altogether, five RU schools with 540 students and nine FZO schools with 830 students were to open with the majority of their students—at least in this initial ukaz—hailing from Kyiv itself. These youth were to range in age from fourteen to eighteen years old depending on gender and the type of industry into which they were mobilized. The youth may have been expected to better tolerate factory conditions than their more savvy elders. But a SNK UkrSSR and Ukrainian TsK resolution dated November 5, 1944, indicates that the government failed to create this republic-wide network of schools.[47] And while the Kyivan Communists would have recognized such schools' success as necessary for reconstruction, they too made little progress in getting them to prosper.

Some children were successfully mobilized to Kyiv but a host of obstacles now stood in the way of keeping them in the city. At the union-level Stalin Ship-Building Factory, for example, a November 13, 1944, memorandum from an instructor, Postnov, of the Kyiv Gorkom's Department of Machine Building to his superiors in the Kyiv Gorkom said, "The preparation of cadres at the factory is at a very low level. The head of the cadres department, comrade Smoliar, and the head of training, comrade Cherniavskaia have become real bureaucrats. Stakhanovite [Preparatory] schools, courses with definite aims and technological minimums are not implemented, and can be found there only formally, on paper."[48]

The same meeting of the Kyiv Gorkom produced a similar resolution about the preparation of young workers at the Lepse Tractor Factory, which now belonged to the All-Union People's Commissariat of Agricultural Machinery. A memorandum by Peremolotova, a coworker of Postnov's, described matters at the factory to the committee: "If the individual method of training of young workers was conducted badly, the other forms of preparing cadres such as Stakhanovite schools, masters' courses, and courses designed to raise one's qualifications were not conducted at all and, as of the present, are not scheduled to be conducted in future."[49] One reason for the lack of training was that there was precious little to occupy these young people, due to the lack of resources dedicated to their factories by the Stalin regime.

Other circumstances made the living conditions for these youth even worse than the dead-end nature of their jobs. At the Stalin Ship-Building Factory, lying on the Dnipro's right bank on the city's southern outskirts, Instructor Postnov reported,

> The workers and the single students numbering some 150 people are housed in a dormitory at 9 Ol'ginskaia Street. The rooms of the dormitory are in a frighteningly unsanitary condition. The central heating and electrical systems are not working. Mattresses, blankets, and pillows are not to be found. Two lengths of wood serve as bedding on which the workers sleep in turn. In the rooms, it is cold and dirty. Personal belongings—dirty foot-cloths, shoes, greasy uniforms, and rags—are thrown haphazardly on the floors and beds. Collective visits to the baths do not occur. One worker, a modeler of the eighth rank, comrade Savin, has not been to the baths for over a month and half. He has dirt and insects on his body. Changes of underwear do not occur. Single workers are not given shoes and clothes. The turner-pupil of shop one, Iumaev, is starving and dressed in rags. He has not been to work in two months. He has no ration cards. He also has not visited the baths in two months. His body and underwear are dirty. And, he has lice on his clothes. When questioned by the head of training, Cherniavskaia, "Why do you not go to work?" the boy burst into tears.[50]

An additional problem was rampant theft at the dormitory due to a lack of places to safely store valuables. Such problems with working and living conditions were the main reasons why, according to Postnov, the factory had fulfilled only 58 percent of its production plan during October 1944. As for the young workers' living conditions at the Lepse Factory, Peremolotova commented on the 150-person dormitory housed on the third floor of the factory's headquarters: "At present, there are 45 people living there. The dorm is not prepared for the upcoming winter. The roof leaks and the bedroom windows are broken and patched only with wood. In the corridors, there are drafts. In the attic, there is no glass in the windows at all. . . . Five rooms are closed off. That is because they are in need of repair. Bedclothes for a complete change are lacking."[51] Such living conditions meant rampant desertion, and that the future conditions for the expansion of production were nonexistent.

Meanwhile, other complaints from the few *orgnabor* youth successfully mobilized to Kyiv found their way to Demian Korotchenko in the Ukrainian TsK. According to a February 3, 1945, report from the assistant people's commissar of the Ukrainian NKGB, Drozdetskii,[52] the letters of young female workers in Kyiv contained the following complaints: from Urits'ka Street, I. D. Miroshnichenko wrote to her relatives in Chernihiv Oblast on December 18, 1945, "They feed us, grandma, very badly. You go to the cafeteria and eat that pickle soup while chasing it down with your tears. And with that, you go to work." On December

2, an M. G. Shcherba wrote to Kirovohrad Oblast from Kyiv's Podil' Raion, "It is difficult for me right now with food. I have nothing to buy anything. The soup they give out is no good. I receive eight rubles a month. Take them and live as you like." Finally, on December 6, a K. O. Natiaga wrote to the Kyiv Oblast town of Kaniv from the Ukrainian capital, "They do not give us much to eat: 500 grams of bread, 400 grams of groats. Take them and make anything you want out of them. We are sitting ten to room in some barracks. This type of life I would not wish upon a dog." These letters suggest how difficult it would be for the city's leaders to count on such youth to help mitigate that major obstacle standing in the way of successful reconstruction: the ever-growing, shielded, and often unorganized population now reassembling in Kyiv.

In the summer of 1945, the Kyiv Gorkom took stock again of the FZOs and RUs dotted among the city's factories. In a resolution of August 17, 1945, Kyiv's leaders noted that the FZOs had produced only one thousand qualified workers for local factories since inception.[53] The resolution also targeted the reason why the number of skilled young workers created at this time was so low, which contributed to a very poor environment for learning: "Labor discipline of the students is located at a low level. During the first half of 1945, turnover at the RU and FZO schools in the city amounts to 386 people. That includes those who, of their own free will, abandon these institutions."[54]

A September 19, 1945, Kyiv Obkom resolution about these schools gives further details on why the creation of skilled laborers was so difficult.[55] Kyiv's RU schools no. 7 and no. 9, for example, found it difficult to prepare seamstresses because there were only nine sewing machines between them for the training of 206 students. Meanwhile, at RU no. 5, located at Leninskaia Kuznitsa, there was not a single machine tool to practice on for the seventy-three students learning to become lathe operators and metal cutters. The resolution continued in this vein: "Other trade schools, for example, at the electro-mechanical factory and the fourth shoe factory do not have any master shops set aside for their students. These youth are practically working in the shops of each enterprise already. The youth eat badly. At the shoe factory's RU they receive their second course served into their hands."[56] This combination of poor food, bad housing conditions, and inadequate or nonexistent training due to a lack of resources led to desertions by many of the student workers. The dead-end world of such factories probably alienated many youth from the Stalin regime's system for a long time to come.

Indeed, at a Kyiv Gorkom meeting in March 1946, a Comrade Teplitskii from the city's Komsomol found only 3,750 of the 20,000 youth employed in Kyiv's factories were members of his organization. But more revealingly, Teplitskii noted that a majority of workers in Kyiv's factories were youth at this time, demonstrating that no matter how unsuccessful, *orgnabor* was still being used, as few among Kyiv's adult population wanted to work at industrial reconstruction in the conditions prevalent then. Even if 20,000 or so adults were employed in Kyiv's factories, they represented only about 3 percent of the city's 600,000-strong population in early 1946. And, according to Teplitskii, there was a lot more ground to be covered before young people could make up the difference. He concluded, "The war ended the study of our youth. Young workers sometimes have an education that spans all of four or five classes.... They cannot become good markers and lathe operators, etc."[57]

In sum, the young people mobilized to Kyiv were not a catalyst for the city's reconstruction. These *orgnabor* laborers lacked support networks in the city to fall back upon, and many abandoned the city to its fate. Local authorities thus hoped for other forms of "compulsory labor" from which it was impossible to desert. Most importantly, they needed laborers to build housing for the *orgnabor* workers of the future.

As outlined in chapter 2, the Stalin regime's idea to meet this need was to use the thousands of German POWs taken captive during the liberation of Eastern Europe. The first POWs assembled in Kyiv were those paraded down the Khreshchatyk on August 16, 1944. This arrival was a result of a July 21, 1944, order from S. Kruglov, the All-Union NKVD Assistant People's Commissar of Internal Affairs, entitled "On the Movement of the Directorate of Camp No. 62 to the City of Kyiv and the Organization There of Eight Camp Branches."[58] It obliged the "All-Union NKVD Directorate for the Affairs of POWs and Internees" to establish a new version of Camp no. 62 in Kyiv for 18,500 POWs under the day-to-day management of the Ukrainian NKVD.

Kruglov's order touched off a flurry of activity. On July 28, 1944, the Kyiv Gorkom passed a resolution entitled "On the Settlement of 10,000 POWs for Work on Improving the City of Kyiv."[59] This resolution hoped to call on the city's main building and communal services trusts to draw up contracts with the All-Union NKVD for the supply of labor to their projects. Among the five different city raions mentioned in the resolution, the centrally located Lenin Raion was supposed to receive the largest number of POWs. There, 2,500 Germans were to be housed in the former premises of Kyiv's *Lombard* (the city's prewar pawn shop), near the shell of the Ukrainian TsK building overlooking the Dnipro. Accommodations for the POWs were supposed to be found in unused schools, factory buildings, and near the republic-level artificial fibers factory in Darnytsa.

Other All-Union NKVD records from 1944 contain orders from Moscow calling for the creation of new campsites belonging to the Directorate of Camp no. 62.[60] One dated September 6, 1944, resolved to open an additional branch housing 1,500 POWs in Kyiv.[61] In this case, the order specifically stated that the POWs were needed "for the construction of houses for the NKGB UkrSSR and the Regional Directorate of Military Supply (Kyiv District NKVD) in the city of Kyiv."

Figure 4.2. German POWs cleaning up and "rebuilding" the Khreshchatyk, October 1, 1944. Reproduced by permission from the H. Pshenychnyi Central State Cine-PhotoPhono Archives of Ukraine.

But it is the findings in a 1944 year-end report from Kyiv's Fourth State Shoe Factory that really demonstrate the significance of the arrival of German prisoners in the city. After mentioning that the factory had received an order from SNK SSSR about equipment headed its way some ten months after liberation, the report stated, "In August of 1944, we signed a contract to receive POW labor from the Directorate [of Camp no. 62]. . . . The rest of our workers lived through the occupation—women and youth—without any qualifications at all."[62] That the Fourth State Shoe Factory's production goals were met indicates what the POW laborers were actually used for.

The Stalin regime held to the idea that accommodations, of some sort, needed to be readied *before* German POWS or internees arrived, which certainly differentiated their experience from the *orgnabor* laborers. Here was the Achilles' heel for housing reconstruction in the city early on. An example of one unsuccessful effort came from aviation factory no. 473 (the future Antonov) belonging to the All-Union People's Commissariat of the Aviation Industry. Its situation is recounted in a "secret memorandum" buried in the protocols of a Kyiv Gorkom meeting pertaining to the resolution "On the Process of Fulfilling the Order of the People's Commissar of March 8, 1945, on the Preparations for the Production of Helicopters at Factory No. 473." Most important was finding enough POWs/internees to build the housing needed for the arrival of 420 production employees scheduled to complete the task. The resolution reads, "For the arrival of the 2,000 internees, the factory is not prepared. The premises on hand for such an occurrence can accommodate only 1,200 people. Supplies of bedding at the factory are absent and the factory is not working on receiving any at the moment either."[63] As usual, the Stalin regime must have feared social disorder if a large group such as the Germans became unhappy with its conditions. But if the convenience of nearby housing was a necessity before such prisoners could be supplied to a building site or factory, reconstruction of any sort must have taken a very long time to begin.

The above memorandum also explains the problems with using POWs at factory no. 473 as it examines conditions at the Air Industry Construction Trust's "Special Construction and Assembly Directorate no. 26" tasked with reconstructing the factory's actual production premises. It reads in part, "There are no deadlines for the construction process set. There is an absence of building materials. There is not enough staff. The camp of POWs transferred into the jurisdiction of Special Construction and Assembly Directorate no. 26 is not used. Of the 800 POWs allotted, only 100 people are working. The territory of the factory, especially the premises no. 1, is littered with garbage and junked airplanes."[64] The absence of materials—whether for housing construction or industrial production—meant there was little for these POWs to do at factory no. 473. This, in turn, likely meant Special Construction and Assembly Directorate no. 26 was probably trying to use the workers on other projects.

Another look at the situation involving the effort to rebuild Kyiv's Technological Institute of the Food Industry (KTIPP) in the summer of 1946 makes the role of newly assembled POWs in Kyiv clearer.[65] KTIPP had offered to SNK UkrSSR that it would house and feed the six-hundred-strong "special contingent" allotted to it by the Directorate of Camp no. 62 for the institute's reconstruction. Originally, these prisoners had been assigned to OSMCh no. 305, belonging to NKZhGS UkrSSR. OSMCh no. 305 later agreed to give them to KTIPP in exchange for housing materials, so that it could finish the housing for the very same prisoners it was giving to KTIPP. But because it had been assigned to over eighty other projects in the city, the labor-starved OSMCh no. 305 failed to allocate enough workers to its KTIPP site and thus the institute was unable to receive the special contingent it had counted on to start reconstruction.

Still, there was no lack of prisoner labor in Kyiv. A September 27, 1945, "Report Note" from the Directorate of Camp no. 62's party organization to the Ukrainian TsK provides a snapshot of POW activity in the Ukrainian capital at that time.[66] The report mentions the camp's twenty-five active (of forty planned) branches dotted around Kyiv, with six branches in the industrial heart of the city, Zhovtnevyi Raion. To operate this massive complex, the Ukrainian NKVD employed 1,351 people with 160 party members and candidates occupying managerial positions. Here at least were jobs with a well-connected employer, although it cannot be said that they helped much with reconstruction. The same could be said for the Germans, as everyone awaited resources.

This, though, makes it clear why there were many people in Kyiv still advocating for *orgnabor* and FZO/RU labor in 1945. After the Fourth Five-Year Plan's announcement and the efforts to seal the city off from unorganized return, however, the idea that future reception of *orgnabor* labor *also* necessitated adequate housing for such people before they arrived became pervasive. In the spring of 1946, for example, a Kyiv Gorkom Department of Construction and Construction Materials "instructor" noted that the city's Artificial Fibers Factory in Darnytsa had supplied three hundred new *orgnabor* recruits with "extremely run-down" living conditions as the Special Construction and Assembly Directorate no. 11 of the Kyiv Industrial Construction (*Kievpromstroi*) Trust worked to rebuild the factory. The instructor reported to his higher-ups that "the roofs have not been repaired. In the rooms, things are damp, dirty, and cold. . . . The workers coming in from work, instead of relaxing, occupy themselves with the search for firewood in order to heat their rooms and dry out."[67]

This memorandum also touched on the food supplies allotted to these workers who were replacements for the German POWs originally scheduled to do this work: "The leadership of the trust, despite the government resolution, was unable to produce stocks of food in a centralized fashion even when a plenipotentiary from the People's Commissariat of Requisitions UkrSSR allocated it a rural raion (the village of M. Kalynivka in Kyiv Oblast)."[68] Such a concentration on improving conditions for *orgnabor* laborers only emerged once the Stalin regime itself refocused on the plight of the rear after its long focus on the front.

As German POWs were under the direction of the All-Union NKVD, their fate in Kyiv was not as harsh as that of the *orgnabor* laborers assembling in in city—especially compared to those young people sent to the Ukrainian capital early on. Still, the Germans were prisoners and there was little risk of them departing for greener pastures. Indeed, they became the most reliable group of workers living in the Ukrainian capital. The majority of Kyivans, as well as the relatively few youth successfully mobilized into the city, simply lacked an incentive to help the local Communists rebuild. What the results were for the city's life is dealt with in the next chapter.

The Reassembled Masses: Demobilized Servicemen

The last ones to return to Kyiv were demobilized servicemen, some of whom already had families in the city. They are considered separately, for they arrived with great expectations due to the special treatment they had received from the wartime Stalin regime. But when conditions did not meet their expectations, these men continued the tradition begun by active-duty servicemen—again like Kostenko, whose letter opened this book—and inundated local authorities with complaints. Although the Kremlin passed further legislation to help them—only adding to their sense of exceptionalism—the arrival of this most demanding of populations was a worry for the Ukrainian Communists as they struggled with reconstruction and unorganized return.

On July 6, 1945, the SNK UkrSSR and Ukrainian TsK adopted a resolution to fulfill the All-Union Supreme Soviet Law on Demobilization passed two weeks earlier. The former said in part, "The law passed by the session of the Supreme Soviet is a shining example of the Stalinist care for the demobilized warrior-victors from the ranks of the army. This law issues forth from the Stalinist directive that of all the valuable capital there is in the world, the most valuable and decisive capital is the people-cadre."[69] A translation of such rhetoric for the Soviet Union's local authorities meant cushioning the front fighters' (*frontoviki*) arrival home as much as possible. Postoccupation realities, however, prevented this from being a smooth process in Kyiv.

Some of the first demobilized to return to Ukraine, for example, met the "welcome" described in an August 18, 1945, report from Rivne Oblast: "In a number of the oblast raions, the arriving demobilized are terrorized by Ukrainian-German nationalists [Banderites]. In Derazhniansk raion, there are occasions where the demobilized arriving from Konigsburg have had their presents taken from them—their new uniforms, awards, and so forth. The demobilized are then invited to join the bandits and, if they do not join, they are told not to in any way partake in social-political life."[70] While Kyiv Oblast had its own "Ukrainian-German nationalists" active in its northerly Chernobol' raion that summer, the stealing of "presents" from the demobilized in the capital was done by criminals without any political motives.[71] As soon as they were outside Kyiv's main train station, for example, some of the demobilized were targeted by muggers during October and November 1945.[72]

If the Supreme Soviet resolution's measures mandating an "organized greeting" of the demobilized had gone off as planned, some of these incidents might have been avoided. A July 26, 1945, memorandum from Shamaev, the head of the Kyiv Gorkom's Military Department, to the Ukrainian TsK outlined this effort for welcoming the *frontoviki* home. Each of Kyiv's raions had been given shifts manning the main railway station (complete with orchestra and flowers), and, if a train was expected, the raikom secretary and the raion soviet chairman were expected to be there too. But according to Shamaev, things had turned out quite differently in practice: "One of the unsatisfactory things about these meetings is that the staff of the railway station cannot report the exact arrival time of a train. Therefore, there are occasions when greeters wait for several hours for the arrival of the demobilized."[73] The inevitable result, Shamaev added, was that some of these greeters left before groups of the demobilized actually arrived, and the results were events like those just mentioned.

The Law on Demobilization also mandated that demobilized servicemen's experiences in the army "be taken into account while they were assigned new work." But according to an October 1, 1945, report of the Kyiv Obkom's Military Department to the Ukrainian TsK, the jobs available in Kyiv were not up to this task. Few of its factories really needed large numbers of skilled laborers, which led Military Department head Makeev to conclude, "A large number of unemployed can be found in the cities, including around Kyiv. Those given jobs number only 37 percent of the total having arrived."[74] But the report's statistics on Kyiv itself were quite a bit worse than for the republic as a whole. In Podil' Raion, for example, only 122 out of 1,259 demobilized returnees had found work by October 1, 1945, while in Zhovtnevyi Raion, the numbers were 120 out of 741.[75] The numbers of unemployed war invalids in the city and oblast were similarly bad, considering the discrimination they faced as reminders of the terrible events of the recent past. According to Makeev, 9,458 of 39,210 demobilized invalids there remained without jobs.

A February 18, 1946, letter from a demobilized Kyivan named M. N. Gorshnov to the Ukrainian TsK reveals more about the employment situation. Some nine months after victory, Gorshnov wrote, "The question of finding work is really difficult. I am an officer, or more correctly, a former officer. In the army, I was the commander of a battery for four years. And here, concerning my request that I be given economic work, I was offered by a Kyiv Obkom employee, the position of courtyard cleaner. This just cannot be happening. It is simply funny."[76] Explaining his efforts to correct this situation, the Ukrainian TsK's Degtiarev wrote to Khrushchev on April 9, 1946, "A check has established that the facts noted in the complaint of comrade Gorshnov have been partly confirmed."[77] With the return of Ukraine's bureaucracy to Kyiv, Gorshnov's desire for white-collar work makes sense, especially since few in the capital were involving themselves with blue-collar work at this time.

Even if they did find work, the demobilized were often frustrated with postwar life. Given Kyiv's multiethnic nature, the question of discrimination based on ethnic lines also emerged during this top-down parceling out of opportunities. A May 10, 1946, letter from a Communist Red Army veteran, Ol'shanetsk, to Khrushchev, for example, noted, "We arrived from the army to our hometowns with an uplifting feeling of patriotism and a desire to take a creative role in the reconstruction of our country. Alas! If you look at where they send Jew-Communists for work the result is that they are all turning into 'suppliers' and 'traders.'"[78] A report from L'viv to the Ukrainian TsK from the head of the

Carpathian Military Region's political directorate dated June 10, 1946, contained more worrying information: "The long wait for work means that among certain demobilized officers unhealthy attitudes that often lead to amoral actions are starting to appear. . . . They systematically get drunk, and occupy themselves with buying and selling, etc."[79]

Initially, local authorities based their efforts to reintegrate the *frontoviki* on the same all-union war-era resolutions that had governed the treatment of tens of thousands of servicemen's families already in the city. But in addressing the needs of at least fifty thousand families, the very title of Makeev's October 1, 1945, report to the Ukrainian TsK suggests the greater importance of these latest arrivals: "On the State of the Reception, Employment, and Supplying of the Demobilized Fighters of the Red Army, [and] of the Help to Families of Servicemen, Invalids of the Great Patriotic War, and Orphans of the Front Fighters around Kyiv Oblast and the City of Kyiv."[80] On October 11, 1945, SNK UkrSSR passed a new resolution in accordance with earlier all-union resolutions emanating from Moscow entitled "On Measures for Offering Help to the Demobilized, the Families of Dead Fighters, Invalids of the Patriotic War, and Families of Servicemen."

This resolution extended the privileges gained by much of the population during the war to others, and then extended them into the postwar era for all. While the needs of the demobilized were reiterated—they were still freed from paying for their children's schooling and given access to low-interest loans for rebuilding—there were also new privileges for those living in the republic's cities. Most notably, the people's commissariats in Ukraine—indeed, all government institutions—were ordered to set aside 10 percent of their newly built and restored housing for distribution by local soviets for the recently demobilized. In addition, the resolution ordered these institutions "to organize . . . the production training of the demobilized that do not have specialties through either individual-brigade apprenticeships or the organization of short courses."[81] There is no record, however, of these latter orders ever having been carried out.

But the earlier points of this resolution were more easily implemented. They called for erasing arrears "from past years" for all who had lost a "breadwinner" at the front, extending the privileges granted during the war years by the June 4, 1943, union-level resolution "On the Privileges of the Families of Military Men Who Have Died or Are Missing in Action on the Fronts of the Patriotic War" through 1946, and extending the privilege of free schooling to the children of dead Red Army men and of first- and second-group invalids of the "Great Patriotic War," which had been granted by the July 2, 1941, all-union resolution "On Excusing from Payment for Studies of Those Children of the Rank and File and Leadership Personnel of the Red Army and Navy."[82]

Figure 4.3. Soldiers' children listen to the news about the victory with the Allies over Fascist Germany, May 9, 1945. Reproduced by permission from the H. Pshenychnyi Central State CinePhotoPhono Archives of Ukraine.

The remainder of the October 1945 resolution targeted the children of anyone related to the military as special recipients for aid. For example, the resolution obliged the Ukrainian People's Commissariat of Trade to provide a "one-time above the norm limit distribution of 490,000 rations to the children of dead fighters, invalids of the Patriotic War, and the needy children of servicemen and the demobilized." The resolution charged the trade commissariat with arranging the sale of these rations through the trade network based on personnel lists. The same was true with the some 120,000 pairs of shoes to be produced for these children. These shoes were "to be sold in the trading network based off of lists drawn up by departments for the state provisioning and material well-being of the families of military men and by the departments of social security, and affirmed by the local city soviets and raion soviets." Matters concluded with: "All of the rights laid out in [this] resolution applying to the children of dead fighters also apply to the children of dead partisans."[83]

The arrival of the demobilized and the extension of privileges to larger and larger numbers of Kyiv's population coincided with an investigation by the Ukrainian Procurator's office into how well resolutions protecting the "rights and interests of enlisted men and their families, the families of dead fighters, invalids of the Patriotic War, and demobilized fighters" were being implemented. After checking

2,357 institutions, charging 27 people with crimes, and disciplining some 75 others, the acting Ukrainian procurator, S. Shuturov, felt confident enough to report on October 15, 1945, that "Incidents of arbitrariness and soulless relations toward members of the defenders of the motherland have become rarer occurrences than before."[84] But reinforcing the privileged position of the demobilized and the families of dead fighters sometimes meant disturbing other people.

Evidence for this comes from a April 24, 1946, "protest" from yet another acting Ukrainian procurator, P. Noshchenko, to SNK UkrSSR about a case in the Dnipropetrovs'k Oblast town of Nikopol' in November 1945 involving a demobilized soldier.[85] The protest's main point was that the demobilized soldier, Podol'skii, based on the resolution of August 5, 1941, should have been returned the whole of the apartment he had occupied at the time of his mobilization by the local Soviet authorities:

> Persons who occupy the living space of servicemen are considered to be temporary tenants and upon return of these servicemen they are obliged to immediately vacate the premises. . . . The fastening to temporary inhabitants of a large part of the apartment of the demobilized Podol'skii (leaving for the two people of his family only one room of 12 square meters) when in the city of Nikopol' the prewar norm of living space has not been changed, is a gross violation of the resolution from August 5, 1941, and the law on demobilization . . . from the Red Army. . . . Even after the demobilized person has been returned his living space and there turns out to be extra space, the question about the confiscation of that excess (in the form of an isolated room) is a decision to be made based on statute 27 of the all-union resolution of October 17, 1937.[86]

Noshchenko's advice to SNK UkrSSR was that all decisions emanating from Nikopol' about this case should be cancelled and that Podol'skii was entitled to all parts of his home. The latter's efforts to secure his housing had most likely begun with a complaint to the local procurator's office.

Later that year, an internal Ukrainian TsK report on the complaints and declarations of workers from Kyiv's Molotov Raion noted that 66 percent of the 1,400 complaints made during the first nine months of 1946 were by demobilized men and the families of enlisted men, and that 89 percent of these concerned housing.[87] The demobilized's complaints had led the Ukrainian Communists at the highest levels to uncover for themselves the fact that there were serious problems with housing distribution in Kyiv. For example, an investigation of the "Apartment Department" within the Molotov Raion Soviet noted: "Until September 1945, the rule that there should be a line for the granting of living space was not observed. Thus, the main document used for computing the category of person putting forth the declaration (invalid of the Patriotic War, demobilized soldier, family of a military server, etc.) was a single registration 'alphabetical' book that registered the order the declaration was received. No other types of operative document on which it might have been possible to correctly judge the line order existed."[88]

While this "alphabetical" book in Molotov Raion reconfirms the idea that arriving early in the Ukrainian capital meant better access to scarce housing, the Ukrainian TsK's investigation may suggest a plan to capitalize on the arrival of the demobilized in order to speed housing reconstruction. For the moment, though, the city was indeed full. In Kyiv Oblast, for example, according to a July 1, 1946, memorandum from the head of the Ukrainian TsK's Military Department, Degtiarov, to Korotchenko, 16,888 people were living in dugouts, 41,431 were living on space belonging to others, and only 6,537 were in newly built housing during the first half of that year.[89] It is quite likely that a high number of those living on "space belonging to others" were the late-arriving demobilized and their families.

Finding food and consumer goods for the demobilized and others with comparable status should have been easier for local Communists, at least before the fall 1946 famine. But matters were complicated by SNK UkrSSR's liquidating private trade in food products in the city in late 1945 after the wartime mix of rationing, state commercial prices, and free market. To counter this policy, SNK UkrSSR ordered that state commercial prices for consumer goods be lowered in the hope that collective farmers would come to the city and sell the proceeds of their private plots for more reasonable prices than the "speculators" who had long dominated that scene. This was a return to the days of "closed trade" that dominated Kyiv in the years just before the Second World War.

The results of such a policy were disappointing, at least according to a meeting about the capital's markets held by the Kyiv Gorkom on January 30, 1946. At the meeting's end, Secretary Aleksei Davydov summarized the food situation: "One would think that it was necessary to mobilize [and] to subordinate everything to this effort, so that [at the markets] things were organized like they should be . . . so that the workers of the capital felt it, [and] so there would be no conversations about the fact that the private sector has been liquidated with nothing organized to replace it. . . . The collective farm worker sees that there is nothing to buy and he has no desire to bring food products into the markets of Kyiv."[90] The heart of the matter was the closure of the private stalls at Kyiv's markets, which had specialized in selling consumer goods to arriving collective farmers in the city. The Kyiv City Soviet had scheduled 222 "trade points" manned by state trading organizations to open in their stead. But by the end of January 1946, only 67 such points were actually working.[91]

But the real reason closed trade failed was that few consumer goods were produced in Kyiv at this time. Davydov summed up the food situation in the winter of 1945–46: despite efforts by the Kyiv City Soviet and the City Trade Department to improve matters, "in connection with the recent changes at our markets there can be felt a certain weakening of production brought in—especially in that prices recently have seriously gone up. . . . Bessarabskii Market is the central market and there is nothing in the place. Only one collective farm is trading there and a kilogram of salted cucumbers costs 18 rubles. That is an intolerable situation. In Kyiv, a kilogram of salted cucumbers costs 18 rubles!"[92] It is unclear from the archives how or whether this lack of counter-trade (peasants selling food in return for the monies necessary to buy industrial goods) was solved. By July 1946, however, a plenipotentiary of the all-union State Plan active in Kyiv could report to the Kyiv Gorkom that prices in the city's markets had stabilized at the same levels they had been the year before, and that for certain staples such as rye bread, salt, sugar, and soap, prices had actually fallen by 50 percent.[93] Such statistics reveal some progress with closed trade, but the famine's arrival put a wrench in the works.

By October 1946, the effects on Kyiv of the disastrous harvest were countered by all manner of efforts to promote the food trade. The most important was the September 16, 1946, all-union resolution to cut state commercial prices on consumer goods. According to a comrade Mukhomorov in Kyiv's Directorate of Markets, this move by SM SSSR did increase peasants' food deliveries to the city's shops, especially pig fat, cooking oil, and fruits and vegetables.[94] But in Mukhomorov's opinion, news of the bad harvest had also created troublesome scenes: "The liquidation of the Galitskii market, which is located in the middle of a very large and densely populated region, has caused the emergence of a large number of 'wild' bazaars that spontaneously locate themselves as semicircles beginning from Dmitrov street on through Turgenev, Gogol', Pavlov, Chakalov and Saksaganskogo streets, as well as on the territory of the Kyiv Wagon Repair Factory. At these little bazaars, up to 2,000 people trade every day."[95]

The impetus for the September 16 resolution may have been the existence of a newly privileged population in places like Kyiv, now only reinforced by the demobilized. Whether or not a steady supply of food began arriving in the city is unknown, however. By November 11, 1946, the Ukrainian TsK and SNK UkrSSR had called on Kyiv's trade and civil catering systems to be "strengthened" with one thousand party cadres as soon as possible.[96] Although only partly implemented by the end of 1946, the fact that a large number of the city's elite were summoned to work in the food distribution network is evidence of grave concern.

The demobilized found the transition into peacetime particularly difficult. But because it was felt that their role in sustaining the USSR was vital, their appearance in the Ukrainian capital spurred a broad official effort to ease their transition into civilian life. That alone makes their experience different from others among Kyiv's masses. Even so, little was actually achieved toward helping them. The Ukrainian TsK's efforts to uncover for itself the problems with the city's housing distribution only indicate that matters went from bad to worse. In Moscow, meanwhile, the Stalin regime was planning the Soviet Union's first postwar ideological moves in the summer of the 1946.

Part Three

Relegitimization

Chapter Five

"The State's Dignity Is Higher Than His Own Dignity"

The Relegitimization of Soviet Power

On November 20, 1943, the Kyiv Obkom established a "Commission of Assistance" to aid the All-Union "Extraordinary State Commission for the Establishment and Investigation of Crimes Committed by the German-Fascist Invaders and Their Accomplices" in its work in the Ukrainian capital. At the former commission's first meeting ten days later in Kyiv, the Extraordinary State Commission's newly arrived leader, Aron N. Trainin, said:

> On arrival here in the territory of Ukraine, the Germans spoke demonstratively about their mission of "liberation." In practice, as is clear from the materials we have familiarized ourselves with . . . they gave directions that were to place Ukraine in colonial dependence. . . . During twenty years of Soviet power, the Ukrainian people had grown to the point whereby the Germans understood that, in order for their colonial plan to work, they would need to work toward complete economic and cultural domination. First, it was necessary to unleash a strike at the heart of Ukraine, to degrade Kyiv, to liquidate its leading role. The Hitlerites' activities around Kyiv ensued from this supposition.[1]

After noting the Germans' export of raw materials bound for Kyiv's industries, their opening of numerous brothels in the city, and their payment of starvation wages to those who worked for them, Trainin said what concerned him most was the massacre at Babyn Iar.

Trainin intended to write a report explaining why the Germans had murdered over 200,000 people in Kyiv, "something far above what we had for Smolensk and other cities." After noting Kyivans' resistance to Nazi efforts to transport them to points west, and suggesting that the city's experiences should be documented for all to read, he concluded:

> When the Germans went after Smolensk they went as the conquerors of Russia. Here, they showed up as the liberators of the Ukrainians. We need to show that in truth all of the Germans' institutions gave directions for the creation of a colonial regime, and we need to show materials that correspond to this truth.

When they conquered Morocco, they said matter-of-factly, "The Moroccans are a lowly race." But they understood that the Ukrainians had a thousand year-old culture and that, as such, they were a people that had to be disarmed, materially and culturally, and then taken bare-handedly.

Having heard Trainin's conclusion, Kyiv Obkom Secretary Serdiuk asked, "The politics of the Germans can be explained based off of materials from Kyiv?" Trainin responded, "Exactly! After all, the Germans' task was to cut off the head of Kyiv, to destroy it, [and] to liquidate its leading cultural role. . . . This will be an answer to any [Ukrainian] nationalist."[2]

Trainin's next tasks were to collect materials on "culture and everyday life" in occupied Kyiv, to begin the accounting (*aktirovanie*) for what was uncovered, and to propagandize about what had happened. Serdiuk's eagerness to take the Germans to task, however, already emphasized a different rationale at the first party meeting in Kyiv on December 27, 1943:

> What the Germans did here will shock many comrades. . . . This is what we should be telling the population. . . . Under the Germans there was no freedom of movement. For that reason people did not socialize with each other. . . . And this is why when the Red Army liberated the city people literally kissed each other out of happiness. Not just because they were happy, but because they had not seen each other. They simply did not know about all the evil the Germans committed. You simply could not talk about it. We need to have them talk about everything. We will account for it, and then show the Germans the bill. That will help with rebuilding. That is why there is a resolution from the government telling us to get this accounting work done quickly.[3]

Investigating the Nazi occupation in order to win economic assistance had now become the imperative. But some ten months later, on September 11, 1944, Nikita Khrushchev, the chairman of the republic-level Commission of Assistance to the Extraordinary State Commission, asked Serdiuk why this *aktirovanie* had yet to be completed.[4] It would take even more time for Khrushchev to publicly announce the commission's final findings, with the economic cost of occupation and the numbers of *Ostarbeitery* lost to Germany remaining the focus.[5]

This change of focus and delay occurred as the Stalin regime started to avoid mention of what had happened at places like Babyn Iar.[6] The anti-Semitism that emerged in the resource-starved Soviet rear was the reason for hushing up the fate of Soviet Jews under the Nazis—a conclusion bolstered by a study of wartime Tashkent where many Jewish evacuees lived.[7] At the same time, the Stalin regime's wartime approval of Ukrainian nationalism to spur support for the Soviet cause was curtailed as the Kremlin encountered resistance to its return in western Ukraine.[8] Perhaps those Communists who returned to Kyiv now also asked themselves how continually reminding people about the fate there of thousands of Jews—and Ukrainians for that matter—during the occupation might help them create a more quiescent city, especially given the nature of the capital's resettlement and the reassembly of its population? In the end, these latter processes had been shaped by the Germans' crimes too. This chapter covers the ensuing attempts by the Ukrainian Communists to relegitimize Soviet power in Kyiv after the Nazis.

Relegitimizing Soviet Power: The Search for a Usable Present

The war destroyed the "alternative reality" constructed by Soviet propaganda during the 1930s. In summer 1941, the rhetoric of building Communism gave way to defeating the Nazis, and the Kremlin remained focused on defeating Hitler through May 9, 1945. Not only did the alternative reality of the 1930s disappear, but so too did the seemingly random terror that had helped bring it to fruition. These circumstances along with the new avoidance of the Holocaust and Ukrainian nationalism, led to the shift away from Trainin's proposal that they contrast themselves with Hitler and his rule. Instead, Soviet power would now mean rulers who could modernize the Ukrainian capital faster and better than anyone else.

Nikita Khrushchev's role in this process was crucial to Kyiv's postwar planning. Apparently, it was Khrushchev who quickly revamped the city's prewar general plan in expectation of reconstruction's planned beginning.[9] Serdiuk's comments made at the December 1943 meeting mentioned above highlight the Ukrainian leader's vision for the city's future: "[Khrushchev] said Kyiv is the capital of Ukraine, the cultural center of Ukraine, and here there should be enterprises of advanced mechanics. Here there should be optical tool and photo apparatus factories, and a radio factory.... Here we need factories of light industry, shoe factories, [and] a factory for the production of bicycles."[10] Already in late 1943, the propagandistic ideal meant creating a modern Ukraine through Soviet industrialization, even as the republic lay in ruins. The first effort to reassert Kyiv's place as the cultural center of Soviet Ukraine focused on the Khreshchatyk, the city's destroyed main street.

Khrushchev quickly changed the city's general plan to accommodate his vision of the Khreshchatyk. Completion of the 1930s-era "Government Square," located alongside the Ukrainian TsK's headquarters on space where the destroyed Mikhailovsky Monastery once stood, high above the Dnipro, was now scrapped. According to I. A. Ignatkin, "One of the insufficiencies in the planning of old Kyiv was the absence of a big central square.... [But] after the occupation, the question of the architectural completion of 'Government Square' was posed in a completely different way. By SNK UkrSSR directive, the central government square now lay immediately on the Khreshchatyk, the main artery of the city of Kyiv."[11]

A June 22, 1944, SNK UkrSSR resolution mandated the drawing up of a preliminary project for the city center. It envisioned the main street "as a trade-business and civic-cultural center as well as a center for mass demonstrations, strolling, and the concentration and division of mass transit flows."[12] From the beginning, the returning Communists must have hoped the Khreshchatyk's reconstruction would prove to the population that Soviet power meant leaders who knew how to lead. But, ideally, these Communists also wanted to show that they understood the thirst of the populace for a successful path to modernization.

The clearing of the Khreshchatyk began before any of these plans were made. When Kyiv's leadership first met regarding the street on February 8, 1944, according to Fedor Mokienko, they set May 1 as the target date for finishing the clearing. "It is really profitable for us to do as much as we can before May 1," he stated. "First, that is how long the workers can be mobilized. Second, because ... in winter, we can take workers from the oblast while in summer they are occupied there with field work."[13] Serdiuk then added another reason for starting this process in winter: "Work on the Khreshchatyk should be getting fired up (*kipet*), such that people see that they [the Ukrainian party members] have started to sort things out. And if they have started to sort things out, that means they are going to build."[14] Many of Kyiv's denizens would already, of course, associate forced modernization with Soviet power, and that association helped the return of these local Communists.

Perhaps Serdiuk's belief that action was necessary was stirred by recollections like those voiced at a July 1944 Kyiv Gorkom plenum by Secretary Mironov of Petriv [later Podil'] Raikom: "On November 22 [1943], the people saw a beaten-up tram on the rails in Petriv Raion.... It was like people were seeing a tram for the first time. And after seeing it they declared, 'Look, real bosses have actually arrived. Ours have arrived. Soviet power has arrived.'"[15] The notion that Soviet power implied men who were "real bosses" and "ours" was another reason why the Ukrainian Communists wanted to start reconstruction in a hurry.

Speaking at a second meeting about the Khreshchatyk on March 9, 1944, Mokienko outlined why Kyiv's Communists hoped to draw ordinary Kyivans into this effort. Noting the work of the *orgnabor*-staffed OSMCh no. 305 on the capital's main artery, Mokienko stated, "They have no [labor] power. There, people do not work and do not have the enthusiasm that we have."[16] To ensure that the Kyivan civilians who voluntarily mobilized for *narodnaia stroika* remained enthusiastic, Mokienko urged better record-keeping of individuals' work, payment for work actually accomplished, and assurance from the raion committees that the loading and unloading of debris continued on pace.

Figure 5.1. Kyivans on the reconstruction of the Khreshchatyk, unknown date. Reproduced by permission from the H. Pshenychnyi Central State CinePhotoPhono Archives of Ukraine.

By July 7, 1944, however, a Kyiv Gorkom resolution noted that the raion leading the way in clearing its area of the Khreshchatyk had fulfilled only 82 percent of the plan. In their conclusion about why work on this project should accelerate, the resolution's authors optimistically declared, "Every Kyivan male and female ... will put forth all their effort toward exhibiting new levels of self-sacrificial and highly productive labor in order to quickly finish the construction of the Khreshchatyk—the beauty, the glory, and the national pride of the great Ukrainian people."[17] The effort to rebuild the Khreshchatyk had become the Kyivan Communists' explicit answer to the Ukrainian insurgents.

But the most pressing task in the city in the summer of 1944 became not the Khreshchatyk but the temporary mobilization of Kyivans for firewood collection so they could heat their homes. At a July 25, 1944, Kyiv Gorkom plenum about the difficulties with this campaign, Serdiuk signaled its importance: "We can no longer explain away things by saying the Germans were here for two years. ... The Ukrainian TsK knew about the prohibitions on mobilizing workers, but it went ahead with the idea, and the decision must be fulfilled by the Kyiv party organization."[18] Apart from Serdiuk's apparent admission here that Kyiv's population was shielded from mobilization by the Stalin regime, the collecting of firewood (although it would have been more important to the city's people in the short term) certainly lacked the political symbolism of rebuilding the Khreshchatyk.

With the reconstruction of the Ukrainian capital already delayed, the party relied on architectural visions of Kyiv's future to legitimize Soviet power. For example, after the June 22, 1944, resolution about the city's main street, dozens of architects and engineers competed to determine what a future Khreshchatyk would look like. Before the SNK UkrSSR declared a winner on March 8, 1945, some of their drawings were publicly displayed at the city's Museum of Russian Art. According to the *Kyiv Truth* (*Kyivs'ka Pravda*) edition of January 9, 1945, more than a thousand Kyivans went to see these drawings, three of which the newspaper published over the following week.

Each of the published drawings is elaborate. All of them portray the city's main Kalinin Square—today's Independence Square (*Maidan Nezalezhnosti*) along the Khreshchatyk—without the prerevolutionary City Duma building that had dominated the area before the war. In the first two, the square is surrounded by large Greek-columned government buildings, huge arches, and large monuments celebrating the liberation of the city.[19] In the third, an even taller set of columned buildings completely surrounds a space that its planners now renamed "Victory Square" with a monument portraying a man on horseback at its center and endless rows of soldiers marching through it.[20]

Another newspaper, *Trud na Kreshchatike* (*Labor on the Khreshchatyk*), published a different drawing from the exhibition on January 26, 1945.[21] There the scene looks away from the now-open space occupied by the former City Duma building across the Khreshchatyk and toward the formidable hill on the opposite side of the street that climbs toward the city's elite Lypky District. At the base of the hill is a huge hall seating five thousand people. Behind it, on the hill itself, is a pantheon with a massive statue of Stalin on top. A wide and curved set of steps from the theater still located on the Khreshchatyk today and to the hall's right leads up to the pantheon.

On March 8, 1945, the SNK UkrSSR resolved that two teams of architects would examine these projects and present their ideas to the SNK UkrSSR Directorate of Artistic Affairs for the compilation of a new resolution by October 1, 1945.[22] The city's chief architect, Aleksandr Vlasov, led one of these teams. In the introduction to his project, he argued that the Khreshchatyk buildings should "show the greatness of the Stalinist epoch and its victories over Fascism, reflect the Stalinist care for the individual through the modern conveniences found in its new buildings, and become an organic part of the general plan for the city's future."[23]

Another document of Vlasov's contains his conclusions about the aims for this project: "The architecture of the Stalinist epoch should forever reflect the power and the greatness of the Soviet people, the fullness of her creative victories, and the eternal glory of the people-victor. One of these monuments to this historic epoch will be the newly reborn center of the city of Kyiv, the Khreshchatyk, and those regions around it destroyed by the German occupants."[24] Vlasov's writings reflect the vague substance of the Ukrainian Communists' legitimizing agenda during this period. Describing the Khreshchatyk as a symbol of the "victorious Stalinist epoch" meant applying the same modernizing vision to the downtown that had been the Ukrainian Communists' mantra since their return.

The other project belonged to architect O. Tatsiia. Like Vlasov's work, a smooth 500-meter long curve connected the two straight sections of the Khreshchatyk to replace the jagged one that had been there before.[25] More spectacularly, the project featured a new Kyiv City Soviet building placed directly along the Khreshchatyk's main curve (complete with a Lenin monument tribune for viewing parades), the placement of moving escalators to glide up the steep Kirov Hill (present-day Mykhailo Hrushevs'koho Street), the digging of three new tunnels—two from the new center down to Podil', and one from Bessarabs'kyi Market at the Khreshchatyk's far end up to Lypky—to ease the movement of trucks through the city center, and the construction of new buildings on the old Government Square.[26]

Perhaps these far-fetched ideas were why SM UkrSSR declared Vlasov's plan victorious on September 17, 1946, and ordered him to create a mock-up for the public at the Museum of Russian Art by February 1947.[27] These efforts, though, should be contrasted with the modest achievements on the Khreshchatyk covered earlier in this volume. The 1,200-meter underground tunnel for sewer pipes and other infrastructure was completed, the asphalting of the 50-meter-wide road and two 14-meter-wide sidewalks was finished, and trees and temporary light posts were installed by fall 1945.[28] But this was all the local Communists could do at this time.

Slow movement downtown meant that the Ukrainian Communists had to propagate other examples of how their return equalled progress for the city. One idea circulating in the Soviet Union at the time argued for the creation of open-air exhibitions to show successes on the country's reconstruction fronts. On February 22, 1944, Karo Alabian, the vice president of the All-Union Academy of Architects, proposed to Khrushchev an "Exhibition of Reconstruction Building in Cities and Villages in Kyiv."[29] Here, Alabian called for the demonstration of recommended building styles as well as the materials used in an attempt to advance reconstruction, save resources, and improve the quality of architecture in areas once occupied by the Nazis. But perhaps because of the lack of building supplies and the resulting political embarrassment it would have created, the exhibition never opened in Kyiv. Khrushchev may have realized this might delegitimize the party's efforts in Ukraine more than anything else. The materials to begin rebuilding outside of "defense-related" industries were not yet there.

The same reasoning probably explains why another idea never advanced: a proposal made to Khrushchev on October 28, 1944, by Grigorii Golovko, the head of the SNK UkrSSR Directorate for Architectural Affairs, to organize an exhibition in Kyiv highlighting the destruction caused by the Germans. This project likely was rejected in part because Golovko wanted to "present materials about the conditions of Kyiv and other cities before the occupation and about what has been done already in the field of reconstruction since the Germans were gotten rid of."[30] As with Trainin's ideas, the government must have deemed it unwise to remind people of the recent past. Instead, they focused on an industrialized, modernized future, for that would help the Ukrainian Communists capitalize on the good will that had met the return of Soviet power to Kyiv in November 1943.

In contrast, the effort to show the Red Army's prowess on the battlefield was politically feasible. One "natural demonstration" in Kyiv was the "Exhibition of Examples of Trophy Arms Captured from the Germans from 1941 to 1944," which opened in the fall of 1944. Moscow-based General Lieutenant R. Khmel'nitskii with GKO's "Trophy Committee" presented the idea in a letter to Khrushchev of March 25, 1944. In his letter, Khmel'nitskii stated that a similar exhibition in Moscow had drawn 2.7 million people since its opening and many positive reviews from visitors. The exhibition's purpose, wrote Khmel'nitskii, was that "a wide showing of the trophies and arms of the enemy should—along with a feeling of surety about the unconquerable nature of Soviet arms—bring to the consciousness of visitors that 'the Red Army awaits a severe battle against a treacherous, tough, and still strong enemy. The battle will demand time and victims, as well as all our powers and the mobilization of all of our resources' (Stalin)."[31] This idea legitimized the return of Soviet power in a more sober manner than previous plans. It focused on positive aspects of the past and hopes for a bright future.

As for restoring the capital's art world, the Ukrainian leadership trod carefully. The Ukrainian TsK and SNK UkrSSR resolved on April 1, 1944, to restore Kyiv's three main museums: the Museum of Ukrainian Art on Kirov Street, and the Museums of Russian Art and of Western and Eastern Art located on Chudnovs'koho Street.[32] Another of the Ukrainian leadership's resolutions from that same day noted, "Have the Directorate of the Affairs of Art with the SNK UkrSSR create a commission to choose works from the picture funds of the museums of Ukraine [located in Ufa and Novosibirsk, RSFSR] so they can be kept in the capital's republican museums."[33]

When this effort failed to fill Kyiv's empty museums, a May 1946 memorandum of L. Petlichenko, the head of the sector of art of the Ukrainian TsK's Department of Propaganda and Agitation, to comrade Raevskii, the director of the Museum of Russian Art in Kyiv, noted that the SNK SSSR Committee for the Affairs of Art in Moscow was ready to "separate out some exhibits so as to fill up the picture galleries of the museum."[34] More than 274 paintings, graphics, sculptures, and drawings, including important works by the likes of Surikov and Shishkin, had already been dispatched from Moscow to Kyiv. In this way, local Communists promoted to Kyivans that Soviet power in Ukraine was closely aligned with the Russian people. After all, Moscow had liberated Kyiv and was now leading the reconstruction campaign.

There were other attempts to symbolize the bright future awaiting Kyiv. In December 1944, Khrushchev received a letter from architect Mikhail Ladyr about building a "Palace of Heroic Youth" on the Khreshchatyk. Ladyr claimed, "Within this celebration, the heroic youth of Soviet Ukraine will find their place—a place achieved by young Ukrainian men and women through the price of suffering, the price of the lives of the best."[35] Ladyr rationalized his efforts: "We need to work on creating a new Soviet classicism. One based on the rich spiritual life of our people, a strong alloy in which there is a super-strong metal that goes by the name of Bolshevism."[36]

While the definition of "Bolshevism" remained somewhat vague, this emphasis on memorializing particularly Ukrainian things must have been deemed inappropriate. While Khrushchev ignored Ladyr's idea, he took seriously a July 5, 1946, letter from two Kyivans, V. Volchkov and I. Tsykovskii, about building an "Alley of Great Names" in the city's May First Garden. The proposed alley "would show . . . those people who fought for freedom, [and] for the flourishing of the culture of our land. . . . On both sides, on pedestals, there should be erected busts of great people. Under these busts there should be inscriptions of their pronouncements about Ukraine, Russia, and the friendship of the peoples."[37] After seeing Lenin, Stalin, and himself among the "great names" to be commemorated (along with everyone from the commanders of the Ukrainian fronts to a mainly Ukrainian collective of artists), Khrushchev duly recommended the idea, and the Kyiv City Soviet eventually approved it, complete with 50 bronze statues costing 700,000 to 800,000 rubles each.

Although Soviet power was increasingly associated with support for the cultural sphere, Khrushchev's approval of a plan to build a subway in Kyiv revealed it to also be closely associated with modernization. By July 1946, the Metro Construction Trust (*Metrostroi*) in Moscow prepared a draft plan of construction that included elevators servicing a planned station in Lypky, a major transfer station called "Opera," and the first of three scheduled lines running from the Bol'shevik Factory to the Dnipro along an east-west axis.[38] While the public did not know these details—and the metro did not actually open until 1960—articles about this futuristic form of transport appeared in *Kyivs'ka Pravda* at this time.

The incomplete publicizing of the Nazis' crimes in Kyiv, the sputtering effort to rebuild the Khreshchatyk, and the escape into fantasy about the city's future all suggest difficulties for the Ukrainian Communists as they tried legitimize their return to the capital, despite favorable conditions at the front. Such challenges meant that they also closely monitored the population's mood about their return and their policies.

Relegitimizing Soviet Power: Monitoring the Mood of the Masses

To grasp the mood of the people at the return of Soviet power, it is helpful to revisit interviews conducted by the Ukrainian Academy of Sciences' Commission for Compiling a Chronology of the Great Patriotic War from the winter of 1943–44, which opened chapter 1. The interviews clarify why the Ukrainian Communists could easily mold the popular mood to their benefit during the first few months after their arrival, as they reveal the timidity of many while the war raged to the city's west.

Organized by the Ukrainian Academy of Sciences' Institute of History, the commission received a description of life in Kyiv before the Red Army's return from Aleksei Bashkulat, an administrator at the city's Shevchenko opera theater: "Before German evacuation, frightening rumors circulated around the city. It was said that all those who had worked for the Germans would be sent to the front. Others would be sent to Siberia. No mercy would be shown."[39] Another commission interview from February 20, 1944, with Isai Vinnitskii, the acting director of Leninskaia Kuznitsa, reveals the mood among those people who remained in the city during the previous winter: "At first the workers were terribly frightened. The Germans had assured them, 'No matter what, the Bolsheviks will shoot you.' I felt a sick atmosphere around me. When you walked up to somebody, they would jump back four steps."[40]

Such timidity is also confirmed by the first "political information" reports sent from Kyiv's Communists to their superiors in the oblast- and republic-level leaderships. Writing on November 30, 1943, to the Kyiv Obkom, Lenin Raikom Secretary Nezhinskii listed questions asked by the population to illustrate what Kyivans thought. After meetings dedicated to studying Stalin's "On the 26th Anniversary of October" speech, Nezhinskii asked these questions: "Were the Germans going to return? Would the fighting end soon? What about the POWs and children taken to Germany?"[41] Later, on December 6, the Kyiv Gorkom's Department of Agitation leader, Urbanskii, mentioned to the Kyiv Obkom that over 70,000 Kyivans had attended 103 meetings about Stalin's anniversary speech since the city's liberation.

But he also added a warning: "In general we have done a lot. But considering the situation around us, this is just not good enough, especially since nothing has been done yet about the organization of an exhibition dedicated to the atrocities committed by the Germans in Kyiv."[42] Then on December 10, 1943, Kyiv Obkom secretary F. Burdeniuk addressed his concern to the Ukrainian

TsK about the political situation in Kyiv: "In the city there are manifestations of Nazi agitation. This is true especially after [Soviet] troops, in accordance with the order of the supreme commander, abandoned Zhytomyr and Korosten'. There are population groups that do not demonstrate activity and who decline to work in enterprises and Soviet institutions."[43] Here might be the only moment during the mid-1940s when publicizing the Germans' crimes in Kyiv was politically correct: that time when local Communists faced the Nazis' possible return.

Circumstances could change on a dime, though, due to events at the front. As German resistance melted away and the All-Union NKVD kept focusing its *massoperatsii* on finding men for the Red Army, it did not take long for the formerly occupied to lose their timidity toward their new masters. And as the more opportunistic among them took advantage of local authorities' loose administration of the city's empty housing, talk about the war's events from those who represented Soviet power in Kyiv was rarely heard. The latter may have realized that time spent dwelling on the occupation period might only further poison relations among the different groups of Kyivans.

The comments of the city's leaders on the mood of the masses following the Ukrainian NKVD's march of thousands of German POWs through Kyiv on August 16, 1944, justifies this conclusion. While some 200,000 Kyivans turned out to see the spectacle, reports about what happened that day reveal the returning Soviets' belief that Kyivans were no longer such an easy group to control. One report from Serdiuk to Khrushchev—about the "reactions of the workers" to the convoy—notes, "Among those workers who pronounced their contempt and hatred, there were also those who expressed their sympathy. For example, 'Not all of them arrived here with the wish to murder, annihilate, etc. but because of the will of Hitler.' When a crying woman was asked why she was crying, she responded, 'Take a look at how hairy, thin, dirty, and shabby they are. They also have wives and children who are waiting for them.'"[44] On the other hand, a separate document reported to Khrushchev that the "general reaction" in the city was that the Soviet government was acting too humanely toward the Germans. Many women, for example, were said to have screamed angrily at the POWs, "What did you do with our prisoners? How you tortured them. Beat them. Do not miss your chance."[45]

But the Ukrainian NKVD head Riasnoi, writing to Khrushchev at the time, maintained a more nuanced perspective: "The movement of the column across the city went on in an organized fashion and was not accompanied by excesses. But when the column passed by hospitals, from the side of the fighters located there recovering as well as from invalids of the Patriotic War there were many attempts to break through the cordon in order to fight the POWs."[46] Whether the "excesses" mentioned here included too much sympathy or too much wrath toward the vanquished Germans, the Ukrainian Communists tried to maintain their vigilance over any foundations for social grievance.

As the Red Army marched into Eastern Europe, loudspeakers announced the Yalta conference communiqué to large crowds. Ovcharenko, the head of the Kyiv Obkom's Organization and Instruction Department, relayed these scenes to the Ukrainian TsK: "There was happiness on the faces of those gathered. Every time the announcer spoke about the devastation of Nazi Germany, those present broke into enthusiastic applause. The Kyivans were especially elated to hear the information about how the timeline and size of the new and even more powerful strikes on Germany were planned at the conference."[47] Later, a May 3, 1945, report from O. Kuroid, the Kyiv Obkom secretary responsible for propaganda and agitation, to the Ukrainian TsK reiterated the "population's comments about the Red Army taking Berlin."[48]

Many of Kuroid's comments reference private conversations, such as one at the Arsenal Factory between an older and a younger worker. After noting the workers' hope for the war's end and for an end to rationing, Kuroid observed, "The old guy responds, 'Do you remember? Before, we bought fine rye bread. One kilogram was enough and now we are buying two [of poor nutritional quality] each day and it is not enough.' The young guy states, 'That is because you are not eating enough pig fat. No matter, after the war everything will be just fine.'" According to Kuroid, the workers then concluded their conversation: "The old man adds, 'I think there will be beer on every street. I really love beer. It will be on the house.' And then he breaks off the conversation, saying things are bad with clothing. To which the young guy responds, 'But they have so many factories. All of them will be sending us stuff.'"[49] Kuroid then contrasted these workers' extravagant visions of the future with a conversation between two women discussing the battle for Berlin in front of the Bessarabs'kyi Market: "'Berlin's taken.' 'They said that once Berlin goes the war will be over.' 'Many Germans have been pounded into the ground.' 'Yes. And quite a few of our loved ones have laid their heads down, too.'"[50] This combination of hope and sadness is something Kuroid wanted Ukraine's leaders to take into account considering their difficulties in achieving their aims in Kyiv at the end of the Second World War.

But those in the Ukrainian TsK's Department of Propaganda and Agitation reading this memorandum saved their thickest red-penciled annotations for these lines: "While filling up a pit with bearing piles, one woman said, 'That corpse of Goebbels, it needs to be hammered like this into a coffin.' Another said, 'Yes, those devils have gotten away.' And the first woman replied, 'Wow! To be able to hammer nails into their corpses.'"[51] Although this report also noted singing and dancing in the streets of Podil', indiscriminate shooting into the air by servicemen all over the city, and happy crowds gathered in front of maps entitled "Western Europe" showing the progress of the Red Army into German-held territory, the sense here is that the ruling Communists compiled and read this document with a mix of hopeful expectation and trepidation considering the city's stalled reconstruction.

Figure 5.2. Bohdan Khmel'nyts'kyi Square in Kyiv on Victory Day, May 9, 1945. Reproduced by permission from the H. Pshenychnyi Central State CinePhotoPhono Archives of Ukraine.

Figure 5.3. Schoolchildren from Kyiv's Stalin Raion prepare to march in the Victory Day parade, May 9, 1945. Reproduced by permission from the H. Pshenychnyi Central State CinePhotoPhono Archives of Ukraine.

Figure 5.4. The people of Kyiv parade on Victory Day, May 9, 1945. Reproduced by permission from the H. Pshenychnyi Central State CinePhotoPhono Archives of Ukraine.

After Moscow finally turned its attention to the homefront, it became important to keep one's superiors aware of the local populace's mood. The effects of one early policy action—Moscow's June 24, 1945, Law on Demobilization—are evident in a report from Kyiv Oblast written at the end of that month. Kyiv Obkom Secretary Burdeniuk reported to the all-union party's Organization Instruction Department head, Mikhail Shamberg, in Moscow with questions from Kyivans: "Why did the Twelfth Session [of the all-union Supreme Soviet] decide the question about the demobilization of the active army but not about the labor army? Which years [of birth] (and when exactly) will be demobilized? When will the question about the length of the working day be decided? Will there be a vacation this year? Why is the war tax still collected if the war has come to an end?"[52] Burdeniuk's summary of responses to demobilization implied his ability to pinpoint what was on the mind of the local population once the latter knew the Stalin regime in Moscow had made a decision.

Burdeniuk included in his report a conversation among some Kyivans living in apartments at 9 Mil'ionna Street. He quoted an engineer, Kuzma Khvoinskii: "Only the USSR can provide for a happy return. [The demobilized] are not threatened with unemployment. . . . A huge amount of construction has gotten underway with us in Kyiv. I work on one of those sites and we are sensing a huge need for cadres—especially qualified ones.... We impatiently await the return of the front fighters (*frontoviki*)."⁵³ This statement contrasts sharply with Burdeniuk's description of the director of the apartment building's contribution: "Nesterenko, Grigorii ... who was standing nearby, responded, 'All of this about demobilization is just talk. They are only writing about it in newspapers. Who is going to come and work in the housing sector for money? They would be better off going to the bazaar to trade than coming here to work.'"⁵⁴ Burdeniuk was highlighting his concerns about how Moscow's decrees might influence his ability to rule the population. After all, Kyiv needed both demobilized soldiers and support for such soldiers if it was to capitalize on their presence and counter the entrenched interests of the formerly occupied.

Such back-and-forth with the provinces may be why the party leadership in Moscow decided to proceed with an extensive three-month campaign for seats in the All-Union Supreme Soviet ending in the elections of February 10, 1946. The Kyivan leaders, like presumably all others across the USSR, sought to represent their city in a way that would make their future as predictable as possible. The campaign began in November 1945 with meetings around Kyiv and its surrounding oblast dedicated to the "Stalin" Constitution of 1936. Such meetings resulted in Secretary Ovcharenko in Kyiv reporting once again to Secretary Shamberg in Moscow. The questions by Kyivans signaled that matters "Soviet" were not yet clearly grasped by the local population: Had the Americans' supposed demand that the collective farms be "cancelled" as of January 1, 1946, been accepted in Moscow? Or, as one worker from Molotov Raion is said to have asked, "What type of elections were there to the [Tsarist-era] State Duma?"⁵⁵

Ovcharenko stressed that the overall mood of the workers was "healthy." But he also included "manifestations of moods of a negative character" as a way of alerting Moscow to the need to act quickly on reconstruction: "In the village of Zavalovka, the collective farmer V. Ovchar said, 'It would be better if in the directorate of the state there was only one person, not one hundred. There would be less expense and we would achieve more. Let us just elect one person. That will be enough.'"⁵⁶ Later, in early December 1945, Ovcharenko wrote to Zlenko, the Ukrainian TsK's secretary for agitation and propaganda, about the seminars and preparatory meetings for the elections held in each of the party's raion committees across Kyiv.⁵⁷ For example, Ovcharenko referenced the exasperation of some of the city's downtrodden workers in late 1945: "At [aviation] factory no. 485 some workers asked, 'Is it really necessary to carry out this agitation in preparation for the elections if we have one party in this country, something that means there cannot be the type of electoral battle like in the capitalist countries?'"⁵⁸

By December 27, 1945, the Kyiv Gorkom secretary in charge of its Organization-Instruction Department, Ratkin, could report to Ovcharenko and Zlenko that precinct commissions were completely staffed and confirmed by the various raion committees and soviets, and that the clarification of the voter lists was now ending. Both Ovcharenko and Ratkin highlighted Kyivans' questions to reveal the local population's confusion about the Soviets' next steps. According to Ovcharenko, the population was asking agitators the "most varied of questions" including, "Why did comrade Stalin pronounce a toast to and especially note the Russian people? How many people died during the Great Patriotic War? Will the German POWs be allowed to vote, and how long will they be working in Ukraine? Can a Soviet republic leave the USSR and be led by its national constitution?"[59]

Although they were designed to signal concern to Moscow, these reports also had to show that the local Communists were masters of the situation. Such a tendency is reflected in the questions Ratkin highlighted: "Do we have a proletariat at the moment? What is a dictatorship, a federation, etc.? Will a special voting region for Jews be organized? Will those citizens without living permits be allowed to vote? Why are those people who served in German institutions during the occupation not deprived of their right to vote?"[60] While some of the confusion might have been due to the vague nature of the Stalin regime's propaganda, these questions testify to divisions within the local population.

The election also signaled the Stalin regime's assertion of something akin to the Soviet power of old. It would have been disingenuous to claim that there was no resistance to this process, and the local Communists wanted to make sure their superiors were informed. Ovcharenko's report mentioned this "anti-Soviet" event: "In the movie theatre at 102 Saksaganskogo Street on November 19, 1945, a group of hooligans in military greatcoats broke up a cultural outing by the workers of the Transportation Signal (*Transsignal*) Factory. . . . The hooligans, before and during the movie, swore, scandalized, and, finally, tore the loudspeaker off of the wall. That broke off the showing of the movie altogether. . . . This occurrence left an unpleasant, sinking feeling, among the workers."[61] Moscow proceeded with the elections and, in early January 1946, meetings of the city's institutions and enterprises selected the representatives for the city's three district electoral assemblies to determine who would represent the city on the ballot on February 10, 1946. According to Ratkin, some 90,000 people attending 500 meetings had nominated 1,600 people for positions in the All-Union Supreme Soviet, and then chosen 2,450 people to select from among these nominees at three district electoral assemblies.[62] The assemblies then determined Kyiv's all-union representatives by the end of the month.

Meanwhile, the "Kyiv Trial" of January 1946, in which a dozen Germans were hanged in Kalinin Square for alleged war crimes committed during the occupation, gave the local authorities a chance to send their superiors an update on the situation in the city.[63] A copy of Kyiv Gorkom Secretary Gorban's political information memorandum to his republic-level superiors notes that Kyivans crowded the streets near the "House of the Red Army" to cheer the sentence, and that nearly 200,000 ventured out at dusk the next day to see the actual hanging.[64] But Gorban added this question from the Lepse Tractor Factory workers: "It is wonderful that they hanged the Germans. But when are they going to judge those who helped them?"[65] These political information reports signaled a frustrated and ultimately divided Kyivan populace.

On February 10, 1946—Election Day—the leader of Kyiv Gorkom sent reports every few hours to the Kyiv Obkom. Turnout was almost universal. As the Pechersk Raikom noted, "Eleven people did not show up to vote. Of those, three showed up twice on the voter lists, two were students on vacation, and six were people who . . . it is not clear where they had gone."[66] But the upbeat nature of the reports dated February 10 changed to a more sober appraisal of matters by March 4 when Gorban wrote a memorandum to the Kyiv Obkom entitled "On the Inscriptions on Bulletins, the Contents of Letters and Notes, Discovered upon Opening the Urns at the Electoral Precincts in the City of Kyiv."[67] Other than actual votes, the information collected from the urns included "quite a few notes of a critical character," which, according to Gorban, "expressed the dissatisfaction and censure of individual voters."[68] While these notes should be considered against a backdrop of many more expressions of gratitude to Comrade Stalin, they also contain a coherent message of the key issues that bothered Kyivans.

The criticisms Gorban cited covered issues mentioned in the preceding chapters: frustration in the face of overlooked privileges, corruption in all facets of housing allocation, and speculation in all facets of the food trade. One letter, dropped into a ballot box located in Kaganovich Raion's 18th precinct, was particularly poignant: "The war ended eight months ago already. It is necessary to rebuild all that was destroyed. No one is arguing about that. But it is necessary to take on everything else, too. First of all, and most important, are the people, or the person. The person is the most valuable capital of all. It is criminal to forget about that."[69]

While it might have been possible in the short term to satisfy such a desire for material support, Gorban also cited notes from two precincts that spoke of a deeper dissatisfaction with Soviet power that might prove more difficult to overcome: "We ask that the government pay attention to the fact that some husbands, especially military men, are getting rid of their wives and families"; "When will Kyiv at last be freed from traitors and speculators?" and "Nikita Sergeevich, when will people be hired based on their talents and not based on local connections, nepotism, servility, and bribery? We await change from you."[70] Such frankness indicates a desire to communicate to the Ukrainian leadership—through the conduit of Kyiv Obkom secretary Serdiuk—a comprehensive list of troubles in Soviet society that had gestated since the period of "peaceful and creative labor" ended in 1941.

Peppered throughout this document are reminders about strained interethnic relations in the city. In his effort to acquaint his superiors with these differences,

Gorban recounted other inscriptions: "I give you my vote, but ask that not a single Jew be in our Ukraine"; "I am not voting, I am a Banderite"; and that "On a bulletin at the eighth precinct in Podil' Raion, [the writer, Pavlo] Tychyna's last name was crossed out and Hitler was written in its place."[71] While these divisions made widespread opposition to the local Communists a relatively remote possibility, such information was included to show the poisonous problems that could be cured only by movement on reconstruction.

Gorban included the opinions of different groups within the city about each other, such as comments by one formerly occupied woman: "My son who is in the Red Army and whom I have not seen in four years . . . writes, 'Mama, have you received your apartment?' . . . He did not hide in the rear, like the enemies of the Russian people did. [Now they] are back here with their wives and screaming, 'We have taken Kyiv. We have taken Berlin,' while the poor wives of Red Army men . . . hear the insult 'German bitches' from these cunning enemies of the people."[72]

Because the Stalin regime had virtually ignored Kyiv's reconstruction since the city's liberation, Gorban also included quotes that illustrated especially negative political positions held by some Kyivans, such as:

> You who have propagated bribes, you who have propagated hunger, you who have given the "Fritzes" more bread than your own, you who have made legal such sayings as "blat [corruption] is more important than the SNK" and "without bribes you are going to go nowhere," you who have villages where no one wants to work while those same people work hard on their individual plots without anyone forcing them to do so, you have made everyone into slaves and then yell that among us labor is a matter of honor. An honest person cannot vote for you bastards. For what did we fight?[73]

And,

> The people have already become indifferent to your agitation. Of course you are afraid. You do not want to fail in this campaign. It is hardly important, however, who is chosen "by the people" from among these so-called deputies or not. I can say only one thing. You have not long left to rule. In the not so distant future, you will be overwhelmed. Just like the party of Fascism was. At that point—make no mistake about it—neither your brutal terror, nor your snake-like agitation will come to your rescue.[74]

As paradoxical as it might sound, Gorban probably included such quotations to illustrate his ability to correctly guide the city through its reconstruction. He concluded his report by remarking that alongside these openly anti-Soviet comments, there were also many "healthy, critical inscriptions and notes uncovering insufficiencies and expressing fair complaints and dissatisfaction," and that the Kyiv Gorkom and its subordinate raion committees had taken measures necessary to satisfy workers' demands.[75] The local Communists were, for the moment, able to successfully manage Kyiv if resources were made available.

The "Law on the [Fourth] Five-Year Plan" announcement in Moscow in March 1946 only reinforced this show of resolve. In the announcement's aftermath, local Communists explained to their leaders that they understood the plan's contents and were trying to propagate those contents to the population. A May 1946 memorandum from the Zaliznychnyi Raikom's Propaganda Department to the Kyiv Gorkom noted that some 1,700 party, soviet, and economic cadres along with 5,000 workers and members of the intelligentsia in the raion were studying the newly passed plan.[76] But this memorandum also contained information about sites where propagandizing was not progressing so smoothly, including the Andreev Railway Depot's party organization, where of the two circles studying the history of the all-union party, one met infrequently and the other lackadaisically. One party member "read the history of the party a long time ago, but he has not read the five-year plan and nothing seems to stay in his head," and the depot's main mechanic responded to a question about the *narodniki* by calling them "'the people who achieved Soviet power,' and then said that he had no time to study."[77] Perhaps the inclusion of these apparent troubles was done to remind superiors of the realities involved in trying to rule over a city without the necessary resources.

Another memorandum of this time entitled "On the State of Study of the Law on the Fourth Five-Year Plan" from the Molotov Raikom to the Kyiv Gorkom highlighted Kyivans' questions about the plan that were asked at meetings following its announcement. A list of them included the following: "1) Will our country be powerful at the end of the five-year plan when compared to the times before the war? 2) Is it possible that we will have more mills and factories than before the war? 3) How and when will the ration cards on bread and other products be pulled from use and will the prices of products be lowered further? 4) Do we have enough labor power after the end of the war?"[78] As was often the case, however, the questions emphasized were actually the lower-level Communists' own concerns about administering Moscow's new initiative than anything else. Such a memorandum reminded local leaders and those above them that they faced a difficult road ahead.

To successfully navigate that road, Ukraine's Communist leaders now capitalized on the concurrent Zhdanovshchina by using the front pages of the Kyivan press to solidify their rule. While the "revivalist" campaign of the time is infamous for its attack on Soviet writers Anna Akhmatova and Mikhail Zoshchenko, its efforts to discipline the Communist rank and file itself are less well-known. The focus in Kyiv would be on tidying up the party's own house after the wartime fight over scarce resources and influence distracted its members. The inexperienced

Communist rank and file would be in need of being propagandized. In the meantime, if the city's masses could be persuaded to trust these men and women, then the idea that Soviet state legitimacy rested on effective leadership would become the local Communists' mantra into the future. Such men and women might find modernizing Ukraine difficult, but at least they could be seen as competent guides through troubled times.

The Relegitimization of Soviet Power: Localizing the Zhdanovshchina

In Kyiv, the Stalin regime's Zhdanovshchina began with a series of articles in the local Communists' newspaper, *Kyivs'ka Pravda*, explaining what party members needed to do to fulfill the Fourth Five-Year Plan. These articles marked a dramatic return—after a five-year absence—of Marxism-Leninism to Kyiv's life. While this print campaign may have shocked the rank and file into taking the plan seriously, it is better seen as propaganda explaining that local Communist leaders were aware that reform was necessary. It implied that the Stalin regime and its local leaders were unafraid to acknowledge that a majority of Kyivans agreed that an authoritarian state was essential for rebuilding. A path toward relegitimizing Soviet power in Kyiv now appeared—just as "building Communism" there recommenced—despite Marx's claim that the state would "wither away" during that process.

Events began on June 11, 1946, when *Kyivs'ka Pravda* reprinted "The Meaning of Ideological Work in Contemporary Conditions," a lead article targeting "cultural workers" from the major union-level party propaganda journal, *Bol'shevik*.[79] The editorial hailed the plan as a "great step forward on the road to the completion of a classless, socialist society and the gradual transition from socialism to Communism." On paper, Ukraine's writers appeared to be responsible for engineering the human beings necessary for this process to succeed.

But when *Kyivs'ka Pravda* published its own article on July 9, 1946, entitled "Ideological Work at a Higher Level," there was an evident change in audience: "The task of the Communist education of all workers becomes of special importance, overcoming the remnants of capitalism in the consciousness of people, and the new increase in the cultural-political level of our people," and these goals could be achieved only if "our party-soviet activists, and our intelligentsia, raise their own ideological-political levels."[80] Now the onus was on rank-and-file Communists to improve themselves as they awaited largesse after the announcement of the Fourth Five-Year Plan. The article continued with a 1930s-era quote in which Stalin argued that if the party had a correctly educated set of members, then nine-tenths of the country's problems would have been solved. Other articles targeted those who had given local leaders the most grief during this period: local Communists leading union- and republic-level factories.

On August 2, 1946, *Kyivs'ka Pravda* reprinted a leader from *Pravda* with the front-page headline "Always and in Everything Be Honest in Front of the State." That the Kyiv Gorkom had already resolved on July 31 that every party organization in the city would hold closed-door meetings between August 5 and 12 to discuss the article's contents signaled its importance. The main argument stated that, "A person, capable of deceiving the party and the state in small matters can also lead people astray in a big way. . . . That is why it is so necessary to educate and strengthen state principles within our cadres, [to create] a feeling of responsibility before the state, a consciousness of one's obligations, and honesty with regard to the state in all affairs big and small. . . . Leaders of the state enjoy the state's full trust. They are given many powers. But, trust does not mean turning off control. Bolshevik rules say, 'Trust, but verify.'"[81] One day later, on August 3, *Kyivs'ka Pravda* published its own story, "The Dignity of a Soviet Person," which told Kyiv's rank and file what they needed to consider to meet the standards of the *Pravda* editorial: "For the Soviet person, the state's dignity is higher than his own dignity. . . . Such an inexhaustible power that illuminates the road, plants belief in the heart, [and] gives life to that well-born fire of dignity, is the teachings of Marxism-Leninism."[82] Due to a lack of constructive ideas, therefore, about how to complete the Soviet Union's historic task, the pointed demand that people place the state's interests ahead of their own marked a new focus for how building Communism was to be accomplished.

But instead of pointing the masses to libraries to read about the Soviet Union's leading ideologues, subsequent articles in *Kyivs'ka Pravda* concentrated on how the city's Communists were to make the state's mission the focus of their lives. They announced a campaign to reemphasize "self-criticism" among the leadership of the city's party organizations (complete with real-life examples from Kyiv), and a renewed effort at the "Bolshevik education" of the young Communists who dominated these party organizations after the war. The message to the masses was plain: the local leaders understood their role and their city's position within the Stalinist state and were pushing to make sure their rank and file also understood how this system worked. This, too, was a signal to readers that their leaders were competent enough to see the city through troubled times.

Kyivs'ka Pravda's August 10 editorial, "Self-Criticism—The Source of Our Power," initiated this campaign. Its argument was couched in terms already familiar to those who had read the aforementioned articles. The main point was that party organizations where leading comrades put their own interests in front of the state's had allowed these "pitiful and ordinary philistines" to "lose their Soviet dignity" and "hinder the victorious movement forward." The article concluded with a far-reaching remedy to ensure that "self-willed solitude, nepotism, and irresponsibility" no longer existed in the city party's frontline organizations: "Criticism and self-criticism help party organizations mobilize the masses for the fulfillment of Stalinist tasks. . . . Widely unleashing self-criticism, regardless of the person and the activities he executes, secures the improvement of internal party work and furthers the development of all branches and fields of our socialist building."[83]

Two weeks later, *Kyivs'ka Pravda* gave an example of a party organization where the lack of self-criticism led to the presence of "that rotten liberalism, that petty-bourgeois lack of discipline, and all that hinders us from moving forward." Entitled "Self-Criticism, the Proven Armor of Bolshevism," it argued that the "most important condition for the wide and brave unleashing of criticism and self-criticism is the independence of party organs." It lamented "the joining together of the party apparatus with the state and economic apparatuses, [and] of leaders in the economy giving monetary awards to party workers and illegally supplying them with food products and industrial goods."[84] Two days later, *Kyivs'ka Pravda* continued this campaign to propagate self-criticism in the Ukrainian capital with an article on a Kyivan party leader who had "lost a Soviet person's dignity" because of corruption. The message people needed was that Soviet power in Kyiv meant competent leaders who put the state first.

In what turned out to be the high point of the campaign, the editorial of August 27, 1946, was entitled "The Moral Face of a Soviet Leader." The code of conduct envisioned here entailed being honest, strictly observing all Soviet laws, making one's behavior an example for others to follow, looking out for the fate of socialist property, helping to maintain severe discipline, and persistently raising one's "ideological level."[85] The article then proffered examples of leaders who did not meet such standards. The first was a Comrade Fleish, the head of Special Construction Assembly Directorate no. 26, who was tasked with reconstructing the city's Darnytsa-based textile factory and accused of seeking a party card "so he could conceal his petty-bourgeois nature. Fleish deceived leading party and soviet organs, passing off false information about construction. When the opportunity offered itself he practiced bribery, 'privatizing' state funds and construction materials." After exposing Fleish, the party organization excluded him from their ranks.[86]

To the masses reading this article, Fleish would have hardly seemed exceptional. That he was highlighted at all was probably to inform readers that the local leaders understood their city well. The article concluded with words of warning: "Member of the party is a high-sounding title. Thus, the party attentively watches so that self-seekers, scoundrels, and the useless do not crawl into its ranks. . . . Guard the cleanliness of the party ranks. . . . Ruthlessly uncover those people who ignore the interests of the people."[87] The local leaders' concern about the quality of leadership in their city, and their desire to improve it, were the main messages they wished to communicate. While Fleish would have seemed like a scapegoat to readers, at least there was some recognition that corruption existed and that something might be done to stem it.

On August 14 and August 23, 1946, *Kyivs'ka Pravda* placed the effort to create better leaders within the context of local party organizations that knew too little about the message that guided them. The intent seems to have been to propagandize to readers that the government understood who was in the party and was making efforts to improve matters. The August 14 article bluntly stated that two-thirds of the Communists in the all-union party in 1946 had joined it during the war.[88] Such clarity about party membership was rare during this period. An article published on August 23, "Raise Cadres in a Loving, Stalinist Manner," admitted that the "placement and preparation of cadres" in Kyiv was problematic, noting that "new people have appeared in many fields of party, soviet, and civilian work" and claiming they lacked "the corresponding preparation and experience. These are people not well-informed about Marxism-Leninism."[89]

While the likes of Fleish needed to be removed from the party—an educational example in itself for others—the main task involved party organizations edifying their own members. If they did not do so, *Kyivs'ka Pravda* implied, the results for the Fourth Five-Year Plan would be disastrous: "The successful fulfillment of these great and important tasks first depends on how well the party organizations organize the ideological-political education of Communists themselves."[90] After years where winning the war, not building Communism, had been Bolshevism's highest priority, it was time to resume the latter effort. The masses' education was of secondary importance. It was now crucial for the reassembled Kyivans to accept the local Communist rank and file as the only people who could create a better standard of living within the super-centralized Stalinist state.

The way toward relegitimizing the Stalin regime in Kyiv was clear: a small coterie of men and women was said to have learned (or be learning) how to guide the state; at the same time, local Communists would resettle and supply the capital's reassembled population. For the Stalin regime, the interplay of central and local messages may have been helpful for the formulation of propaganda in the years ahead. "Soviet Patriotism's" paradoxical focus on allegiance to an authoritarian state as it worked at building Communism probably became quite natural considering the potential for social disorder all around in places like Kyiv.

The Zhdanovshchina also colored Kyiv's rulers' response to the 1946–47 famine.[91] Official word of trouble with the harvest emerged from the implementation of the all-union resolution of September 16, 1946, that was introduced in the last chapter.[92] This resolution contained four key points: postponement of the cancellation of the ration card system for food products, an increase in state ration prices for staples like bread and sugar, a decrease in state commercial prices for food and industrial goods, and an increase in the salaries of low- and average-wage workers. Kyivans' reactions to this resolution and subsequent efforts to control the food supply in the city reveal Soviet power's problems three years after the Nazi occupation.

Kyiv's local leaders learned about the population's reactions to this resolution from "political information" reports produced by the city's raikoms after the resolution was made public. According to a report penned by Istomin, a member of the Podil' Raikom on September 16, 1946, the workers at the Stalin Ship-Building Factory supported the resolution, for they saw it as a temporary phenomenon due to that summer's drought.[93] The author, though, was careful to point out the give-and-take involved in the reaction at the factory. For example, he quoted a "demobilized, non-party comrade Vavulin" as saying, "We have got to help the state. . . . We understand all of this and know that this is only done so that in the future we will live better."[94] But he then added his own words: "At the same time the workers of the factory ask that there be bread all the time in the commercial shop on the factory premises."[95]

Alongside this equivocation, Istomin reported "a number of negative and incorrect judgments" about the resolution. Such "judgments" at the Second Power Station, for example, involved statements about excess bread allegedly being sold abroad, and that only speculators would benefit from the decrease in state commercial prices. This was hardly a surprise considering the questions asked by workers in the past. But Istomin's inclusion here of one worker's reaction to the events of September 16 did suggest difficult times lay ahead. A laborer by the name of Buriak had remarked, "Let them work, those who publish this law, for I am not going to work. . . . Who did we elect? Who is Molotov? . . . The rich have become revolutionaries and have changed their last names."[96] With the prospect of ration cuts on the horizon, the realization that living conditions in the Ukrainian capital might deteriorate further likely spurred local leaders to seek scapegoats among the rank and file who might be publicly deemed incompetent so as to protect their image.

The result was indeed turmoil and turnover within the local party at this crucial moment, although whether people were removed from its ranks or simply transferred to other posts is difficult to tell. On September 17 and 18, 1946, the Kyiv Gorkom held a meeting about the mid-August Ukrainian TsK resolution "On the Selection, Determination, and Education of Party and Soviet Cadre in the Ukrainian Party Organization." The resolution announced that 42 percent of Kyiv's *nomenklatura*—555 people—had been removed for "failing in their work" since the beginning of 1945.[97] At the meeting about this resolution, Secretary Gorban pointed to behavior that needed to change: "In Podil' Raion there is an unobtrusive fuel-making office, a part of the local trade directorate. The manager is a comrade Ivanov. A comrade Fuchsman is working as his assistant. . . . [He] hired a few relatives, and those relatives hired in turn some of their relatives and it works out that a shop director, a first seller, a second seller, and a second accountant (all of these people), are close relatives. This in turn leads to people covering up for each other and to abuses of power in office."[98] In building this argument, Gorban also touched on a case that the newspaper *Soviet Ukraine* (*Radians'ka Ukraina*) covered in late May 1946 and about which the Kyiv Gorkom had already passed a resolution on July 31.

That case involved the leader of the Kyiv City Directorate of Catering (*Obshchepit*), who had ordered illegal food distribution, embezzled funds, and, along with other authorities, sold "food without the use of ration cards. All of this—and many other facts of selling and stealing—became systematic in the [Directorate]."[99] Gorban then announced that the Kyiv Gorkom had excluded two of the officials involved from the party. He also admitted that there had been "signals" about this matter for "a long time" before the *Radianska Ukraina* article, and in its aftermath, "the circle of abuses had only gotten wider." He concluded, "The noted insufficiencies and mistakes in the area of the selection and distribution of cadres have led to the fact that in several organizations, in leading roles, there are people who do not breed political trust and who, through their criminal activity, have brought colossal damage to our state."[100]

Gorban's next example must have shocked the rank and file with its magnitude. This was another case from Molotov Raion: "During 1945–46, 30 million rubles of yeast were stolen at the Kyiv Yeast Factory under comrade Iakubovich's leadership. More than 100 people have been arrested in this affair. In 1945, Molotov Raikom had on hand signals about abuses at the Main Beer Directorate (*Glavpivo*) from the side of workers Butenko and Grushko, but it did not react as it should have done, in a Bolshevik manner."[101] Such examples likely gave the party rank and file a warning about what was, and was not, possible if they contemplated theft from within Moscow's economy of scarcity.

The final part of Gorban's speech addressed the rebirth of the "bourgeois-nationalist views of Hrushevs'kyi and his school [of historians]" among the local intelligentsia during the war.[102] Here was another signal to the local Communists: Ukrainian nationalism was expressly forbidden now that the war had ended. Gorban did his best to achieve the Zhdanovshchina's goal when he concluded, "First and foremost, responsibility for [the intelligentsia's mistake] lies with the Kyiv Gorkom and with us, the secretaries, before the city party organization."[103] Self-criticism by a local leader—whatever the line—was a signal of the Stalinist state's return to building Communism.

Soon the Kyiv Gorkom cracked down on the city's intelligentsia. On September 20, 1946, local Communists passed a resolution about improving the work of the Ukrainian Union of Soviet Writers' party organization. Noting that only 40 to 50 percent of that organization's Communists bothered to show up for meetings, and that only two theoretical conferences had been held in 1946, this resolution sounded the death knell for the wartime theory "concerning the right of writers to make ideological mistakes" that some Ukrainian authors had voiced as recently as a month earlier.[104] There would be no arguing with Moscow's line now that the Stalin regime had decided on the Fourth Five-Year Plan.

On November 15, the Kyiv Gorkom passed a resolution about the work of the party organization of the Shevchenko Opera. Its Department of Agitation and Propaganda conducted the investigation of the theater and then reported to Gorban: "We need to select themes of lectures in such a way that they beat on the painful spots that exist in these artists' psychology, on their customs, [as well as] on their narrow-minded petit-bourgeois (and other no-good) traits that are too developed and that contradict the present-day interests of the theater's work." The task of the opera's party organization would be to orient it "toward modern times, [and] to mobilize the whole collective for the unconditional fulfillment of the Ukrainian TsK resolution that the opera theater in the 1946–47 season put on no less than two to three operas on modern Soviet themes."[105] Those in power in Kyiv wanted their underlings—in whatever sphere they managed—to recognize that the future demanded leaders who understood that Moscow had taken its decision and that it was up to them to improve the city's life.

To emphasize this point, the Kyiv Gorkom also passed a resolution about Kyiv State University's party organization and the ideological education of its students. After noting that some of its academic departments had not held party meetings for six-month stretches, the resolution claimed that the "bourgeois-nationalist conceptions of Hrushevs'kyi" could be found in its departments of Ukrainian history and literature.[106] To remedy the situation, the Kyiv Gorkom offered up the following "practical measures" as suggestions for raising the standard of Marxist-Leninist education at the university: "During November, examine the plans for scholarly research work of the departments of the social-economic disciplines (the dissertations prepared, the attempts at passing qualifying exams), as well as the measures [taken by] all the departments concerning the strengthening of students' ideological education."[107] Sound leadership meant dissociating oneself from Ukrainian nationalism as much as maintaining a watchful eye over corruption.

Meanwhile, "practical measures" directed at the city's workers by the Kyiv Gorkom merely reminded them that their state and its leaders were guided by Marxism-Leninism. One instructor from that organization's Industrial Department visited the Bozhenko Furniture Factory and found the study of Marxism-Leninism infrequent and unenthusiastic.[108] This visit shows that the Zhdanovshchina was implemented across the city's party organizations with Communists in the economic sphere receiving just as much, if not more, of a push toward vigilance as their comrades in the cultural sphere. Indeed, a number of factory directors were removed from their positions and, in a few cases, the party itself for their poor management of the city's industry. This crackdown attacked white-collar corruption and hapless management just enough to show the rank and file and the masses at large who was—or was not—the correct type of leader.

The local Communists' subtle additions to the Zhdanovshchina's focus on the state's role in building Communism had made the Stalin regime's propaganda in Kyiv more effective, which may have played a role in "Soviet Patriotism's" paradoxical creation later. This book's concluding chapter examines this argument from the population's perspective. They wanted—and received—leadership, at least in part. But the question of whether they challenged their leaders' hegemony must also be examined. No doubt most among the masses were content with the efforts of the Ukrainian Communists within the necessary state confines. But could that have been because life in this "regime city of the first category," no matter how centralized and hierarchical the Stalin regime's command and control system, was a byproduct of the relationship between the elites and the more confrontational members among the reassembled masses?

Chapter Six

"Tashkent Partisans" and "German Bitches"

Relationships with Soviet Power

During the summer of 1944, the Ukrainian NKVD conducted an investigation of Genia Brand, a returnee from Osh (Kirghiz SSR) accused of spreading ethnic hatred after confronting those she believed had stolen her property during the occupation. On July 13, Brand told her investigators:

> Having heard from my neighbor Mazur that the organs of Soviet power were to exile those railroad workers who had lived on occupied territory, I declared that meant there were going to be many free apartments. As for the witness's saying that I said for every dead Jew, thirty Russians would be shot, I said that in this context. I believe it was while I was at the bazaar. I was standing there with Chernysheva—who lives with me—and someone else and someone was talking about how during the occupation "they" had led an old Jew down the street and mocked him. I then said not to worry, as "they" will pay for it. What I meant was the Germans would pay for it, not the Russians.[1]

While Brand spoke of "Russians," she likely meant "Ukrainians," for few trumpeted the latter's interests during the civil war to the city's west. There can be little doubt, however, that some returnees desired revenge against the formerly occupied thought to have taken advantage of an empty Kyiv. The Ukrainian capital's relentless population growth created a vicious cycle of rumors and made the local Communists' efforts to lead more difficult.

At a session of Kyiv's Ukrainian NKVD Military Tribunal on August 3, 1944, Brand's neighbor, Sophiia Mazur, had her testimony to the investigation read out: "In April 1944, Brand told me the whole population who lived through the occupation would be exiled from Kyiv and from Ukraine itself and that the population that had not lived under the occupants would be settled here. With such conversations, Genia terrorized everyone in the building."[2] Testimony from one of Brand's acquaintances, Anna Rozhdestvenskaia, contained a similar message: "She told me and other inhabitants of our house that soon there would be many free apartments. . . . After these conversations, the inhabitants of our building began to worry about the possibility of eviction. Brand, in an insulting manner, made references about Russians: that all Russians are thieves; that they steal Jews' property; and that for that they will pay."[3] Whether or not Rozhdestvenskaia was referring to Russians or Ukrainians here, Genia Brand's arrest suggests that Kyiv's authorities wanted to put a spotlight on the problem of unorganized return. Rival groups among the reassembled masses were now sparring with each other. But if one side were favored by the Ukrainian Communists, might that choice help to shape the Stalin regime's politics after the war?

This chapter uncovers Kyivans' relationships with their leaders during the mid-1940s. It first examines the anti-Semitism surrounding the arrival of returnee Jews, a phenomenon that resulted largely from the wartime laws involving housing. The focus then turns to street crime, in which many of the criminals were connected with the Red Army in some way. Third, the chapter looks at investigations of dissolute behavior among the Kyivan elite itself as it tried to take advantage of its position.

In order to successfully lead Kyiv, the Ukrainian Communists adapted to these phenomena. Politics in Kyiv would still be the byproduct of the compromises the Stalin regime had made during the resettling and reassembling of its masses. But understanding how to deal with the unorganized return of a large Jewish minority, with incessant crime committed by those related to the Soviet military, and with the corruption of all sorts within their own ranks would also be necessary for political survival. The relationships that subsequently emerged between state and society would now combine with the local Communists' promotion of themselves as leaders of the state to help relegitimize Soviet power in Kyiv after the Nazis.

Anti-Semitism and Soviet Power

Anti-Semitism among the Stalin regime's highest circles emerged before the war.[4] A summary of Stalin's subsequent politics toward Jews, however, indicates the Germans' attack prevented the spread of anti-Semitism during the war.[5] But such chauvinism did touch Kyiv's elite after the war. In a letter of February 10, 1944, for example, a former researcher at the Ukrainian Academy of Sciences' Institute of Geological Sciences, Kalman Bronshtein, wrote to the Ukrainian TsK's Directorate of Propaganda and Agitation about the academy's return from evacuation in Ufa (RSFSR). Bronshtein charged, "One must establish that there were manifestations of chauvinistic-anti-Semitic tendencies during this process. Among those left behind are over 80 people, a huge majority of whom are Jewish."[6] Claiming that it was impossible that only Jews could be among those considered the least qualified for work in Kyiv, Bronshtein concluded, "Here, we are face to face with a completely intolerable introduction of 'percentage norms.' This is a violation of the constitution and a violation of the policies of the party and the government."[7] In a place where association with Ukrainian nationalism had meant a death sentence in the 1930s, Bronshtein's effort to grab the Stalin regime's attention made perfect sense.

Bronshtein was not alone. Writing on April 7, 1944, to Georgii Aleksandrov, the All-Union TsK's secretary in charge of propaganda and agitation in Moscow, Anatoli Kabalkin noted an earlier declaration he had written about "rude violations of the nationalities policy" taking place in Ufa, and added, "As far as I know, a number of other declarations about the above should have arrived in the ensuing eight months as well."[8] But given Stalin's reluctance to publically marginalize Jews during the war, such accusations probably reflect opportunism within the Soviet elite resulting from wartime scarcity, rather than a planned effort from above. In turn, such intra-institutional turf battles probably also reflected an understanding, as mentioned earlier, of the masses' wartime embrace of anti-Semitism.[9] It was the lack of resources needed for survival, combined with the return of Genia Brand and many more like her that would also make such an attitude possible. And with Jews accounting for almost 20 percent of Kyiv's 704,609 people by late 1946, the sources for seemingly credible talk about their marginalization from above were definitely there, too.[10]

Various letters to the Ukrainian TsK about ethnically charged rumors show that Ukrainian leaders quickly tried to snuff out this challenge to their authority. Rakhil' Karpman, an economist employed by the Ukrainian Council of Invalids' Cooperatives (*Ukoopinsovet*) and recently summoned back to her hometown from Cheliabinsk Oblast (RSFSR), wrote, "In the first days of August 1944, I was returning from the Kyiv City Procurator's Office, when alongside the building of Ukoopinsovet, I met an employee there, comrade Sara Blomberg, who began asking me about what was going on with me and how was I doing. I thought her question concerned my apartment and I answered that I had all the sanctions I needed from the higher bureaucratic organs in order to receive one but that I could not settle into one because no one 'locally' was helping me out."[11] Karpman then added that she had contemplated writing a second letter to Khrushchev about the return of her prewar apartment, but refrained because she had heard a rumor at the Kyiv City Procurator's office that Khrushchev had departed the city and that "comrade Malenkov had arrived" from Moscow.

According to another letter, from Vasilii Davydov (the head of party organization of *Ukoopinsovet*) to the Ukrainian TsK, Sara Blomberg then asked him as well as two other of the organization's employees (Shcherbakov and Shumeikov) about these possible "imminent changes in the makeup of the government." Davydov recapped these conversations: "To [Shumeikov], Blomberg reported that Khrushchev, Korniets, and a number of workers from the Ukrainian NKGB had been recalled from Ukraine because Jews were marginalized, and that these changes would be spelled out in the press. To Shcherbakov, Blomberg reported about the question of where she had heard this and she answered somewhat unclearly saying that some sort of writer had especially visited the city about the matter."[12] The writer in question was Itzik Fefer, a member of the Jewish Anti-Fascist Committee who visited Kyiv in June 1944 to hear from the Jews about the city's resettlement.

The Ukrainian leadership duly requested letters from the local intelligentsia who had met with Fefer during his visit. The writer Khaim Tokar wrote on September 22, 1944, to the Ukrainian TsK's Organization-Instruction Department: "In my conversation with [Itzik] Fefer, while he was here, he told me that when he was in the United States, the president of the Zionist organization, [Chaim] Weizmann, told him and [the actor Solomon] Mikhoels, that all Jewish hope for after the war (if you are speaking of postwar Europe) lay with the USSR and on comrade Stalin, who had so brilliantly solved the national problem in the Soviet Union."[13] Fefer's visit to Kyiv had catalyzed Jews to voice their displeasure with how the Stalin regime was resettling the Ukrainian capital.

Nikita Khrushchev responded to this challenge by having the Ukrainian NKGB launch an investigation. Savchenko, still the local NKGB leader, likely produced his September 13, 1944, report on "Anti-Semitic Manifestations in Ukraine" to protect the Ukrainian TsK's image in Moscow. Khrushchev, of course, was the Stalin regime's man in Kyiv. While Savchenko declared the main reason for the increase in anti-Semitic incidents in Ukraine was "German propaganda and the work of Ukrainian nationalists," he also concluded that provocative statements by Jews in Kyiv had fanned the flames of anti-Semitism in the city.[14] The Ukrainian TsK's own report concluded that the anti-Semitic incidents in Kyiv had been of "coincidental-like character" and had emerged "on the basis of hooliganism or apartment and other everyday questions."[15]

A main focus in this report was on unorganized returnees overrunning the city and causing problems. Soviet power could do much more to prevent their return, and this was what the Ukrainian Communists wanted from Moscow. Although Khrushchev's and Savchenko's efforts were what likely led GKO to issue the November 1944 resolution that tried to stop unorganized return to Kyiv, such legislation was full of holes as far as the local Communists were concerned.

There were soon other dramatic appearances of anti-Semitism. For example, on September 4, 1945, a Jewish Ukrainian NKGB officer shot and killed two Red Army soldiers in the city's Kaganovich Raion.[16] A Ukrainian NKVD Military Tribunal later sentenced the officer, Iosif Rozenshtein, to death for these murders.[17] Rozenshtein had retaliated after being called a Jew, labeled a "Tashkent Partisan," and suffering a beating by Nikolai Mel'nikov and Ivan Grabar, the two men he then later chased down and shot. Rozenshtein had also called the two "German hides" (*nemetskie shkury*).[18] But the aftermath of this murder reveals further attempts to compel the republic's hierarchy into forcing someone in Moscow to put a stop to unorganized returnees coming to the city.

In a memorandum circulated within the Ukrainian TsK, Alidin, the head of that institution's Organization-Instruction Department, argued that "some of Grabar's anti-Semitic feelings" stemmed from the fact that his mother's apartment had been recently awarded to a Jew returning from evacuation. "Why are we fighting when my apartment is occupied by the Jews?" were said to be his final words to the Kaganovich Raion procurator just a few days before he was murdered.[19]

The initial report by the Kaganovich Raikom to the Ukrainian TsK painted this scenario: "After a certain amount of time, near the house where the murders took place, there gathered a crowd of around a thousand people. From the crowd there rang out anti-Semitic shouts. Here, too, the crowd beat up the wife of Rozenshtein as well as two other Jews who happened to be nearby."[20] The report's conclusion noted that the crowd only disbanded after the secretaries of the Kyiv Gorkom, Gorban, Davydov, and Moskalets, as well as the secretary of Kaganovich Raikom, Kornitskii, had personally driven out to the scene.

Alidin's report also contained information about the moments just before and after the murders took place, focusing on the words and deeds of Rozenshtein's wife and his friend, Spektor, that led to the crowd's taking revenge: "From the testimony of witnesses it has been determined that Rozenshtein's wife, having chased her enraged husband into the courtyard where Grabar lived, approached one of the women in the court yard and yelled, 'Tell me, you German bitch, where have you hidden the bandits?' . . . Spektor, standing in the crowd, at the sound of Grabar's mother shrieking, 'They have killed the son, they will kill the mother too,' allegedly said, 'Well, let them kill.'"[21] Instead of sympathy for the returnees, the formerly occupied are portrayed here as victims by language that equates them with the "Ukrainian-German nationalists" fighting Soviet power in Ukraine's western oblasts.

The populace's reaction to the funerals of Grabar and Mel'nikov kept this issue at the forefront of the Ukrainian leadership's concern. Writing on September 8, 1945, Ukrainian NKVD chief Riasnoi told Secretary Korotchenko in the Ukrainian TsK about his organization's observations as the three-hundred-people strong funeral procession wound its way from the October Hospital to the Luk'ianiv Cemetery: "We saw the following manifestations: on the corner of Pushkin Street and Shevchenko Boulevard, unidentified persons from the number taking part in the procession beat up two Jewish citizens heading toward the funeral procession; while proceeding along Dmitrov Street, those persons walking behind the coffin, noticed a Jewish female looking out the window and threw stones at her."[22] Riasnoi then claimed he would strengthen patrol service in the city, with "special attention" reserved for its bazaars as well as those places where large numbers of people were known to amass, and at the houses of Grabar and Mel'nikov. All of this was due to the "excited condition of certain layers of the city population that has appeared in the aftermath of the spread of false rumors about, and agitation directed against, persons of the Jewish nationality."[23] Again, the general line was that such rumors could easily be avoided if Kyiv's passport regime was observed and, implicitly, the city was not so open to returnees.

Another view of what happened on September 7 can be found in an October 1945 letter addressed to Stalin, Lavrenty Beriia, and Petr Pospelov, the editor of Moscow-based *Pravda*, and eventually returned to the Ukrainian TsK. In this case, the authors—four newly arrived, demobilized Jews—claimed that Rozenshtein's act started a "Jewish pogrom" with one hundred Jews beaten (a number that led to thirty-six hospitalizations and five deaths), and that after those incidents, "The atmosphere in Kyiv became even more explosive. The pogromists began preparing an even more 'solid' pogrom to fully meet the size of this capital city. But the local organs have, as of now, prevented this from occurring."[24] It hardly seems surprising, given the intelligentsia's claims that these Jews cited the reason for the pogrom as the "new crooked line allowed by our party concerning the national question."[25] But while such an argument would have made sense in the 1930s, the Nazi invasion and the Stalin regime's efforts to repel the Germans meant such reasoning had now lost its resonance.

Their letter ended with rhetoric that they hoped would help the Stalin regime to notice Jews' rapidly emerging second-rate status in postwar Kyiv: "Who is working on this special form of national politics through the selection of cadres and the planting of the seeds of anti-Semitism other than the Ukrainian TsK and the SNK UkrSSR? It is enough to look at the statistics concerning these cadres for it to become clear that the majority of them stayed in Ukraine under the Germans, actively collaborated with them, and now like before they find themselves in leading roles."[26] Such an argument was timely, but Moscow's return of this letter was probably designed to help the Ukrainian Communists recognize that unorganized return was a fact of life for the foreseeable future. The implicit message from Moscow was that the Ukrainian party needed to make sure Jewish interests in Kyiv were not compromised while nationalist favoritism toward Ukrainians was kept in check.

But the readdressing of another anonymous letter from the all-union party in Moscow back to the Ukrainian TsK in March 1946 seems to mark the point where the Kremlin's position on anti-Semitism in the Ukrainian capital changed. This was almost two years before the murder of JAFC leader Mikhoels at the hands of the All-Union MGB—the event that historians have traditionally marked as the moment of Moscow's adoption of an anti-Semitic line to reinforce its political thinking and the beginning of the "Black Years" for Soviet Jewry. That Mikhoels' longtime lobbying for Jewish interests was now misplaced given newly independent Israel's joining the United States's side at the outset of the Cold War is still seen as the main reason for the Jews' new second-class status in the USSR.[27]

Figure 6.1. N. S. Khrushchev, F. V. Mokienko, General A. A. Hrechko, and P. H. Tychyna (far right) at the celebrations of the twenty-eighth anniversary of the October Revolution, November 7, 1945. Reproduced by permission from the H. Pshenychnyi Central State CinePhotoPhono Archives of Ukraine.

The events in Kyiv recounted here, however, seem to have left the Stalin regime in March 1946 with little choice but to ratify the marginalization of Jewish interests in that city. Although it had limited the purging of Jews among the intelligentsia and covered up the Holocaust in the occupied territories to stem rising anti-Semitism, the Kremlin's position on anti-Semitism in Kyiv seems to have changed because of battles there over housing and this was position that it wanted known that it recognized while plotting postwar reconstruction.

The letter that was readdressed from Moscow to Kyiv began with a question: "What is going on here in Ukraine? Now the Jews own all of Ukraine. It is they, with their Jewish snouts, taunting the Russian people in Ukraine. For money, they have bought many people, even the leaders of raions and cities of Ukraine. Who sells passports at the market? Jews. Who is trading awards? Jews. Who is killing the Russian people? Jews. Who is throwing people out of their apartments in winter in Kyiv? Jews." It concluded in part, "What needs to be done? 1) Exile, to the last man, all Jews to Siberia and then take some Siberians and bring them here so they can taste life."[28] Despite such a conclusion, this letter signaled to the Ukrainian Communists that Moscow expected them to devise a more practical way of overcoming the divisions present among the reassembled population. And

Ukrainian NKGB chief Savchenko's subsequent investigation of this letter does indicate a change in thinking among the Ukrainian Communists. Sides would need to be taken if this conflict was to end.

Initially, Savchenko's "special report" to Khrushchev declared the letter's plans to be a "hoax" dreamed up by a demobilized officer recently excluded from the party. But hoax or not, the letter's brutal tone leaves a clear impression that anti-Semitism in Kyiv could no longer be hushed up. Savchenko's report thus contained a warning to Khrushchev: "The author writes, that he is expressing the opinion of a group of Communists—numbering twenty people—who met at the home of the letter's author and 'steadfastly resolved to wage a merciless battle with these parasites' (meaning the Jews) for to go on living like this is impossible."[29] Khrushchev's Moscow-inspired response was to allow the Ukrainian population in Kyiv to say what it wanted about the minority Jews as long as Ukrainian nationalism was kept in check.

That anti-Semitism became legitimized in Kyiv by the end of this period can be seen by what happened in the summer of 1946. On August 21, *Radians'ka Ukraina* printed a feuilleton by Ukrainian writer Ostap Vishnia entitled "Allow Me to Make a Mistake." Of course, the Zhdanovshchina had condemned the Ukrainian intelligentsia for propagating the idea that the party should allow writers to make ideological mistakes as they attempted to interpret the center's new line on propaganda. Although Vishnia's article mocked such writers, what really prompted numerous letters to *Pravda* that later found their way to the Ukrainian TsK's Department of Letters was his description of the relationship between returnees and the formerly occupied in Ukraine's capital.

The line in the article that drew the most questions from readers said, "It was already clear to a certain extent, who fought at the front, and who in Fergana and Tashkent, who returned as rebuilders and restorers, and who to trade in beer and soft drinks and win back apartments."[30] This anonymous response sent back from Moscow about Vishnia's writing is typical: "What he wanted to say [overall], I do not quite understand. But I do understand what he said in the paragraph that I underlined. . . . These are words I heard first on the street from a hooligan anti-Semite after I arrived here in Kyiv from the hospital as an invalid of the Patriotic War. . . . I just cannot understand why an organ of the Ukrainian TsK allows such things to be printed. Can this really be done with their permission?"[31] Another response was written by a demobilized veteran named M. Vaslits now residing in Kyiv: "While criticizing in that feuilleton several of our writers . . . he incidentally writes several lines that have no relation whatsoever to the feuilleton but that bear all relation to that anti-Semitic lie. . . . In any case, that is how I understood it and that is how it was understood by the whole of Jewish society."[32]

There were no written instructions to the local leadership about how to deal with Vishnia's commentary. Although *Pravda* printed an article criticizing the tone of Vishnia's essay on August 29, and the article was reprinted the next day in *Radians'ka Ukraina*, the Ukrainian leadership's only public statement was an accompanying editorial that claimed Vishnia's work was petty and mistaken.[33] But the facts that none of the Ukrainian leaders were punished for Vishnia's article, and that numerous meetings of the city's writers and cultural workers about this "ideologically mistaken" work now ensued, show the Stalin regime was more worried about any sprouting of Ukrainian nationalism in Kyiv than the treatment there of its minority Jews.

The Vaslits letter well explains what Jewish returnees, now taunted about having "saved themselves in Fergana [Uzbek SSR] and Tashkent," faced on return to Kyiv when it came to housing: "The majority of those who returned on the basis of the law of August 5, 1941, concerning the return of the apartments of military men and of the families of military men, began working on retaking their apartments, which those who had been here with the Germans had already in most cases succeeded in settling. The effort to evict these settlers has led to the spread of anti-Semitism everywhere and in everything."[34] Vaslits's letter says directly that the main reason for anti-Semitism spreading in Kyiv was because of the housing question. But the letters' return was the Kremlin's effort to make sure the Ukrainian Communists understood that taking sides along ethnic lines was now perfectly all right if they wanted to maintain their legitimacy in Kyiv.

The letters also portray Jews as solid Soviet citizens caught up in the social turmoil following the destruction of Ukraine. One letter dated August 23, 1946, and written by three engineers, Burmenko, Fel'dman, and Babenko, from the Kyiv office of the City Construction trust (*Gorstroi*), stated, "Soviet laws stipulate that people returning from evacuation, amid certain conditions, have the right to the return of their living space.... Cannot a reevacuated person, demanding his apartment back, also be a rebuilder and useful to the country? Or, can the latter only be those who remained here during the occupation and did not lose their apartments?"[35] These men were no doubt right to see the likes of Vishnia as an example of anti-Semitism in Kyiv, a fact that the local Communists needed to make sure did not lead to the spread of Ukrainian nationalism.

Another letter, written by the engineers Vasilii and Zinaida Zaitseva, touched on similar ideas but also reflected the authors' opinion that Vishnia was closely tied to the Ukrainian TsK. The return of such letters signaled that the Kremlin wanted the likes of Vishnia reined in to make sure that siding with the Ukrainian majority did not lead to excesses in the cultural sphere. The Zaitsevs had written, in part,

> We need to remind honest people less about where they were during the war— they were needed everywhere—and more about where Ostap Vishnia was before and during the war and how he helped the *frontoviki*.... They have no need for Ostap Vishnia and have no desire to read his feuilletons about their loved ones.

That very day, in the newspaper *Pravda* of August 21 there was printed a resolution of the all-union TsK about the journals *Zvezda* and *Leningrad*. . . . It follows that a decision of the newspaper *Radians'ka Ukraina* should be to carefully study that resolution and to answer us on its own pages.[36]

Kyiv's leaders would only have needed to remember the bloody conflict the Stalin regime was waging with the nationalists to the city's west to see that Vishnia's arguments might be taken too far.

A final returned letter continued Moscow's effort to educate its Kyivan underlings about its policy. The author, a demobilized Red Army officer, L. Lev, noted Vishnia's positions and then declared, "I am not talking about some sort of shortsightedness exhibited by the party leaders, but an ideology that is gathering speed and that, step-by-step, is starting to convince the unstable elements of the country. If an official organ of the Ukrainian TsK can write this stuff, what can unofficial representatives in unofficial conversations be talking about?"[37] Lev correctly saw a new ideology emerging. Many ordinary Jews had seized on the Zhdanovshchina as a chance to cure the Ukrainian capital of anti-Semitism. The new line, however, paradoxically meant that Jews would need to swallow the fact that Ukrainians' interests were more important than their own to the regime. Moscow's challenge to its underlings and their "culture builders" in Kyiv was to make sure that no one took advantage of this new ideology to destabilize the regime.

Anti-Semitism in Kyiv after the Nazis developed from battles over apartments between returnee Jews and a primarily Ukrainian population that lived through the occupation. Initially, the local authorities told the Stalin regime that unorganized return damaged their ability to maintain leadership over the city. When Moscow did not do anything substantive about the numbers of returnees, events in Kyiv finally moved the Kremlin to allow its Communist leaders in Kyiv to take sides in favor of the majority Ukrainian population to maintain their legitimacy. It may even be that the Stalin regime made this important decision after it had examined how the local Communists in Kyiv interacted with the question of unorganized return. After all, it had been the city's position within the Stalin regime's planned economy, as well as the manner in which the city was resettled, that shaped the relationships between the Kyivan leaders and the various segments of the city's population and their resulting policies. Such relationships may be another reason then why anti-Semitism later became an integral part of the Stalin regime's propaganda playbook.

Street Crime and Soviet Power

In October 1944, Kyiv's chief of police, V. Komarov, reported to the Kyiv Gorkom about increases in street crime.[38] Organized gangs of criminals, many composed of enlistees or deserters from the Soviet armed forces, were the core of the problem, according to Komarov. Such groups had committed many of the most violent of the 1,561 "criminal manifestations" registered that year, including 33 murders and 47 armed robberies. Of the 383 criminals later cited for these crimes, 171 were tied to the military in some way, which put the local Communists in a difficult position. They tried again—as with anti-Semitism—to pin this problem on unorganized return.

From the start, the city's militia considered fighting street crime of secondary importance because of the *massoperatsiia* to staff the Red Army. The militia did, however, spend some energy right after liberation trying to stop theft of "socialist property." In his report, Komarov described efforts to stop "the stealing of food and industrial goods at the enterprises of public catering, departments of workers' supplies, warehouses, supply houses, procurement and building organizations, as well as the abuses of ration cards, and speculation."[39] He concluded that 807 people had been brought to justice for stealing socialist property with 1,040,000 paper rubles, 205,100 rubles' worth of gold, 5,637 kilograms of bread, and 589,650 rubles' worth of industrial goods confiscated during the first nine months of 1944.[40]

One case involved the July 11, 1944, arrest of six injured soldiers, who were supposed to be recuperating at one of the city's many war hospitals, at the Galitskii Bazaar. The report on the case describes these men: "While living in Kyiv . . . they did not occupy themselves with socially useful labor, instead they practiced speculation. Every day they were found at the market. From the money they earned through speculation, they got together for binge drinking sessions with the aftermath being their participation in hooligan actions that included the beating of citizens." Another case concerned the July 17 arrest of three patients of Military Hospital no. 2563 who, "Having gone AWOL from the hospital . . . stole the boots off of an injured man and sold them. . . . They then drank away the monies received. On their return to the hospital, there was debauchery. They called the service personnel 'kikes' after which they went AWOL again and showed up at 4 Victims of the Revolution Street where they smashed several windows and went after citizens with their walking sticks."[41]

But the main reason Komarov cited for these incidents was the "everyday influx of population into the city of Kyiv together with which penetrate criminal offender elements."[42] Such a conclusion points to the powerlessness of the local authorities, for unorganized return could only be stopped by a comprehensive policy out of Moscow. Komarov's hope must have been that if in-migration could be somehow curtailed, he might be able to find a way of controlling the servicemen already inhabiting his city.

This approach led to incredible scenes in Kyiv. On October 4, 1944, for example, the head of the Kyiv Cinema Directorate, Dobrovol'skii, wrote to the

Kyiv Garrison commandant about the behavior of servicemen in the city's movie theatres.[43] He included a legal document (*akt*) about an incident in the city's "October" theater to illustrate his argument:

> On September 29, 1944, at 19:00 in the evening, a handicapped (*bol'noi*) and drunk man barged through ticket control and attacked a male audience member with a stick. The [theater] director emerged from his office, tried to defend the man, and took the stick away from the drunk. To the scene came the militia officer, Zhuk. The drunk then dove at the director with a knife in his hand. The director took the knife away from him and together with the officer brought him to his office with the goal of learning his last name and the number of his hospital. The drunk, however, escaped, and then ran outside yelling, "Cripples get over here!" Another three drunk and handicapped individuals then appeared and they began to throw cobblestones at our glass door. After breaking down the door and smashing its glass, they burst into the foyer and threw themselves on the director, with one of the cripples pulling out a dagger in the process. After he was beaten to the point of unconsciousness, the director was extracted from the theater by his employees. The man from the militia did nothing to try and capture the drunks. Two servicemen appeared from within the hall and tried unsuccessfully to escort them out of the theater. But the drunks remained. By that point, there had yet to appear anyone from the garrison. All of the audience ran out of the theater. As soon as the robbers heard the commandant had been called, the head of the gang took off his [hospital] robe, ran into the street, jumped onto a passing tram heading in the direction of the Kirilov hospital and left. Inside the cinema, there remained the other three who had taken part in the beatings. We asked the commandant's men to remove the drunks from the hall. The hall's lighting was turned on and the three could be observed, but the head of surveillance, a comrade Orlov, did nothing to take them way.[44]

Dobrovol'skii concluded by asking that those guilty be caught and put in front of a military tribunal, and then have their sentences sent to him to be prominently hung in each of his movie theaters. Whether Dobrovol'skii's demands were met is not known, but Kyiv's leaders needed to be seen doing something about such "manifestations" if their legitimacy among the reassembling population was to be maintained.

In a rare attempt to show their concern, *Kyivs'ka Pravda* published an article on November 25, 1944, about a Kyiv Garrison Military Tribunal trial involving a Red Army deserter named G. Mironov. The article began by noting that a Lenin Raion court had convicted Mironov of "hooliganism" earlier that year, but that it "gave Mironov a chance to correct himself, choosing in the end to send him to the front to defend the fatherland. Mironov, however, deserted from the army, was caught, and was sent back to his unit for a second time. He then deserted once again. On November 7, 1944, the accused beat up and knifed a citizen, Mel'nichenko." The article then concluded, "The majority of males have gone to the front. . . . But those like Mironov hinder the work of those laboring in the rear. They damage Soviet society." Mironov was later sentenced to "the highest form of societal defense: death by firing squad."[45]

That hooliganism could mean a death sentence was obviously the message the local leaders wanted to get across. But the term implies a whimsical approach toward crime by local authorities. The term's association throughout this period with ever-increasing levels of violence hints again that they found criminal activity by those associated with the military somewhat justifiable.

Komarov's report did lead directly, however, to the November 28, 1944, Ukrainian TsK and SNK UkrSSR resolution "On Strengthening the Battle with Crime and Hooliganism in the City of Kyiv."[46] That resolution obliged Ukraine's NKVD, its Procurator's Office, its People's Commissariat of Defense, and the Kyiv City Soviet to stop the increase in street crime in the Ukrainian capital. But although this resolution made the battle against street crime the Kyivan militia's primary focus, it seems to have been mainly an attempt to oblige the military to better regulate itself.

Comrade Gerasimenko, the Ukrainian People's Commissar of Defense, for example, was required to organize a battalion of soldiers to patrol the city and strengthen guard posts on the city's edges and at its markets, train stations, shops, restaurants, theaters, and cinemas. The resolution also obliged the SNK UkrSSR Directorates for the Affairs of Art and of Cinema to organize separate box offices for servicemen, to distribute tickets to the commandant's office to be sold directly to servicemen stationed in the city, and to organize "cultured leisure" for those waiting for films to begin such as "speeches of lecturer-reporters, popular song presentations, [and] cultured games (chess, checkers, dominos)."[47] Finally, it demanded that the new chairman of the Kyiv City Soviet, Fedor Mokienko, reestablish around-the-clock surveillance of each apartment building by its own inhabitants, to identify where each youth discovered on the streets was supposed to be at any given moment, to hang the passport regime statute in prominent places, and to implement a nine o'clock p.m. curfew for anyone under sixteen.[48]

That Kyivans approved of these ideas is apparent from a letter addressed to Khrushchev and received by the Ukrainian TsK on November 30: "We the inhabitants of Zaliznychnyi Raion ask that you be merciless toward thieves during this time of war. For thieves: the death penalty. In wartime, how difficult it is morally as you worry about your beloved fathers, mothers, children, and friends of our union. But then you have to wait for thievery like the coming of daylight, and if you raise a finger to try and stop it then you can say good-bye to your life. I am not making this up. This is a cry from the soul of a sick person." After noting several murders and robberies, the letter concluded, "There are not enough militia

Figure 6.2. The Ukrainian Soviet Socialist Republic's People's Commissar of Defense, V. F. Gerasimenko, reads an *ukaz* from Comrade Stalin to the troops of the Kyiv garrison during the parade of May 1, 1945. Behind him stand Khrushchev, Korotchenko, and party leader M. S. Hrechukha. Reproduced by permission from the H. Pshenychnyi Central State CinePhotoPhono Archives of Ukraine.

members at this time to check the documents of male deserters. We ask for your help."[49] Khrushchev duly responded by sending the letter on to Kyiv Obkom Secretary Serdiuk with the instructions, "Report to me on this. What are you doing about it?" Serdiuk passed it on to Gorban in the Kyiv Gorkom. By February 24, 1945, Gorban had responded to confirm the anonymous letter's contents as correct, and to say that measures were being taken to find the criminals.[50]

A lot of paper about crime was generated during this period, but its prevalence and the identity of those committing it seems to have stayed the same. The Directorate of Kyiv Oblast's Ukrainian NKVD, for example, sent reports to Gorban and to Babchenko at the Ukrainian People's Commissariat of Justice every ten days during December 1944 about the "battle with hooligan manifestations in the city of Kyiv." The Ukrainian NKVD reported that from December 1 to December 9, seventeen trials concerning cases of hooliganism had taken place resulting in sixteen guilty verdicts. As for December 10 to December 20, the numbers there were ten cases and seven guilty verdicts.[51]

The report listed a number of cases as most characteristic. The first involved "the case of Zhylyns'kyi. He committed debauchery in the restaurant Radians'ka

Ukraina hitting a woman with his crutch while also attempting to strike the maître d' of the restaurant. The court sentenced him to one year of jail time." The second was "the case of the accused citizen Saranch, M. L., who pretended to be an employee of the Ukrainian NKVD. At the October Market he committed debauchery and began swearing at citizens. The chamber in Podil' Raion sentenced Saranch to one year in prison."[52] Such actions may have come from a general sense—as reconstruction ground to a halt—that individuals needed to take matters into their own hands if they wanted to survive. And for those who were somehow involved with the Soviet armed forces, such as Zhylyns'kyi and possibly Saranch as well, they might have come to the realization that they had more leeway, given their status as saviors of the Soviet state.

The results were more incredible events like one at the Kyiv Circus, described by an employee of the Ukrainian TsK's Department of Propaganda to his superior, the secretary responsible for propaganda on August 23, 1945. His report reveals that the arrival of more and more servicemen probably made things even tenser in the city:

> At the beginning of the show, on the right side of the arena, and sitting in the first row were some invalids of the Patriotic War—about ten to twelve of them—in hospital clothes and with crutches (almost all of them were missing a leg). At the intermission, a commandant's surveillance patrol numbering 25 to 30 men appeared in the hall. One man approached the invalids and asked them to leave. The invalids refused. Thus, the surveillance patrol began to remove them by force from the hall. The invalids fought back using their crutches in the process. A serious brawl began then and there. The commandant's patrol began to take away the crutches and succeeded in extracting some of the invalids from the circus building. However, servicemen from the audience rushed to the aid of the invalids and began to disarm the surveillance patrol. Others wanted to come to their aid but their wives restrained them. Then fights broke out within and among the audience members themselves, most of the time between servicemen. The result of all this was that a lot of noise could be heard coming from the circus building. It was a disgusting scene. The patrol did not manage to remove the invalids. It itself was kicked out of the building based on the demands of the servicemen in the audience. At that point, many invalids began to cry. When everything had calmed down and the performance started up again, the patrol once more entered the hall and occupied all the exits. But then the members of the audience began to hide the invalids. By show's end they were all wearing civilian clothes, leaving the theater under escort, and avoiding arrest.[53]

Such "disgusting scenes" continued, however, for no one would challenge the soldiers who had sacrificed so much for a Soviet state that could now do so little for them.

The movement of trains carrying the demobilized through the Ukrainian capital led to other "characteristic acts of hooliganism" such as an incident at Kyiv's Darnytsa railway station described in a November 23, 1945, Kyiv Gorkom resolution about the Southwestern Railroad. According to the resolution, a group of military men "fought amongst themselves and then tried to beat up a number of railroad workers, breaking windows in the station and in buildings nearby. The commanders of that shift of railroad workers at Darnytsa not only did not undertake any efforts to try and stop this hooligan act in order to restore order at the station, but actually left their posts too. The result was that the work of the station for the acceptance and dispatch of trains stopped for forty minutes."[54] It was only because of the "timely intervention" of Moiseev, the Darnytsa Raikom secretary, that matters were eventually brought under control. Hooliganism that could shut down the biggest rail junction in the city for almost an hour was something local power had to respond to.

The only response however was to mandate again that the Soviet armed forces better regulate themselves. On September 22, 1945, for example, the Kyiv Military District issued an order entitled "The Announcement of a Conviction by Military Tribunal in the Case of the Elder of the Seventh Auto Regiment, Paliev, Who Has Been Sentenced to Be Shot." The order recounted the case and then stated the district's stance on what was to happen in the future to those who committed such crimes:

> On September 8, a group of soldiers from the seventh motorized regiment, numbering five people and under the leadership of Paliev, showed up drunk to a dance at Berdychiv's Second Infantry School. There they started to express themselves using censurable words, tossing insults at the girls and the wives of officers who were present at the club, and threatening the students of the school as well. Paliev then started a fight with one of the students, Aleksandrov. When the duty officer of the school, Lieutenant Kashinov, showed up at the scene to reestablish order, Paliev unleashed a blow to his face with brass knuckles. After Paliev was confined to the premises of the guardhouse of the school, he went on a rampage and tried to escape. On September 13, 1945, the Chernihiv Garrison Military Tribunal convicted Paliev as a malicious hooligan, as someone whose level of dissoluteness permitted him to attack a Red Army officer, to the highest form of punishment: death by firing squad. . . . Only people who have lost their resemblance to human beings, who do not respect the laws of the Red Army, and who do not agonize in their souls about the need to strengthen the military might of our dear motherland, the Soviet Union, maraud, and commit acts of fighting, debauchery, and hooliganism. People like Paliev can neither be tolerated among the ranks of the Red Army, nor among the Soviet people itself."[55]

The Kyiv Military District by no means meant for the above order to remain secret. It was printed on thousands of small fliers for the troops to read. The argument, though, about curtailing hooliganism so as to "strengthen the military might of our dear motherland" must have rung hollow in the face of the great victory over Germany.

It took another anonymous letter from the capital to provoke the Ukrainian TsK to do something about crime in Kyiv. The letter, complete with five unidentifiable signatures, was received by the TsK's Bureau of Letters and Declarations on November 13, 1945, and addressed to Khrushchev:

> Comrade Khrushchev we have a request of you. Pay attention to what is going on in our Soviet capital, especially on the edges of the city.... With impunity, the bandits mock the peace-loving population. They rob apartments, murder tenants as well as those passing by, and we have no defense out here at all. On the edge of the city, there is no militia. Even night watchmen do not exist.... We peaceful citizens ask you, as if you were our own father, to pay attention to how we suffer at the hands of these hooligans and murderer-bandits. Those, who, especially at night, take power into their own hands.[56]

These lines must have provoked a sudden response from Khrushchev, for already on November 27, Riasnoi of the Ukrainian NKVD reported back to the Ukrainian Communists' leader "about the strengthening of battle with criminality" in the city. His report commented, "The increase in the numbers of criminal manifestations during the last three months in the city of Kyiv is based upon the following conditions: a) The commission of criminal activities by those criminal elements liberated from their places of incarceration due to the amnesty b) The increasing penetration of the criminal element among those workers recruited by enterprises and building organizations for work in the city c) The increased participation in these emerging criminal manifestations of servicemen—from the numbers of morally unstable elements who have penetrated the Red Army."[57] What is most startling here is Riasnoi's parroting of Komarov's conclusion from a year earlier, that increases in crime in the Ukrainian capital were mainly connected to the city's openness to returnees. While servicemen are directly mentioned as a problem, they had been misled by the "morally unstable."

Perhaps Riasnoi and Komarov's worries about returnees were justified given the prevalence of bribery involved in securing living permits in Kyiv. Although the republic-level leadership eventually curtailed in-migration to the Ukrainian capital, it was probably the Kyiv City Militia, due to its role in the living permit issuance process, that suffered most in the fallout surrounding the uncovering of 250,000 or so people illegally residing in the city. On November 30, 1945, Ukraine's acting procurator, Dirin, wrote to the Ukrainian TsK about Riasnoi's report to Khrushchev. Dirin wanted to strengthen the passport regime in order to "uncover, bring to justice, and to banish from Kyiv those persons who are living here without a determinate place of living and employment."[58]

The real reason for the hooliganism epidemic was still the presence of men connected to the Soviet armed forces, and often legally entitled to be in Kyiv. For example, on December 4, 1945, Diatlov, Riasnoi's assistant at the Ukrainian NKVD, wrote to Khrushchev about an act of hooliganism involving servicemen residing in the city:

> The most socially dangerous of these emerging crimes have the following make-up. . . . Amid the population of the Solomenka and Batyeva Gora [Zaliznychnyi Raion], there is an alarmed mood due to the undignified behavior of servicemen of the military units quartered there. . . . The head of the first section of the Directorate of Construction-Restoration Work of the Southwestern Railroad, the engineer-major comrade Ivanov reported this on October 10, 1945, at the eleventh militia station, "During the night of October 10, 1945, at the women's dormitory of the first section of the [Directorate] at 131 Uritskaia Street, there appeared a group of five unknown people who proceeded to terrorize the women inhabiting that building." . . . On October 12, 1945, during the night, an operative group of militia did a check of said dormitory. In it there were discovered seven servicemen from the airport construction-battalion. We found two of them hiding under some of the women's beds, covered with blankets. It has been determined that the servicemen of said battalion systematically come to the dormitory to visit girls familiar to them. And despite the protests and shock of a large portion of the women living there, they remain overnight and behave in an obscene manner. . . . On November 25, 1945, around 20:00 hours, at the women's dormitory of the [Directorate] there knocked at the door a group of servicemen asking to be admitted inside and purporting themselves to be from a commandant's surveillance patrol. After they were denied entry, the servicemen started to break down the entrance doors, letting off in the process two random shots from their rifles outside and a round from a machine gun once they were inside. The women living in the dormitory broke a window and ran out into the night. An investigation has determined that servicemen of a unit located near the dormitory committed this outrage.[59]

In light of the anonymous letter just mentioned, Diatlov's report about these activities on Urits'ka Street was probably why the Kyiv Gorkom passed a resolution on December 28, 1945, entitled "On the Condition of, and on the Strengthening of, the Battle with Criminality and Hooliganism in the City of Kyiv."[60]

In that resolution, local Communists acknowledged that crime and hooliganism had "in the last few months, significantly grown as problems." After noting a rise in "audacious manifestations," the resolution read, "What is typical about all of this is that the crimes are committed not just by formal criminals liberated from incarceration by the amnesty, but by a significant number of students and working youth and servicemen." The resolution then observed that through December 20, 1945, the Kyivan authorities had rounded up some 724 groups of criminals. Such an increase in numbers compared to earlier in 1945 was accompanied by the announcement that, although 72 of these groups were students, 84 of them were invalids from the Patriotic War and another 220 comprised active-duty servicemen.[61]

While Kyiv's openness to returnees was again the scapegoat for the city's problems, little was said in response to the misbehavior of those already there. Points 5 and 7, for example, read, "Oblige the executive committees of the raion soviets to establish full-time watchmen in apartment houses, shops, cafeterias, warehouses, and in other places, to staff all courtyard caretaker and watchman vacancies, and to look over the staffs already in place to replace those who are not fit to be working in such professions," and "Oblige the administrations of theaters, clubs, and cinemas, restaurants, cafeterias of institutions, and places of learning, to strengthen the order within institutions they have jurisdiction over."[62]

This report recognized that life in postoccupation Kyiv had forced local Communists to compromise with their past efforts to arrest, purge, and exile. But with the elections for the All-Union Supreme Soviet around the corner, the local Communists probably sensed Moscow's stirring meant they and their system would survive into the future.

The resolution also obliged *Kyivs'ka Pravda* to "cover widely in print the sentences of the courts and the tribunals of cases of hooliganism, burglaries, and other acts of criminality." And although the Kyiv Obkom's and Gorkom's public mouthpiece published four short articles about such subjects during the first six months of 1946, the articles only detail an effort to apply tougher sentences to civilians. One, from March 20, describes how the leader of a gang of recidivists was shot and his accomplices given ten years in "far way camps" for, among other things, forcing women to undress on Mel'nykova Street and stealing their clothes.[63] Another article from May 25 describes a three-day show trial of eight young "hooligans" at the city's Bread-Baking Industry House of Culture that ended with similar sentences.[64]

The Kyiv City Soviet resolved to take new measures in the battle against street crime on March 12, 1946.[65] But these measures amounted mainly to increasing the militia's numbers and strengthening the passport system in a city that was witnessing the arrival of significant numbers of *orgnabor* workers for the first time. Ukrainian NKVD chief Riasnoi's report of November 27, 1945, was actually the first to mention efforts at "strengthening" the passport regime in the city: "While battling against criminal elements, the organs of the Kyiv City Militia, alongside their undercover work and policing measures, conducted roundups and mass operations to check places where criminal and suspicious elements congregate and arrested those concretely tied to crimes."[66]

The Ukrainian NKVD's *massoperatsii* were now again efforts to find "criminal elements," as they had been in the 1930s, and not just attempts to find people to fight for the Red Army. But as crime in the city continued to go up, they appear more as a sign of weakness by the Ukrainian police than of strength. Their eagerness to end unorganized return always seems to have masked their recognition that fighting criminality too vigorously in the Ukrainian capital might actually make matters worse. Their run-ins with servicemen recounted here probably reinforced such thinking.

When the Kyiv Obkom passed a resolution on November 10, 1946, entitled "On Strengthening the Battle with Criminality and Appearances of Banditry in the Raions of Kyiv Oblast," all the Kyiv Gorkom and its raikoms were supposed to do was purge the ranks of the Ukrainian MVD in their city of "unfit" and "compromised" elements, and to replace them with "Communists and Komsomols demobilized from the Red Army."[67] While a rising number of violations of "socialist legality" committed by militia employees themselves had been uncovered during 1946, the "battle" against street crime failed to challenge those actually committing it in Kyiv.[68] Things remained very much up in the air as the makeup of the actual law enforcement bodies now came into question.

Throughout much of this period the local Communists argued that unorganized return was a main reason for the rise in street crime in Kyiv. In their zeal to try and rein in one of their central problems, they allowed the criminal actions of invalids, deserters, and enlisted men in the Soviet armed forces (the ones actually running amok in the city) to continue by and large. Over time, the idea that the local authorities recognized the legitimacy behind at least some of these frustrated young men's actions probably helped the Communists gain new legitimacy among Kyiv's population—most of whom, of course, were related to someone involved with the Soviet armed forces. The result was a Ukrainian capital in the mid-1940s that experienced violent episodes the likes of which are almost unimaginable in the twenty-first-century West. Such was the price of building legitimacy for the local Communists if they wanted to lead Kyiv's reassembled population into the postwar era.

Communist Rank-and-File Dissolute Behavior and Soviet Power

Dissolute behavior among Kyiv's Communist rank and file emerged as a byproduct of the power and privilege they enjoyed after wartime. Bribery, theft, and moral debauchery among those running the Ukrainian capital were ubiquitous even as local Communists propagandized about shoring up their numbers, and their legitimacy, following the Fourth Five-Year Plan's announcement.

Word of such behavior, however, only amplified the desire of envious members of the bureaucracy to make further revelations about bad conduct. That few were punished for their actions—and that the Ukrainian leadership itself tried to stamp out these reprisals—meant that by the end of this period, the phrase "morally degenerating" (*moral'nyi-razlozhivshii*) could safely describe quite a few in the city's elite. As with anti-Semitic language and the violence of veterans, dissolute behavior among its leaders became a social norm after the war.

It took Moscow's interference, however, for the Ukrainian Communist leaders to recognize what had become of their rank and file by war's end. In October 1945, Georgii Aleksandrov, the head of the All-Union TsK's Department of Propaganda and Agitation, forwarded an anonymous letter about Kyiv's "school of propagandists" to the Ukrainian TsK.[69] At the top of the letter, penned a month earlier, Aleksandrov told his underlings in Kyiv to pay the "most serious of attention" to this matter. The letter's author, discussing the precursor to the higher party schools where young Communists would be taught Marxism-Leninism during the Cold War years, commented:

> In Kyiv, there is a year-long school of propagandists at 4 Pokrovskaia Street.... The director and the head of the academic section are rarely sober. The students do not study much; they spend most of their time in the parks. The result is that fifteen of them have become pregnant; some have had abortions, others await the aftermath.... The director of the school cannot be taken seriously. In the school, he is known as "the little braggart." He is a person who is morally coming apart at the seams. He has been married several times.... He often visits the women's dormitory and like a little boy tries to catch [the women] by their breasts. In dormitory number 23, due to the above behavior, a scandal erupted. Pugachev [the director] meets with the women students in his office and fondles their breasts and then they go and tell their girlfriends about it all.... The teaching of party history is done very badly. In general, the school resembles a tavern.... Ivanov-Potemkin (the head of the academic section) has made several heinous offers to women to sleep with him. I ask you to ask Chumes (the History of the USSR office head) about this question, as well as the teacher Zhurba.... The above facts can be added to more completely and be confirmed by teachers and students (Kichko, Mozhaev, Seredenko) and others as they are only a hundredth of what has occurred here.[70]

By November 5, the Ukrainian TsK had "acquainted" itself with the situation at the school. The reason, it concluded, for the "unhealthy moods and shameful appearances" such as "theft, hooliganism, deception, drunkenness, [and] revenge" was the "openly compromised behavior" of the director.[71]

The Ukrainian TsK official's report finds the testimony of women teachers and students at the school to be essential to this "acquainting" process:

In the school, facts of dissipation and cases of amoral behavior by individual students of both sexes have occurred.... Those who spoke at the closed women's meeting on September 24, 1945, noted such facts. The student Sirota noted that beliefs in superstition, dreams, and fortune-telling, etc., are widespread among the women of the school. Vinogradova, Maksimenko, and others, noted instances of prostitution among the girls. Also telling were the contents of the notes sent forward to the presidium at that meeting. For example, in one of them it says ... "What can explain the fact that our leading workers and bosses, cultured and educated, having read and taught about morality and ethics to others, cannot follow these rules themselves? Having upstanding wives and good families, they have mistresses and are secretly cheating on their spouses." ... Completely absent from the school is any care about the professor-teacher and administrative-technical staff. The assistant director of building services, comrade Parkhomchuk, has a reputation in the school as a bum and boor. He swears unstintingly and embarrasses the teachers and the students.... He was defended by Pugachev, and the party organization could not rid themselves of him. The leadership of the school has completely compromised itself. At the women's meeting, comrade Vinogradova noted that during conversations with women students in his office, the director allows any and all "familiarities" to take place. If a cute girl comes in to see him, he will not let her leave for a long time. One of the women students in the school also acts a little too uninhibited these days. She takes people under her wing and orders others around. When I asked, "Who is that girl?" The answer I received was that the girl is "close to the director" at the moment.... The above facts give credence to a clearly unhealthy atmosphere in the school of propagandists; one that can be sorted out only by a complete renewal of leadership.[72]

While a "complete renewal of leadership" was promptly undertaken by the Ukrainian TsK, local Communists were likely caught off guard by this signal from Moscow. No one from above had remarked on the subject of social dissipation among the local elite since the return of Soviet power. *Kyivs'ka Pravda* had printed only three articles about "bribery and the stealing of socialist property" during the first two years after the return.[73] The result, as with the revelations about anti-Semitism and servicemen's criminality, was a host of self-serving investigations of various levels of official corruption in the city by Kyiv's elite, the first of which appeared later in November 1945.

That report, written by D. Chernenikii, the Kyiv Obkom assistant secretary responsible for the food industry, concentrated on the workings of two Kyivan organizations, City Trade Department (*Gortorgotdel*), and Kyiv Consumer Goods Trade (*Kievpromtorg*), which played major roles in how consumer goods were bought and sold in the Ukrainian capital.[74] First, Chernenikii commented on how Gortorgotdel managed the distribution of consumer goods through ration coupons: "A large number of coupons were received by just a few institutions and trading organizations (and those with relatively small numbers of employees).... Gortorgotdel also handed out [coupons] to persons based on notes and other types of illegal orders (sometimes without even writing down the people's names, their addresses, or places of work)."[75]

Chernenikii then included an example of goods being distributed based on nepotism: "Based on a note that reads, 'I ask that you help out our friend from home,' from the assistant chairman of the Stalin Raion Soviet in Stalino [Donetsk], comrade Ananchenko, to the head of Gortorgotdel, comrade Kuznetsov, a new suit and pair of boots was issued to a comrade Dul'skii who arrived in Kyiv from Stalino on a business trip." The report also covered Gortorgotdel's management of Kyiv's markets where, according to Chernenikii, collective farmers bringing their goods to market were "instantly surrounded by resellers" who, "in wholesale fashion, without doing any weighing, and on the cheap, purchase all the food." Such "speculators" then sold this food at a 50 to 100 percent markup, and the results were "large numbers of butchers with turnovers of 10,000 rubles a day."[76]

The situation at Kievpromtorg was little different. Chernenikii continued, "A major portion of the plan for commodity turnover was fulfilled through the selling of commissioned goods and the buying of random items from the population at market prices."[77] Some of these commissioned goods came from Kyiv's Lombard, an institution that, according to a second report by Chernenikii, was illegally selling Kievpromtorg items evacuated in 1941 at state commercial prices because their dead or absent owners were no longer around to claim them.[78] According to this report, such goods were either resold in "open trade" at much higher prices or "things were not given over for sale in a shop but given out to various people based on directives from the director of the Lombard, comrade Pritsker and others, or the head of the base, comrade Ostapovskii, immediately on the premises of the base itself."[79]

While the local economy was a complicated one, with different pricing systems and forms of trade, such investigations revealed severe levels of corruption among the local elite. That Chernenikii also claimed such phenomena were possible because some employees of Gortorgotdel had occupied leading positions with the Germans introduced a new scapegoat—similar to the Jews mentioned earlier—into the local lexicon.[80]

A January 23, 1946, Kyiv Obkom resolution revealed this corruption to a wider audience. It helped to downplay local authorities' culpability by saying of the leaderships of Gortorgotdel and Kievpromtorg: "They gave leadership roles in certain responsible sectors to persons who should not have been given control, and to persons who during the temporary occupation of Kyiv actively worked in responsible positions in the German administrative organs." The resolution then listed more examples of how these organizations operated. In the case of

Kievpromtorg, the organization had "illegally realized the most valuable of industrial goods in 4,469 orders to a sum of over 500,000 rubles at state prices" during the first ten months of 1945. Meanwhile, the Gortorgotdel-subordinated Kyiv Department Store (located then, as today, on the Khreshchatyk) "squandered through notes and surrogate orders, 5,239 types of severely scarce goods as well as 64,000 textile pieces costing over 2,150,000 rubles."[81]

Although the employees who had occupied "responsible positions" with the Germans may have lost their jobs, their directors were only warned that if they did not fix this situation, the most stringent party punishments would be meted out against them. Such levels of corruption were now on the radar of local authorities. Despite their revelations, Chernenikii's reports bolstered local Communists' arguments that they could effectively lead the state amid terrible scarcity.

Building that argument, however, meant allowing the issue of corruption among the city's ruling bureaucracy to arise time and again after it had gone uncommented upon for so long. New investigations of Kyiv's Gortorgotdel by the Ukrainian Ministry of State Control saw that organization's problems noted in an August 1946 memorandum from the Kyiv Gorkom's assistant secretary responsible for industry, Tkachenko, to his superiors. Tkachenko revealed that "There has been an illegal realization of a huge amount of severely rationed goods to the detriment of workers and white-collar employees of enterprises and organizations in Kyiv, as well as the illegal distribution through notes and individualized orders of the most in deficit, rationed goods (wool, woolen cloth, textiles, and shoes)." Then he became more specific about how Gortorgotdel operated: "These goods were handed out most of the time to leading and responsible workers in the city, including those workers who receive consumer goods limits and for whom there exist special shops with their exclusive inventories, as well as to workers of trading and selling organizations."[82]

A list of concrete facts followed: "Out of 40,300 coupons that comrades Kuznetsov and Khrynin [the organization's directors] fulfilled during the first ten months of 1945 and the first quarter of 1946, workers of industrial enterprises received only 543 of them (or 1.3 percent). The rest of the coupons were given out to individuals at their own discretion." Tkachenko's memo concluded by noting the issuance of a severe reprimand to Kuznetsov by the Ministry of State Control. In the end, the Kyiv Gorkom on September 20, 1946, passed a resolution "On the Aftermath of the Check of the Work of Gortorgotdel in the City of Kyiv" which removed Kuznetsov from his job.[83]

Additional cases of corruption were uncovered in the summer of 1946 by other investigative organs. One case, touched on already in chapter 5, involved Kyiv's Yeast Factory. The Military Procurator of the Dnipro River Basin, Vinogradov, wrote about this case to the Kyiv Gorkom: "It has been established that over the period of 1944–45, more than 150 tons of different types of yeast were stolen from the Kyiv Yeast Factory. The result is that there has been a loss of 30 million rubles inflicted on the state.... There have been brought to criminal account more than 100 people. Of those, 55 have been arrested."[84] But the head of the Molotov Raikom, as well as the chairman of the Molotov Raion Soviet, received only "severe reprimands" for their negligence involving these crimes committed two years before.[85] While the lengthy investigations into Kuznetsov's dealings did result in his losing his position, the pattern that emerges is of damning revelations revealed to highlight corruption in the city while local leaders took few steps to punish negligent party officials.

But such investigations likely meant opening a Pandora's box of competing interests within resource-starved institutions in the capital, which led to more revelations about corruption than was necessary. Vinogradov, for example, had discovered the "Yeast Affair" while conducting another investigation into thefts within institutions subordinate to the Ukrainian Ministry of Food Processing. That investigation was probably responsible for an anonymous letter to Khrushchev from that ministry's employees about its assistant minister for cadres, a certain Makhinia. In saying they were afraid to state their names due to Makhinia's "connections in the Ukrainian TsK," these workers brought forth the "Yeast Affair" to explain why "this adventurer should long ago have been sitting on the bench of the accused." Their anonymous letter began, "The former director of the yeast factory, Iakubovich (at the moment under arrest) gave Makhinia large bribes. Besides that, Makhinia discharged large amounts of yeast from the factory to various persons from whom he received sums of money including his own chauffeur (now also arrested for these dealings). Iakubovich is an extremely suspicious person. During the occupation, he was located here in Kyiv. As soon as Makhinia arrived, he immediately named Iakubovich the director of that factory."[86] As local procurators began to look into wartime corruption, some Kyivans seized on the chance to rid themselves of colleagues they did not like. Here, again, the fact that someone had prospered during the occupation was a convenient argument to discredit them while maintaining the legitimacy of a system quite profitable for those on the inside.

Ukraine's leadership, however, certainly did not want this campaign to be taken over from below. For example, the Ministry of Food Processing employees continued on about why Makhinia should be "unmasked" as a major criminal in this fashion: "In 1943, when the Red Army was taking Kyiv, Makhinia sent his close friend Lozenko to the city (today he is the main engineer at the Kyiv Beer Factory) to be the plenipotentiary for the All-Union People's Commissariat of the Food Processing Industry. Lozenko showed up in the city on the same day it was liberated and threw himself in the direction of the food processing enterprises (like the beer factory, the tobacco factory, and the food bases).... In this way, Lozenko managed to make a profit of over one million rubles."[87]

In response to these accusations, the Ukrainian TsK's Department of Cadres wrote to Korotchenko and claimed that a "survey of the workers and white-collar employees" at the Kyiv Beer Factory had failed to uncover any "direct proof" of the illegal selling of beer. Then the TsK's main staffing department concluded, "All of this refers to the period at the end of 1943 and the beginning of 1944 when at Kyiv's factories there was no established order. Therefore, to try and make things more precise is impossible."[88] Although the TsK did take up the question of the stolen yeast, the only penalty Makhinia received was a "severe reprimand" for his unsatisfactory selection of cadres. Thus, the anonymous workers' efforts to use Makhinia's past against him did not work. Considering all that went on in other institutions and enterprises during the war years, almost any Communist in the city was probably on shaky ground in 1946.

What happened at Kyiv's Auto-Repair Factory no. 1 that year is a good example of the rivalries within the local rank and file that leaders needed to keep an eye on as they investigated the issue of corruption. This factory had been transferred from the All-Union Ministry of Defense to the All-Union Ministry of Automobile Transport in early 1946, and its director, a comrade Mazanov, had been dismissed in the process in alleged agreement with the party committees responsible for appointment to such a *nomenklatura* position. After Mazanov protested his dismissal in a letter to Khrushchev, the correspondence was returned to the factory's new party organization leadership for perusal. This prompted that organization to pass a resolution seeking Mazanov's exclusion from the party. This exclusion was then seconded in an October 12, 1946, Podil' Raikom resolution that announced:

> Through a closed party meeting of the party organization of the Automobile Repair Factory no. 1 on October 5, 1946, and a check of the Podil' Raikom, it has been established that a group of Communists at the factory (Mazanov, Ganzha, Petrov, Maksimenko, and Kiri'anov), men closely connected by their ties of power and personal friendly relations, began to create an antiparty group to cover up their abuses of power.... They tried to compromise the Podil' Raikom, the new leadership of the party organization recommended by the same raion committee and elected into office by secret vote, and the new leadership of the factory itself, which had tried to uncover their crimes.... [This] distracted these organizations from fulfilling their tasks put forth by the Fourth (Stalinist) Five-Year Plan.... The former director of the factory, Mazanov, compromised himself at the factory with his criminal inactivity. [Such activity includes] his showing up at work drunk, his intimate ties with women who were subordinate to him, his drinking sprees, his systematically receiving food products from the factory's Department of Workers' Supply without any records kept or payment received, ... his playing cover for those bilking the Directorate of Workers' Supply, ... his looting (the contraband shipment of a personal car back from Germany as well as a piano, a radio, rugs, clocks, and other things), and finally

his attempt—through deception, ganging up upon (*grupperovshchina*), and anti-Semitic outbursts—to return to the factory and avoid the party's punishment.⁸⁹

While this resolution reveals a panoply of bad behavior common across the city at this time, the Kyiv Gorkom's investigation decided that Mazanov had been unjustly removed from his position without the approval of any party organization.

An assistant to the Ukrainian Minister of Automobile Transport, Minin, allegedly said to the investigation, "When they found out that Mazanov had written to Khrushchev, these people pursuing his removal collected compromising materials on him so as to fend off any unpleasantness surrounding his illegal firing."⁹⁰ The Kyiv Gorkom finally issued a new resolution of January 23, 1947, that reinstated Mazanov into the party—albeit with a reprimand for 52,000 missing rubles from the Directorate of Workers' Supply and a promise that he would receive "responsible work within the system of Ukrainian Automobile Repair." While Mazanov did not return to his former job, the other accused Communists had their names cleared.

This could not have been easy to do, as many letters were now being written by dissatisfied party members describing how Kyiv's elite lived at the Zhdanovshchina's beginnings. On June 1, 1946, for example, Khrushchev received a letter from P. Enakiev, a Ukrainian Ministry of State Security (MGB) employee, about a fellow employee named Medvedev who led that organization's counterintelligence directorate. The letter begins, "I find that if I associate Medvedev with that category of people who are dissolute and who have lost their consciousness . . . then there is a fair amount of truth in doing so."

Enakiev justified his accusation with the following narrative: "Medvedev, already and for a long time, has a family and has slept with employees of the Ukrainian MGB who do this not out of feelings of love, but for material gain. . . . Thus, he has placed around him private 'adjutants' from among the operatives who secure goods and gifts for him and his girls." According to Enakiev, for some of these "adjutants," their new stature had also gone to their heads: "[Take] Zhuralev. At one point, in a drunken state, he cruised around the city shooting indiscriminately before he got drunk with some random women within the confines of the ministry." But it was among his fellow comrades, Enakiev concluded, that Medvedev's behavior was particularly poisonous: "There are many occasions when due to the ignorance of this egoistic boor, employees of the Ukrainian MGB have cried after seeing him about bad news in their lives. When these people went for sympathy to the party committee, they received this answer, 'What can we do? That is Medvedev you are talking about.'"⁹¹ In response to Enakiev's letter, the Ukrainian TsK's Department of Cadres undertook an investigation into Medvedev and then reported to A. A. Epishev, a TsK secretary, about what it had uncovered.

After stating that an "un-party-like, callous attitude toward people" could be seen throughout Medvedev's work history, the report turned to its subject's personal life, which now encompassed two families (one in Gorky [RSFSR], the other in Kyiv) as well as numerous affairs within the ministry that had included "all sorts of coaxing (presents, food, clothing, and political-control seats in the theatre)."[92] The so-called adjutants existed as well, and they were known for both their "obsequiousness and toadyism" and "systematic drinking parties, debauchery in public places, one-night stands with women, and, as a result venereal diseases." The report concluded ominously: "Efforts by the [Ukrainian MGB] party committee to discuss the behavior of Medvedev have gone nowhere because the Minister of State Security, comrade Savchenko, has declared in a speech that he has no pretensions toward Medvedev's work and that any sort of talk about him is inconsequential." It is not clear what happened to Medvedev, but other Communist employees of the Ukrainian MGB received only reprimands from the Kyiv Gorkom for theft and "polygamy" in the summer of 1946.[93]

An investigation of a similar affair in the Ukrainian MVD, which ended with a similar outcome, suggests that these investigations were, more than anything else, an effort to signal to the city's population that the elite's bad behavior had been recognized by those at the top. A former employee of the Ukrainian MVD's Department of Counterintelligence, a comrade Volgozhanin, had written to Stalin about his being unjustly fired and excluded from the party in May 1946. This had happened, he declared, because he claimed that the head of counterintelligence at the Ukrainian MVD, Elizarov and his assistant, Terekhova, used their positions for their own gain and had quashed all criticism. According to a December 1946 memorandum to the Ukrainian TsK's Department of Cadres from TsK Secretary Epishev, Volgozhanin's appeal to Moscow was confirmed as true but that "a check has determined that [he] did behave in an undignified manner in his daily life: he spread provocative rumors, he discredited the organs of the Ukrainian MVD, and revealed the methods of Chekists' work. For this the department's party organization excluded him from the candidates of the party. The party committee of the Ukrainian MVD discussed this question on December 9, 1946, and, in a change from its prior decision, gave Volgozhanin a party penalty—a reprimand."[94] Following this investigation, Volgozhanin was also called in to the Ukrainian TsK's Directorate of Cadres where he admitted his "insufficiencies and mistakes" and was, per his own request, reassigned to the All-Union MVD Department of Cadres located in Moscow.

Like that of his comrades in the Ukrainian MGB, Volgozhanin's disruptive behavior only merited a reprimand, not exclusion from the party. Again, this decision was because of local leadership's recognition of how ingrained dissolute behavior had become as a result of the war. Only those who had become too involved with the wartime encouragement of Ukrainian nationalism were purged in great numbers at this time.

After the Ukrainian Communists decided to distribute resources in a way that favored formerly occupied Ukrainians, they pinned blame for the ensuing ethnic disturbances in Kyiv on late-arriving Jews in a vain attempt to close the city off from the world. The Stalin regime signaled that the marginalization of Jewish interests would be allowed to continue there as long as Ukrainian nationalism was held in check. Likewise, unorganized return was initially blamed by local Communists for the city's crime wave, in an effort to curtail population growth. This allowed the antisocial behavior of those related to the Red Army in Kyiv to take on new legitimacy. It may even be that the local Communists' own legitimacy was enhanced among Kyivans due to their supposed leniency in this process. The same might be said after these leaders recognized, but did little about, social dissolution and corruption within the elite. In fact, the openly anti-Semitic, violent, and dissolute content of everyday life in Kyiv characterized a "regime city of the first category," where the horrors of the Second World War had become the signature events of its past.

Conclusion

The return of Soviet power to Kyiv, Ukraine, to rule over the city's formerly occupied population during the Second World War came at a time when the Stalin regime was single-mindedly focused on defeating the Nazis. Thus, the Ukrainian NKVD's *massoperatsii* worked to find men for the Red Army rather than cleanse Kyiv of the "socially dangerous" as in the past, while returning party officials worked to build trust with the formerly occupied so the latter would start contributing to the needs of the front and begin reconstruction. Meanwhile, the all-powerful Moscow-based GKO began to shield Kyiv's population and, eventually, even Kyiv Oblast's agriculture-based population who lived surrounding the capital, from most of the horrors of *orgnabor* in hopes that they would also help.

Before acknowledging that housing reconstruction was a far-fetched idea given the lack of resources, the Stalin regime also allowed the forced mobilization of young Ukrainian adults to Kyiv in 1944. But when *orgnabor* desertion in the Donbas and war with the Ukrainian nationalists to the city's west left the republic's "defense-related" industries short of people, this idea was curtailed. By the end of 1944, the Stalin regime had changed to mobilizing primarily German POWs toward Kyiv. Even then, when these prisoners ended up on the production floor of the city's labor-starved industries instead of building the living premises necessary to attract and keep *orgnabor* laborers, the city's housing reconstruction almost ground to a halt. That Kyiv was to be essentially ignored after the occupation in terms of centrally mandated allocations of labor power and materials was something its Communist leaders only belatedly realized.

They did, however, realize that the resettlement of huge numbers of unorganized returnees from the east might challenge their ability to successfully lead the city after the occupation. By the time the Stalin regime announced the Fourth Five-Year Plan in March 1946, such resettlement meant Kyiv's postoccupation population had tripled to 600,000 with a Jewish minority almost as large in percentage terms as it had been before the war. The Stalin regime's wartime insistence on keeping the partially destroyed Ukrainian capital open for resettlement by members of its victorious armed forces trumped local Communists' desire for it to be closed off from the world.

The fact that unorganized returnees who successfully returned to the city could then exploit the August 5, 1941, All-Union Supreme Soviet ukaz bonding servicemen's housing to their families for the length of their military service resulted in great tensions. This was because many of the formerly occupied Ukrainians, in a capital that had lost only 20 percent of its housing space during the war, were now settled in housing these unorganized returnees rightfully believed to be theirs. But the genesis of such tension was actually the fact that the Ukrainian leadership had allowed itself and the already reassembled formerly occupied population to take advantage of an almost empty capital right after the liberation. The leaders' refusal to enforce the law about servicemen's rights to their prewar apartments now returned to haunt them.

Such a scenario was only exacerbated by the Ukrainian leadership's later decision to allow hundreds of Kyivan enterprises and reassembled workforces the right to rebuild partially destroyed buildings across the city. This occurred even though many of the apartments within them must have legally belonged to the some 500,000 Kyivans still absent from the city, such as the families of those who had served or were serving at the front. It was the opportunism of the locals involved here—to the point that Ukrainian authorities' arguments about these apartments being "unassociated with any individual" present in the city evoked memories of the Holocaust that had claimed the lives of fifty thousand Jews from the city—that may have sown some of the seeds for how the Stalin regime chose to propagandize about itself in the 1940s.

The possibility for opportunism probably increased as it became obvious to everyone that the Stalin regime's economy, forged by the Great Breakthrough and its methods of controlling the population through the Great Terror, no longer made sense after years of unparalleled death and destruction. Quality employment in Kyiv's industries did not exist at this time. And the arrival of a quarter of a million people—some legally and others illegally—to a partially destroyed but politically important capital city in plain view of the Stalin regime meant potentially dangerous levels of social dislocation. Although this was apparently ignored by the Stalin regime, it was the fact that unorganized returnees were now returning to scenes of economic devastation very different from the relative optimism of Soviet life in the 1930s that made these local authorities wary. Their understanding was that the passport system created during that decade was no longer enough to guarantee against outbreaks of social disorder, which in turn might cost them their positions.

In Kyiv, these phenomena combined with the opportunistic misdistribution of housing resulted in the politically unchallenged local representatives of the Stalin regime allowing all manner of pathologies, including anti-Semitism, to become social norms. Later, as Moscow rolled out the revivalist Zhdanovshchina campaign in the summer of 1946, these same authorities found themselves emphasizing in the local press that they recognized it was necessary now to put the state's interests before their own. Such a focus emerged in Kyiv because almost everyone there now recognized that the only alternative to the local Communists was the possible breakdown of social order, which the former had ironically helped to generate in the first place.

Across the Soviet Union, this allegiance to the all-powerful state was set to become a paradoxical focal point for how the Stalin regime would continue "building Communism." Meanwhile, rather than witnessing the disappearance of nationalist feeling after the crushing of capitalism that was believed to have created it, as Marx had predicted, the marginalization of the Jews now became an tool essential for the Stalin regime. But the road to such contradictions may have been chosen because in places like postoccupation Kyiv, the authorities' record in overcoming the challenges they faced as representatives of an all-powerful and arbitrary regime were so mixed.

Officials in the Kyiv Obkom and Gorkom, for example, were unable to compel their colleagues in the local *nomenklatura*—the city's all-union factory directors—to allocate resources that might have helped with housing reconstruction and consumer goods production, perhaps addressing the dual problems of unorganized return and misdistribution of housing. But such officials were able to limit coveted access to their ranks thanks to the Stalin regime's decision to limit party growth in 1944. Their subsequent marginalization of the *okruzhentsy* as "cowards" and the unofficial resistance fighters as liars, combined with Moscow's resurrection of Andrei Zhdanov's prewar idea that only the "best people" could join the party, helped these leaders to build legitimacy among a fractious and frustrated reassembling population. The idea of treating almost everyone with equal distrust—at least when it concerned access to party membership—bought Kyiv's authorities time to devise ways to overcome the city's problems.

To relegitimize their rule, the returning Communists also effectively created propaganda in line with the Kremlin's wartime wishes. An initial focus on exposing Nazi crimes quickly fell by the wayside once the Red Army headed westward and fears of the Germans' return receded. Indeed, the Ukrainian Communists effectively limited talk about what had gone on in the city after September 19, 1941, because the social and political ramifications of the Nazi invasion, such as the misdistribution of housing, continued long after Soviet power returned. Instead, the line became that it was Soviet power that could most quickly place the Ukrainian capital back on the road to modernity. Almost fantastical ideas about the Khreshchatyk and the city's future subway followed as leaders like Nikita Khrushchev trumpeted the populist idea that improved infrastructure equated to modernity.

While the city- and oblast-level Communists were unable to transform the ruined Khreshchatyk into that image of the future, their successful efforts to identify the mood of the masses helped them to accurately shore up their interest vis-à-vis their bosses in the republic- and union-level party apparatuses. Here they also bought time through the Supreme Soviet elections of February 1946, with many reports to the Moscow-based regime relaying critical questions from the masses, to show that the city's leadership could effectively run the city should resources actually be sent their way. While the Ukrainian leadership sealed the city off from in-migration following the Fourth Five-Year Plan's signal that the Stalin regime's economic system was to remain unchanged, perhaps it was their difficulties helping that most privileged of groups—the demobilized *frontoviki*—navigate the city's housing crisis that may have finally led the Stalin regime's representatives in Kyiv to take a new tack toward relegitimizing Soviet power there.

The focus of the Stalin regime's Zhdanovshchina revivalist campaign in the Ukrainian capital was not on an intelligentsia gone astray but on the party elite's need to put the state first. The Ukrainian Communists thus conducted a campaign suggesting that they recognized what types of leadership were necessary to succeed in the Stalin regime's state system. No other political alternatives, of course, existed, nor were they desired by most people given terrible living conditions.

Explained away for years in self-serving fashion by the Ukrainian Communists as a byproduct of unorganized return that would disappear if the city was closed off, anti-Semitism in Kyiv was finally deemed politically correct following a signal from the Stalin regime in Moscow. Because of the lack of reconstruction, the housing interests of Kyiv's early arriving Ukrainian majority over those of its late-arriving Jewish minority thus became virtually sacrosanct as long as any talk of nationalism remained curtailed. The legitimization of violence by those related to the Soviet military also resulted from the Kyivan authorities' purposely associating such acts with illegal entrance into the city in the vain hope of preventing unorganized returnees from arriving there. Corrupt and dissolute behavior among the local Communists' own elite also became enshrined as legitimate, for while some cases of bribery needed to be revealed to the masses as part of the city's Zhdanovshchina campaign, little or nothing was done behind the scenes to punish the leaders involved. The unprecedented scale of the war's destruction, and the social situation resulting from it, may even have allowed such language and behavior to appear just to many Kyivans.

Ultimately, the historical processes covered in this book help clarify why Stalin's Communist regime made the statist and anti-Semitic idea of "Soviet Patriotism" its new ideology in the second half of the 1940s. Although the Soviet state was destabilized during the war, so were its people, and with the latter battling among themselves for their own interests, even such a regime could justifiably claim that its strengthening would be a good thing. But while they approved of most things Soviet and accepted the hegemony of all things Russian, the Ukrainian majority asserted its interests as it battled with a large Jewish minority over scarce resources.

Although Kyiv was still labeled a "regime city," the Ukrainians helped transform it into a postwar Stalinist capital that served their interests first—a notable turn for the Soviet Union's long-run future. And while the Stalin regime was still in full control in Kyiv, the implementation there of the very same statist and anti-Semitic ideas that Moscow eventually used to strengthen itself at the beginning of the Cold War, suggests that the war's events in this regime city helped from below to determine how this totalitarian state would rule from above.

Notes

Introduction

1. Tsentral'nyi Derzhavnyi Arkhiv Vyshchykh Orhaniv Vlady Ukrainy (hereafter TsDAVOVU), fond. r-2/7/ 1818, fol. 32. Unless otherwise indicated, translations are my own.
2. Hamm, *Kiev*, 233.
3. Meir, *Kiev*, 317.
4. Hillis, *Children of Rus'*, 14–15.
5. Pauly, "Tending to the 'Native Word,'" 251–72.
6. Yekelchyk, "The Making of a 'Proletarian Capital,'" 1241.
7. Smishko, *Vozrozhdennyi Kiev*, 9.
8. Yekelchyk, "The Civic Duty to Hate," 537. For the number of Jewish dead, see the testimony of occupation survivor Vladimir Davydov, given to the Ukrainian People's Commissariat of State Security (Ukrainian NKGB) in November 1943 at TsDAVOVU, 4620/3/243b, fol. 28.
9. Pastushenko, *V'izd repatriantiv do Kyieva zaboronennyi*, 19.
10. Berkhoff, *Harvest of Despair*, 167–86.
11. Khlevnuik, "The Reasons for the 'Great Terror': The Foreign-Political Aspect," 160–69.
12. McLoughlin, "Mass Operations of the NKVD, 1937–8," 118–52.
13. Kuromiya, *Voices of the Dead*, 23.
14. Shearer, "Social Disorder, Mass Repression, and the NKVD during the 1930s," 85–117.
15. Shearer, *Policing Stalin's Socialism*, 2.
16. Kuromiya, *Stalin's Industrial Revolution*, 316.
17. Filtzer, *Soviet Workers and Stalinist Industrialization*, 255.
18. Ivanova, *Labor Camp Socialism*, 70.
19. Liber, *Soviet Nationality Policy, Urban Growth, and Identity Change*.
20. Zinchenko, "Razom z narodom," 64; Subtelny, *Ukraine*, 419.
21. Getty, *Origins of the Great Purges*, 106.
22. Cynthia Kaplan, "The Impact of World War II on the Party," 158–59.
23. Osokina, *Our Daily Bread*, 152–53.

24. E. A. Rees, "The Great Purges and the XVIII Party Congress of 1939," 208.
25. Zinchenko, "Razom z narodom," 65.
26. Exact statistics on the city's population and its number of industrial workers for the years 1925 through 1939 can be found in Institut Istorii Akademii Nauk UkrSSR, *Istoriia Kieva v dvukh tomakh*, vol. 2, 175–232.
27. Ibid., 198–200.
28. Osokina, *Our Daily Bread*, 36–37.
29. Institut Istorii Akademii Nauk UkrSSR, *Istoriia Kieva v dvukh tomakh*, Vol. 2, 213–14.
30. Ibid., 217–18.
31. Osokina, *Our Daily Bread*, 134.
32. Institut Istorii Akademii Nauk UkrSSR, *Istoriia Kieva v dvukh tomakh*, reports 846,293 people living in Kyiv in 1939; see Vol. 2, 232. For the statistics on housing, see Vol. 2, 241.
33. Tsentral'nyi Derzhavnyi Arkhiv Hromads'kykh Obied'nan Ukrainy (hereafter TsDAHOU), 1/23/4913, fol. 3.
34. Fitzpatrick, *The Russian Revolution*.
35. Kotkin, *Magnetic Mountain*, 198–237.
36. Brooks, *Thank You, Comrade Stalin!*, 238.
37. Davies, *Popular Opinion in Stalin's Russia*.
38. Rigby, *Communist Party Membership in the U.S.S.R.*, 236–56.
39. Kostyrchenko, *Tainiia politika Stalina*, 108–10.
40. Veidlinger, *The Moscow State Yiddish Theatre*, 15–18. A "Jewish Autonomous Region," with its capital at Birobidzhan, did exist in the Russian Soviet Socialist Federative Republic's Far East from 1934 onward, but the numbers of Jews who chose to move there remained miniscule.
41. Brown, *A Biography of No Place*, 18–133.
42. Berkhoff, *Harvest of Despair*, 205–31.
43. Shearer, "Social Disorder, Mass Repression and the NKVD during the 1930s," 92.
44. Hagenloh, "'Socially Harmful Elements' and the Great Terror," 300.
45. McLoughlin, "Mass Operations of the NKVD, 1937–8," 142–43.
46. Hagenloh, "'Socially Harmful Elements' and the Great Terror," 286.
47. Danilov and Pyzhikov, *Rozhdenie sverkhderzhavy*, 8.
48. Ibid., 162.
49. Lewin, "Rebuilding the Soviet Nomenclatura, 1945–48," 219–51.
50. Veidlinger, "Soviet Jewry as a Diaspora Nationality," 4–29.
51. Brandenberger, *Propaganda State in Crisis*, 251.
52. Berkhoff, *Motherland in Danger*, 220–21.
53. Filtzer, *Soviet Workers and Late Stalinism*, 7.
54. Bordiugov, "The Popular Mood in the Unoccupied Soviet Union," 61.
55. Zubkova, *Poslevoennoe sovetskoe obshchestvo*, 23.
56. Jones, *Everyday Life and the "Reconstruction" of Soviet Russia*.

57. Qualls, *From Ruins to Reconstruction*.
58. Weiner, *Making Sense of War*, 21.
59. Pinkus, *The Soviet Government and the Jews, 1948–1967*, 86.
60. Such research is summarized in Joshua Rubenstein's introduction to *Stalin's Secret Pogrom*, 1–61.
61. Marples, *Heroes and Villains*, 311.
62. Institut Istorii Akademii Nauk UkrSSR, *Istoriia Kieva v dvukh tomakh*, Vol. 2, 499–519.
63. Institut Istorii Akademii Nauk UkrSSR, *Istoriia gorodov i sel Ukrainskoi SSR v dvadtsati shesti tomakh, Kiev*, 375–79; Institut Istorii Akademii Nauk UkrSSR, *Istoriia Kieva v trekh tomakh, chetyrekh knigakh*, Vol. 3, 355–63; Smishko, *Vozrozhdennyi Kiev*.
64. Pavlenko, *Narys istorii Kyieva*, 418.
65. Mitsel', *Evrei Ukrainy v 1943–1953 gg.*, 14.
66. Pastushenko, *V'izd repatriantiv do Kyieva zaboronennyi*, 68.

Chapter One

1. Arkhiv Ministerstva Vnutrishnykh Sprav Ukrainy (hereafter AMVSU), 3/1/22, fols. 67, 68.
2. AMVSU, 3/1/22, fol. 80.
3. AMVSU, 3/1/22, fol. 83.
4. TsDAHOU, 166/2/179, fols. 13, 15. For more on the Commission on the History of the Patriotic War in Ukraine, see Berkhoff, "Ukraine under Nazi Rule, 1941–1944," 98–99.
5. TsDAHOU, 166/2/243, fol. 25.
6. TsDAHOU, 166/2/243, fol. 29.
7. Berkhoff, *Harvest of Despair*, ch. 8.
8. Khrushchev, *Khrushchev Remembers*, 216.
9. TsDAHOU, 1/23/633, fols. 11, 12.
10. Derzhavnyi Arkhiv Kyivs'koi Oblasti (hereafter DAKO), p-1/3/23, fol. 87.
11. TsDAVOVU, 4620/3/243b, fol. 28.
12. For a memoir of these events, see David Budnik and Iakov Kaper, *Nichego ne zabyto*.
13. Altshuler, *Soviet Jewry on the Eve of the Holocaust*, 225.
14. DAKO, p-5/2/141, fols. 25, 27.
15. Derzhavnyi Arkhiv misto Kyieva (hereafter DAmK), r-17/1/36, fol. 31. On the fate of the *Ostarbeitery*, see Ben Shephard, *The Long Road Home*.
16. Armstrong, *Ukrainian Nationalism*, 89; Pastushenko, *V'izd repatriantiv do Kyieva zaboronennyi*, 19.
17. Yekelchyk notes that the last time such a number was announced in public occurred in the March 1, 1944, editions of *Radians'ka Ukraina* and *Kyivs'ka Pravda*,

where the number of Nazi victims in Kyiv was estimated at 195,000. See "The Civic Duty to Hate," 537.

18. Ibid., 538.
19. See also DAKO, p-1/3/ 2, fol. 9.
20. The numbers for Kharkiv were 833,000 to 246,000 and for Rostov 510,000 to 224,000. See Gosudarstvennyi Arkhiv Rossiiskoi Federatsii (hereafter GARF), 9415/3/1408, fol. 12.
21. For the 220,000 number, see Berkhoff, *Harvest of Despair*, 317.
22. TsDAHOU, 1/23/685, fol. 157.
23. GARF, 9415/3/1408, fol. 28.
24. GARF, 9415/3/1408, fol. 15.
25. DAKO, p-5/2/2, fol. 46.
26. DAKO, p-1/3/37, fol. 125.
27. There is no mention in the archives of the boxes marked "U.N.K.V.D." inviting denunciations to be placed on Kyiv's streets as had been done in Khar'kiv in previous months, and which Alexander Werth mentioned in his *Russia at War, 1941–1945*, 567.
28. DAKO, p-5/2/21, fol. 40.
29. DAKO, p-5/2/21, fol. 41.
30. TsDAHOU, 1/23/685, fols 205, 206.
31. The ukaz was entitled "On the Measures of Punishment for Those German-Fascist Evil-doers Found Guilty of Murdering and Torturing the Soviet Civilian Population and Red Army Prisoners, [as Well as] for Those Spies and Traitors of the Motherland from among the Soviet Citizenry and Those Who Aided Them." For a published copy, see the appendix of Abramenko, *Kyivs'kyi protses*.
32. DAKO, p-1/3/1, fol. 36.
33. DAKO, p-5/2/69, fol. 12.
34. This process began in May 1942 when GKO stopped conscripting workers from the railway industries into the Soviet armed forces. During 1942, other "defense-related" industries saw their workers "reserved" from conscription amid a centrally directed effort to standardize labor administration. See Barber and Harrison, *The Soviet Home Front*, 151–58.
35. TsDAHOU, 1/23/951, fols. 75, 76.
36. Barber and Harrison, *The Soviet Home Front*, 60–63.
37. Somov, *Po zakonam voennogo vremeni*, 148.
38. TsDAHOU, 1/23/ 633, fol. 33.
39. DAKO, p-1/3/2, fol. 60.
40. TsDAHOU, 1/23/632, fol. 1.
41. TsDAHOU, 1/23/632, fol. 19; DAKO, p-1/3/104, fol. 17.
42. TsDAVOVU, r-2/7/592, fol. 178.
43. DAKO, p-5/2/3, fol. 30.
44. AMVSU, 3/1/33, fol. 22.
45. DAKO, p-5/2/3, fol. 60.

46. DAKO, p-5/2/7, fol. 86. On the necessity of feeding members of the armed forces first during the war years, see Moskoff, *The Bread of Affliction*, ch. 6.
47. TsDAVOVU, r-2/7/966, fol. 124.
48. DAKO, p-1/3/104, fol. 30.
49. DAKO, p-5/2/3, fol. 62.
50. TsDAHOU, 1/23/633, fol. 31.
51. DAKO, p-1/3/2, fols. 40–45.
52. DAKO, p-5/2/141, fol. 181.
53. DAKO, p-5/2/141, fol. 241.
54. TsDAHOU, 1/46/361, fols. 3, 4.
55. Vrons'ka and Kul'chyts'kyi, "Malovidomi storinky istorii," 6–7.
56. DAKO, p-1/3/45, fol. 68.
57. Yekelchyk, "The Making of a 'Proletarian Capital,'" 1235.
58. Hagenloh, *Stalin's Police*, 301. A longer list of "Regime II" locations was also compiled just before the war. While "Regime I" locations such as Kyiv were off limits to all who had once crossed the Stalin regime, "Regime II" locations were off limits "only" to those convicted of political crimes, banditry, repeat hooliganism, speculation, murder, brigandage, espionage, and some forms of robbery and theft. See Hagenloh, *Stalin's Police*, 421, note 49.
59. Barber and Harrison, *The Soviet Home Front*, 66.
60. DAKO, p-1/3/45, fol. 74.
61. DAKO, p-1/3/45, fols. 76, 77.
62. DAKO, p-1/3/45, fol. 78.
63. DAKO, p-1/3/45, fol. 79.
64. DAKO, p-5/2/394, fol. 14. *Limitchiki* was Russian slang in the 1930s for people not allowed to live within the limits of those areas deemed politically important to the Stalin regime.
65. GARF, 9415/3/1412, fols 1–18.
66. TsDAHOU, 1/46/361, fol. 1.
67. TsDAVOVU, r-2/7/789, fols. 50–95.
68. TsDAVOVU, r-2/7/789, fol. 65.
69. See DAKO, p-1/3/37, fol. 132v.
70. TsDAVOVU, r-2/ 7/ 973, fols. 28, 29.
71. TsDAVOVU, r-2/7/789, fol. 94.
72. TsDAVOVU, r-2/7/789, fol. 74.
73. TsDAVOVU, r-2/7/789, fol. 90.
74. TsDAVOVU, r-2/7/966. fol. 7.
75. TsDAVOVU, r-2/7/966, fols. 97–107.
76. TsDAVOVU, r-2/7/789, fols. 82, 83.
77. TsDAVOVU, r-2/7/789, fol. 83.
78. TsDAVOVU, 4620/3/281, fol. 20. For more on Pronicheva, see Berkhoff, "Dina Pronicheva's Story of Surviving the Babi Yar Massacre," 291–317.
79. TsDAVOVU, r-2/7/789, fol. 77.

80. TsDAVOVU, r-2/7/789, fol. 77.
81. TsDAVOVU, r-2/7/789, fol. 77.
82. TsDAVOVU, r-2/7/789, fol. 62.
83. TsDAVOVU, r-2/7/789, fol. 67.
84. TsDAVOVU, r-2/7/789, fol. 50.

85. For commentary on the housing shortage in Kyiv that government bureaucrats faced upon arrival in the city after it was made the Ukrainian capital in 1934, see Yekelchyk, "The Making of a 'Proletarian Capital,'" 1233–44.

86. TsDAVOVU, r-2/7/789, fol. 72.
87. TsDAVOVU, r-2/7/789, fol. 78.
88. TsDAVOVU, r-2/7/789, fol. 88.

89. Almost everywhere else in Ukraine, the heads of the oblast departments of the militia were ordered to register the reevacuated populations in the places of their permanent residence and in places where they had been sent by the plenipotentiary of the SNK UkrSSR and Ukrainian TsK in Kharkiv. See TsDAVOVU, r-2/7/979, fol. 2.

90. TsDAHOU, 1/23/3858, fol. 4.
91. TsDAHOU, 1/23/3858, fol. 7.
92. TsDAVOVU, r-2/7/997, fol. 69.
93. TsDAHOU, 1/23/1377, fols. 8, 9.
94. TsDAHOU, 1/23/1377, fols. 8, 9.
95. TsDAHOU, 1/23/1377, fols. 6, 7.
96. TsDAHOU, 1/23/1377, fols. 1, 2.
97. TsDAHOU, 1/23/1377, fols. 4, 5.
98. DAKO, 1/3/43, fol. 71.
99. TsDAVOVU, r-2/7/1009, fol. 95.
100. The GKO resolution was numbered 6944c. See DAKO, p-1/3/158, fol. 40a.
101. Filtzer, *Soviet Workers and Late Stalinism*, 13–40.
102. DAKO, p-5/2/10, fol. 108.

103. For assertions of the Kyiv Komsomol's leading role on the Khreshchatyk during winter 1943–44 see, for example, *Istoriia Kieva v dvukh tomakh*, Volume 2, 514.

104. DAKO, p-5/2/190, fol. 9.
105. DAKO, p-1/3/26, fol. 317.

106. The first raids on Darnytsa's railway junction and the pontoon bridge over the Dnipro leading to it occurred on January 5 and 23, 1944, with an unknown number of casualties. See AMVSU, 3/1/33, fols. 22, 50. Another raid on Darnytsa on April 8, 1944, is known to have left three hundred people dead and four hundred injured. See AMVSU, 3/1/33, fols. 206–7. The last Nazi bombs to fall on Kyiv came on June 23, 1944. See AMVSU, 3/1/33, fol. 302.

107. For more on the phenomenon of the Special Construction and Assembly Unit, see Goncharov, "Voina i trud," 433–34.

108. TsDAVOVU, r-2/7/969, fol. 133; TsDAVOVU, r-2/7/975, fol. 29.
109. TsDAVOVU, r-2/7/974, fol. 65; DAKO, p-1/3/136, fols. 44, 45.
110. DAKO, p-1/3/23, fol. 4.

111. DAKO, p-1/3/32, fol. 17.
112. DAKO, p-1/3/30, fol. 137.
113. TsDAHOU, 1/23/951, fol. 76.
114. TsDAHOU, 1/23/951. fol. 76.
115. TsDAVOVU, r-2/7/987, fol. 57.
116. TsDAVOVU, r-2/7/999, fols. 88, 89.
117. See Marples, *Heroes and Villains*, chs. 1 and 5, for background on the historiography of the fighting between the returning Soviets and the Ukrainian nationalist resistance, which began during the Second World War and lasted into the 1950s.
118. DAKO, p-5/2/209, fol. 22.
119. DAKO, p-5/2/239, fol. 27; DAKO, p-1/3/104, fol. 87.
120. DAKO, p-1/3/36, fol. 88.
121. TsDAVOVU, r-2/7/1003, fol. 25. For a detailed description of how these institutions worked, see Filtzer, *Soviet Workers and Late Stalinism*, 34–39.
122. DAKO, p-5/2/305, fol. 17.
123. TsDAVOVU, r-2/7/1003, fols. 110, 111.
124. TsDAHOU, 1/23/2614, fol. 1.
125. TsDAVOVU, r-2/7/974, fol. 173.
126. TsDAVOVU, r-2/7/980, fol. 7.
127. TsDAVOVU, r-2/7/981, fol. 5.
128. TsDAVOVU, r-2/7/988, fol. 3, 8.
129. TsDAVOVU, r-2/7/979, fol. 106.
130. TsDAVOVU, r-2/7/999, fol. 100.
131. TsDAVOVU, r-2/7/999, fol. 100.
132. TsDAVOVU, r-2/7/1011, fol. 115.
133. TsDAVOVU, r-2/7/1015, fol. 33.

Chapter Two

1. TsDAHOU, 1/23/1249, fol. 17.
2. GARF, 9415/3/1411, fols. 54–55.
3. TsDAHOU, 1/23/1249, fol. 13.
4. GARF, 9415/3/1411, fol. 96.
5. TsDAHOU, 1/30/71, fols. 269, 270.
6. For an explanation of the Stalin regime's ever-widening interpretation of what "defense-related industry" was during the war years, see Filtzer, *Soviet Workers and Late Stalinism*, 161–62.
7. TsDAHOU, 1/46/308, fol. 54.
8. TsDAHOU, 1/23/1244, fols. 2–9.
9. TsDAHOU, 1/23/1244, fol. 2.
10. TsDAHOU, 1/23/1244, fol. 2.

11. TsDAHOU, 1/46/308, fol. 44.
12. TsDAHOU, 1/46/308, fol. 49.
13. TsDAHOU, 1/46/309, fol. 2.
14. TsDAVOVU, r-2/7/1001, fol. 47.
15. TsDAVOVU, r-2/7/985, fol. 16.
16. TsDAHOU, 1/46/308, fols. 14–15.
17. TsDAHOU, 1/46/308, fol. 20.
18. TsDAVOVU, r-2/7/2091, fol. 30.
19. TsDAVOVU, r-2/7/2091, fol. 30.
20. TsDAHOU, 1/23/1288, fol. 25.
21. TsDAHOU, 1/23/1288, fol. 31.
22. TsDAHOU, 1/23/1288, fol. 31. These "organized groups of bandits" were most likely members of the Organization of Ukrainian Nationalists loyal to Stepan Bandera. After the German retreat, such "Banderites" fought for many years against the new Red Army "occupiers," as well as the troops of the Ukrainian NKVD, for their dream of an independent Ukraine. For more on the Banderites and Bandera's position in the Ukrainian resistance, see Subtelny, *Ukraine*, chs. 22 and 23.
23. TsDAHOU, 1/23/1288, fol. 21.
24. TsDAHOU, 1/23/1288, fol. 29.
25. DAmK, r-1/4/44, fol. 15.
26. DAKO, p-1/3/158, fol. 40a.
27. TsDAVOVU, r-2/7/2662, fol. 76.
28. TsDAVOVU, r-2/7/2662, fol. 64.
29. TsDAVOVU, r-2/72662, fol. 62.
30. TsDAVOVU, r-2/7/2662, fol. 62.
31. TsDAVOVU, r-2/7/2662, fol. 58.
32. DAKO, p-1/3/180, fols. 249, 250.
33. Arzamsakin, *Zalozhniki vtoroi mirovoi voiny*, 43–66.
34. DAmK, r-1262/1/4, fol. 1.
35. By comparison, Stalin Oblast in the Donbas—which had lost over 250,000 people to Germany during the war (the most of any region)—had only 83,500 people return by the end of 1945. See TsDAHOU, 1/23/2614, fol. 68.
36. TsDAHOU, 1/23/2993, fol. 73.
37. TsDAHOU, 1/23/2993, fol. 74.
38. TsDAHOU, 1/23/3022, fol. 59.
39. TsDAHOU, 1/30/209, fol. 199.
40. TsDAHOU, 1/23/1807, fol. 42.
41. TsDAHOU, 1/23/1807, fol. 51.
42. TsDAHOU, 1/23/1807, fols. 52–53.
43. TsDAHOU, 1/23/1807, fols. 98–100.
44. TsDAHOU, 1/41/5, fol. 196.
45. TsDAHOU, 1/41/5, fol. 202.
46. TsDAHOU, 1/41/5, fol. 203.

47. TsDAHOU, 1/41/4, fols. 161, 161v.
48. TsDAHOU, 1/41/4, fol. 167.
49. DAKO, 1/3/185, fol. 6.
50. DAKO, 1/3/185, fols. 70, 71.
51. DAKO, p-5/2/958, fols. 7, 8.
52. DAKO, p-1/3/ 275, fol. 192.
53. DAKO, p-1/3/275, fol. 190.
54. TsDAVOVU, r-2/7/3291, fol. 5.
55. TsDAVOVU, r-2/7/2189, fol. 109.
56. TsDAHOU, 1/23/1745, fols. 103, 104.
57. TsDAHOU, 1/23/1745, fol. 116.
58. TsDAHOU, 1/23/1807, fol. 126.
59. TsDAVOVU, r-2/7/3061, fol. 128.
60. TsDAHOU, 1/23/4716, fol. 168.
61. GARF, 9415/3/1417, fols. 3–6.
62. GARF, 9415/3/1417, fols. 10, 11.
63. TsDAHOU, 1/23/3712, fol. 1.
64. TsDAHOU, 1/23/3712, fol. 2.
65. Rebecca Manley, *To the Tashkent* Station, 261–62.
66. TsDAHOU, 1/23/3712, fols. 11–21.
67. TsDAHOU, 1/23/3712, fol. 12.
68. TsDAHOU, 1/23/3712, fol. 15.
69. TsDAHOU, 1/23/3712, fol. 17.
70. TsDAHOU, 1/23/3712, fol. 18.
71. TsDAHOU, 1/16/50, fols. 50–61.
72. DAKO, p-1/3/270, fol. 124.
73. DAKO, p-1/3/270, fol. 259.
74. TsDAVOVU, r-2/7/3345, fol. 34.
75. TsDAVOVU, r-2/7/3291, fol. 52.
76. TsDAVOVU, r-2/7/4046, fol. 22.
77. TsDAHOU, 1/23/2614, fol. 68.
78. DAmK, 1262/1/7, fol. 3.
79. DAmK, 1262/1/7, fols. 11v, 12v.
80. DAmK, 1262/1/7, fols. 11v, 12v.
81. DAKO, p-1/3/280, fols. 2–4.
82. TsDAVOVU, r-2/7/3215, fol. 63.
83. TsDAVOVU, r-2/7/3215, fol. 64.
84. TsDAVOVU, r-2/7/3215, fol. 73.
85. TsDAVOVU, r-2/7/4046, fol. 91.
86. TsDAHOU, 1/30/371, fol. 155.
87. TsDAHOU, 1/30/371, fols. 155v, 156.
88. TsDAHOU, 1/30/371, fol. 165.
89. TsDAHOU, 1/30/371, fols. 153, 154.

90. TsDAHOU, 1/23/3382, fol. 28.
91. TsDAHOU, 1/23/3712, fol. 23.
92. TsDAHOU, 1/23/3712, fol. 34.
93. TsDAHOU, 1/23/3712, fol. 30.
94. TsDAHOU, 1/3712/37, fol. 37.

Chapter Three

1. DAKO, p-5/2/422, fols. 71, 71v.
2. DAKO, p-1/3/32, fol. 14.
3. DAKO, p-1/3/2, fol. 36.
4. DAKO, p-1/3/180, fol. 31.
5. DAKO, p-1/3/289, fol. 15.
6. TsDAHOU, 1/23/3022, fol. 59.
7. On party growth during the war years, see Rigby, *Communist Party Membership in the USSR*, 236–56.
8. TsDAHOU, 1/46/1515, fols. 13, 14.
9. DAKO, p-1/3/104, fols. 17, 24.
10. TsDAVOVU, r-2/7/966, fol. 80.
11. DAKO, p-1/3/104, fol. 1. This factory may have produced water softener.
12. DAKO, p-1/3/104, fols. 28–30.
13. DAKO, p-1/3/104, fols. 225–27.
14. DAKO, p-1/3/104, fols. 21–22.
15. DAKO, p-1/3/158, fol. 41.
16. TsDAHOU, 1/23/3382, fol. 173.
17. TsDAHOU, 1/23/3382, fol. 66.
18. TsDAHOU, 1/23/3382, fol. 175.
19. DAKO, p-1/3/27, fol. 125.
20. TsDAVOVU, 4620/3/6, fol. 143.
21. TsDAVOVU, r-2/7/1005, fol. 97.
22. TsDAVOVU, r-2/7/1005, fols. 98–100.
23. DAKO, p-1/3/177, fol. 206.
24. DAKO, p-1/3/185, fol. 5.
25. DAKO, p-1/3/185, fol. 6.
26. TsDAHOU, 1/46/804, fol. 16.
27. DAKO, p-1/3/269, fol. 9.
28. DAKO, p-1/3/270, fol. 46.
29. DAKO, p-1/3/273, fol. 124.
30. TsDAVOVU, r-2/7/969, fol. 120.
31. TsDAHOU, 1/23/1856, fols. 53–56.
32. TsDAHOU, 1/23/1856, fol. 58.
33. TsDAVOVU, r-2/7/1950, fols. 10–14.

34. DAKO, p-1/3/183, fol. 12.
35. TsDAVOVU, r-2/7/2206, fol. 90.
36. TsDAHOU, 1/23/2407, fol. 20.
37. TsDAHOU, 1/23/3382, fol. 28.
38. TsDAHOU, 1/23/2407, fols. 14–18.
39. DAKO, p-1/3/277, fol. 5.
40. DAKO, p-5/2/1141, fol. 80.
41. Smishko, *Vozrozhdennyi Kiev*, 9.
42. TsDAVOVU, r-2/7/619, fols. 84–86.
43. DAKO, p-1/3/155, fol. 9.
44. DAKO, p-1/3/155, fol. 9.
45. DAKO, p-1/3/155, fol. 9.
46. TsDAVOVU, r-2/7/1013, fol. 6.
47. DAKO, p-1/3/173, fol. 194.
48. DAKO, p-1/3/173, fol. 195.
49. DAKO, p-1/3/158, fol. 114.
50. TsDAVOVU, r-2/7/1789, fols. 38–39.
51. TsDAVOVU, r-2/7/1001, fol. 35.
52. TsDAVOVU, r-2/7/1001, fol. 35.
53. TsDAVOVU, r-2/7/589, fol. 69.
54. TsDAVOVU, r-2/7/ 973, fol. 25.
55. Moskoff argues that these stores and restaurants were created at a time when pressure on the food supply was easing. They were also meant to stem inflationary pressures in the food market while allowing the state to profit, like collective farmers had been doing since the beginning of the war at their daily farmers' markets. See *The Bread of Affliction*, 166–69.
56. TsDAVOVU, r-2/7/981, fol. 45.
57. TsDAVOVU, r-2/7/990, fol. 106.
58. DAKO, p-1/3/144, fols. 25, 25v.
59. DAKO, p-1/3/144, fols. 25, 25v.
60. TsDAVOVU, r-2/7/991, fols. 115, 118.
61. DAmK, r-1/4/11, fol. 276.
62. DAKO, p-1/3/347, fol. 44.
63. TsDAHOU, 1/23/2697, fols. 20, 21.
64. Rossiskii Gosudarstvennyi Arkhiv Sotsial'no-Politicheskoi Istorii (hereafter RGASPI), 17/88/650, fol. 91.
65. TsDAHOU, 1/30/7, fols. 6–8.
66. *Kommunistychna partiia Ukrainy v rezoliutsiiakh i rishenniakh z'izdiv, konferentsii i plenumiv TsK*, 36–37.
67. TsDAHOU, 1/23/2697, fol. 21.
68. TsDAHOU, 1/23/2697, fol. 21.
69. TsDAHOU, 1/23/2697, fols. 188, 189.
70. DAKO, p-5/2/1139, fol. 151.

71. DAKO, p-5/2/1139, fol. 223.
72. DAKO, p-5/2/173, fols. 2, 3.
73. DAKO, p-1/3/36, fol. 119.
74. DAKO, p-5/2/874, fols. 18, 19.
75. DAKO, p-1/3/271, fols. 19, 20.
76. DAKO, p-1/3/268, fols. 20, 21.
77. RGASPI, 17/88/650, fol. 91.
78. DAKO, p-5/2/4, fol. 7.
79. DAKO, p-1/3/26, fol. 112.
80. DAKO, p-5/2/1139, fol. 19.
81. DAKO, p-5/2/849, fol. 58.
82. DAKO, p-5/2/1139, fol. 7.
83. DAKO, p-1/3/162, fols. 40, 42.
84. DAKO, p-1/3/162, fol. 47.
85. DAKO, p-1/3/162, fol. 49.
86. DAKO, p-1/3/162, fol. 6.
87. DAKO, p-1/3/162, fols. 9, 10.
88. DAKO, p-1/3/162, fol. 16.
89. DAKO, p-1/3/164, fols. 194, 195.
90. Rigby, *Communist Party Membership in the USSR*, 277–78.
91. DAKO, p-1/3/164, fols. 198–203.
92. DAKO, p-1/3/164, fols. 198–203.
93. DAKO, p-1/3/164, fol. 204.
94. TsDAHOU, 1/46/1515, fols. 15, 16.
95. DAKO, p-1/3/179, fols. 50–52.
96. DAKO, p-1/3/179, fols. 52, 53.
97. DAKO, p-1/3/182, fols. 113–15.
98. DAKO, 1/3/265, fol. 3.
99. DAKO, p-1/3/265, fol. 4.
100. DAKO, p-1/3/265, fol. 4.

Chapter Four

1. TsDAHOU, 1/46/807, fols. 1, 2.
2. TsDAHOU, 1/46/157, fols. 4, 5.
3. Danilov, *Sovetskoe gosudarstvo v Velikoi Otechestvennoi voine*, 181.
4. DAKO, p-1/3/36, fol. 4.
5. TsDAVOVU, r-2/7/1763, fol. 49.
6. TsDAVOVU, r-2/7/1763, fol. 51.
7. TsDAVOVU, r-2/7/991, fols. 2, 3.
8. TsDAVOVU, r-2/7/1007, fol. 145.
9. TsDAVOVU, r-2/7/966, fol. 124.

10. TsDAVOVU, r-2/7/966, fol. 124.
11. DAKO, p-1/3/104, fols. 170, 171.
12. DAKO, p-1/3/104, fol. 120.
13. TsDAVOVU, r-2/7/1011, fol. 66.
14. DAKO, p-1/3/36, fol. 8.
15. DAKO, p-1/3/36, fol. 88.
16. DAKO, p-1/3/41, fol. 191.
17. TsDAVOVU, r-2/7/2189, fols. 108, 109.
18. DAKO, p-5/2/273, fol. 39.
19. TsDAVOVU, r-337/26/23, fol. 50.
20. TsDAVOVU, r-2/7589, fol. 63.
21. TsDAVOVU, r-2/7/589, fol. 63.
22. DAKO, p-1/3/155, fol. 9. The full text of this resolution is at TsDAVOVU, r-2/7/617.
23. DAKO, p-1/3/173, fol. 195.
24. DAKO, p-1/3/155, fol. 11.
25. DAKO, p-1/3/173, fol. 194.
26. TsDAVOVU, r-2/7/993, fol. 8; TsDAVOVU, r- 2/7/1013, fol. 7.
27. See Institut Istorii Akademii Nauk USSR, *Istoriia Kieva v trekh tomakh, chetyrekh knigakh*, Vol. 3, 362.
28. DAKO, p-5/2/394, fol. 94.
29. TsDAVOVU, r-2/7/1001, fol. 76.
30. TsDAVOVU, r-2/7/1013, fol. 6.
31. TsDAHOU, 1/23/1380, fol. 12.
32. Manley, *To the Tashkent Station*, 262.
33. Vrons'ka, *V umovakh viiny*, 58–64.
34. TsDAVOVU, r-2/7/589, fols. 69, 70. In his outline of the ration-card system during the Second World War in the Soviet Union, Moskoff argues that only those people in the legal labor force were officially entitled to receive cards. He also argues that this system of rationing was of course "impossible to execute" due to the shortage of food at that time. See *The Bread of Affliction*, ch. 7.
35. TsDAVOVU, r-2/7/592, fol. 2.
36. TSDAVOVU, r-2/7/592, fol. 145.
37. TsDAVOVU, r-2/7/974, fol. 177.
38. DAKO, p-5/2/394, fol. 94.
39. TsDAVOVU, r-2/7/996, fols. 91, 92. In his survey of why the collective farm market was a necessity in the USSR during World War II, Moskoff points out that Moscow started to suppress the peasants' hold on the market for food as soon as the state's ability to provide the population with enough food was restored, during 1944. See *The Bread of Affliction*, ch. 8.
40. TsDAVOVU, r-2/7/994, fols. 62–64.
41. TsDAVOVU, r-2/7/1002, fol. 40.
42. TsDAVOVU, r-2/7/1005, fol. 99.

43. TsDAHOU, 1/23/2252, fol. 69.
44. TsDAHOU, 1/23/4913, fol. 3.
45. TsDAHOU, 1/23/4913, fol. 3.
46. TsDAVOVU, r-2/7/1003, fols. 25–30.
47. TsDAVOVU, r-2/7/1011, fol. 129.
48. DAKO, p-1/3/40, fol. 244. Alexei Stakhanov's record-breaking coal-mining shift in 1935 and the awards he received for it remained the Stalin regime's model for Soviet workers to emulate after the Second World War.
49. DAKO, p-1/3/40, fol. 248.
50. DAKO, p-1/3/40, fol. 245.
51. DAKO, p-1/3/40, fol. 248.
52. TsDAHOU, 1/23/2359, fols. 22, 22v.
53. DAKO, p-1/3/183, fol. 10.
54. DAKO, p-1/3/183, fols. 10, 11.
55. DAKO, p-5/2/935, fols. 38–40.
56. DAKO, p-5/2/935, fols. 38, 39.
57. TsDAHOU, 1/23/3382, fols. 106, 107.
58. GARF, 9401/1a *Sbornik Sovershennykh Sekretnykh Prikazov NKVD USSR za 1944 god*, s no. 00651 po no. 00900 (Order no. 00775).
59. DAKO, p-1/3/32, fols. 86–88.
60. GARF, 9401/1a, *Sbornik soveshennykh sekretnykh prikazov NKVD USSR za 1944 god, s no. 00170 po no. 001330* (Order no. 001296).
61. GARF, 9401/1a, *Sbornik soveshennykh sekretnykh prikazov NKVD USSR za 1944 god, s no. 00170 po no. 001330* (Order no. 001116).
62. TsDAVOVU, 4620/3/6, fols. 146–55.
63. DAKO, p-1/3/176, fol. 38.
64. DAKO, p-1/3/176, fols. 36, 37.
65. TsDAVOVU, r-2/7/3215, fols. 63–65, 73.
66. TsDAHOU, 1/46/803, fol. 3.
67. DAKO, p-1/3/270, fol. 259.
68. DAKO, p-1/3/270, fol. 260.
69. TsDAHOU, 1/23/1807, fol. 4.
70. TsDAHOU, 1/23/1807, fol. 227.
71. TsDAHOU, 1/46/358, fol. 62.
72. TsDAHOU, 1/46/804, fol. 25.
73. TsDAHOU, 1/23/1807, fol. 67.
74. TsDAHOU, 1/23/1754, fol. 9.
75. TsDAHOU, 1/23/1754, fols. 14, 15.
76. TsDAHOU, 1/41/7, fol. 255.
77. TsDAHOU, 1/41/7, fol. 258.
78. TsDAHOU, 1/41/11, fols. 37, 38.
79. TsDAHOU, 1/23/3022, fols. 19, 20.
80. TsDAHOU, 1/23/1754, fols. 6–41.

81. TsDAVOVU, r-2/7/2212, fols. 1–5.
82. TsDAVOVU, r-2/7/2212, fols. 1–5.
83. TsDAVOVU, r-2/7/2212, fols. 1–5.
84. TsDAHOU, 1/23/1754, fol. 313.
85. TsDAVOVU, r-2/7/4046, fols. 18, 19.
86. TsDAVOVU, r-2/7/4046, fols. 18, 19.
87. TsDAHOU, 1/30/369, fol. 2.
88. TsDAHOU, 1/30/369, fol. 4.
89. TsDAHOU, 1/23/3712, fol. 28.
90. DAKO, p-1/3/347, fols. 10, 11.
91. DAKO, p-1/3/347, fol. 3.
92. DAKO, p-1/3/347, fols. 1, 2.
93. DAKO, p-1/3/347, fol. 13.
94. DAKO, p-1/3/347, fol. 18.
95. DAKO, p-1/3/347, fol. 16.
96. DAKO, p-1/3/295, fol. 6.

Chapter Five

1. DAKO, p-5/2/21, fols. 4, 5, 6.
2. DAKO, p-5/2/21, fol. 15.
3. DAKO, p-1/3/2, fols. 48, 49.
4. DAKO, p-5/2/21, fol. 17.
5. Yekelchyk, "The Civic Duty to Hate," 539.
6. Berkhoff, "Total Annihilation of the Jewish Population," 111–15.
7. Ibid., 115–16, Kostyrchenko, "The Genesis of Establishment Anti-Semitism in the USSR," 183. On wartime anti-Semitism in Tashkent and Central Asia in general, see Manley, 230–33.
8. Yekelchyk, *Ukraine*, 145–46.
9. Matushevych, *Khreshchatyk*, 72.
10. DAKO, p-1/3/2, fol. 57.
11. Ignatkin, *Kyiv*, 16–18.
12. Matushevych, *Khreshchatyk*, 115.
13. In the last work of the Soviet era published on Kyiv's history, V. P. Smishko admitted the city's rebirth "by enthusiasm alone" after the war was not possible. See *Vozrozhdennyi Kiev*, 59–60.
14. DAKO, p-1/3/45, fols. 66, 67.
15. DAKO, p-1/3/23, fol. 92.
16. DAKO, p-1/3/45, fol. 104.
17. DAKO, p-1/3/32, fol. 20.
18. DAKO, p-1/3/23, fols. 200–204.
19. *Kyivs'ka Pravda*, January 9, 1945, 2; January 12, 1945, 1.

20. *Kyivs'ka Pravda*, January 14, 1945, 1.
21. TsDAVOVU, r-2/7/1949, fol. 97.
22. Matushevych, *Khreshchatyk*, 92.
23. TsDAVOVU, r-2/7/1949, fols. 21, 22.
24. TsDAVOVU, r-2/7/1950, fol. 38.
25. TsDAHOU, 1/23/1921, fols. 1, 2.
26. Matushevych, *Khreshchatyk*, 93.
27. TsDAHOU, 1/23/1921, fols. 3, 7.
28. TsDAHOU, 1/23/1921, fol. 19.
29. TsDAHOU, 1/23/883, fol. 2.
30. TsDAHOU, 1/23/883, fol. 22.
31. TsDAHOU, 1/23/883, fol. 10.
32. TsDAVOVU, r-2/7/974, fol. 21.
33. TsDAVOVU, r-2/7/974, fol. 23.
34. TsDAHOU, 1/41/4, fol. 2.
35. TsDAHOU, 1/23/632, fol. 40.
36. TsDAHOU, 1/23/632, fol. 40.
37. TsDAHOU, 1/41/7, fol. 36.
38. TsDAHOU, 1/23/3426, fols. 1–12.
39. TsDAHOU, 166/3/243, fol. 42v.
40. TsDAHOU, 166/3/243, fol. 12v.
41. DAKO, p-5/2/69, fols. 16, 17.
42. DAKO, p-5/2/108, fol. 25.
43. TsDAHOU, 1/23/633, fol. 38.
44. TsDAHOU, 1/23/940, fol. 4.
45. TsDAHOU, 1/23/940, fol. 10.
46. TsDAHOU, 1/23/940, fol. 33.
47. TsDAHOU, 1/46/758, fol. 7.
48. TsDAHOU, 1/23/1755, fol. 2v.
49. TsDAHOU, 1/23/1755, fol. 2.
50. TsDAHOU, 1/23/1755, fol. 2v.
51. TsDAHOU, 1/23/1755, fols. 3, 3v.
52. RGASPI, 17/88/449, fol. 4.
53. RGASPI, 17/88/449, fol. 6.
54. RGASPI, 17/88/449, fol. 6.
55. RGASPI, 17/88/667, fols. 247–50.
56. RGASPI, 17/88/667, fol. 251.
57. TsDAHOU, 1/30/351, fol. 81.
58. TsDAHOU, 1/30/351, fol. 83.
59. TsDAHOU, 1/30/351, fols. 76, 77.
60. TsDAHOU, 1/23/351, fols. 90, 91.
61. TsDAHOU, 1/23/351, fol. 78.
62. TsDAHOU, 1/23/351, fol. 18.

63. According to L. M. Abramenko, the fifteen Germans were tried for war crimes, convicted, and sentenced in accordance with the April 19, 1943, ukaz of the Presidium of the Supreme Soviet of the USSR. Twelve were later hanged on what is today Independence Square in Kyiv. None of them were involved in actual crimes that took place in Kyiv during the Nazi occupation. Some had been captured in fall 1943 near Kyiv. Others were captured only in May 1945 in central Europe. Proof that the massacre at Babyn Iar had taken place came in part from a document drawn up on November 27, 1943, by the Kyiv Oblast Commission of Assistance to the Extraordinary State Commission for Establishing and Investigating the Crimes of the German-Fascist Occupiers and Their Accomplices and the Damage Caused by Them to Citizens, Societal Organizations, State Enterprises and Institutions of the USSR. For a survey of the trial and copies of the document and verdict mentioned here, see *Kyivs'kyi protsess*.

64. DAKO, p-1/3/329, fols. 55–56.
65. DAKO, p-1/3/329, fols. 55–56.
66. TsDAHOU, 1/30/351, fol. 146.
67. TsDAHOU, 1/30/351, fols. 153–72.
68. TsDAHOU, 1/30/351, fol. 164.
69. TsDAHOU, 1/30/351, fol. 167.
70. TsDAHOU, 1/30/351, fols. 164, 165.
71. TsDAHOU, 1/30/351, fols. 170, 171, 173.
72. TsDAHOU, 1/30/351, fol. 166.
73. TsDAHOU, 1/30/351, fol. 170.
74. TsDAHOU, 1/30/351, fols. 170, 171.
75. TsDAHOU, 1/30/351, fol. 173.
76. DAKO, p-1/3/330, fol. 13.
77. DAKO, p-1/3/330, fols. 136, 136v.
78. DAKO, p-1/3/330, fol. 158.
79. *Kyivs'ka Pravda*, June 11, 1946, 1.
80. *Kyivs'ka Pravda*, July 9, 1946, 1.
81. *Kyivs'ka Pravda*, August 2, 1946, 1.
82. *Kyivs'ka Pravda*, August 3, 1946, 1.
83. *Kyivs'ka Pravda*, August 11, 1946, 1.
84. *Kyivs'ka Pravda*, August 25, 1946, 1.
85. *Kyivs'ka Pravda*, August 27, 1946, 1.
86. *Kyivs'ka Pravda*, August 27, 1946, 1.
87. *Kyivs'ka Pravda*, August 27, 1946, 1.
88. *Kyivs'ka Pravda*, August 14, 1946, 1.
89. *Kyivs'ka Pravda*, August 23, 1946, 1.
90. *Kyivs'ka Pravda*, August 14, 1946, 1.
91. Donald Filtzer argues that the famine was the result of the Stalin regime's own policy because, instead of releasing food from its emergency reserves, the regime sought to wait out the crisis by curtailing consumption. See *Soviet Workers and Late Stalinism*, ch. 2.

92. DAKO, p-1/3/347, fol. 59.
93. DAKO, p-1/3/347, fol. 59.
94. DAKO, p-1/3/347, fol. 59.
95. DAKO, p-1/3/347, fol. 60.
96. DAKO, p-1/3/347, fol. 61.
97. DAKO, p-1/3/330, fol. 11.
98. DAKO, p-1/3/330, fols. 12, 13.
99. DAKO, p-1/3/282, fols. 145, 146.
100. DAKO, p-1/3/330, fol. 13.
101. DAKO, p-1/3/330, fols. 14, 15.
102. DAKO, p-1/3/330, fol. 19.
103. DAKO, p-1/3/330, fol. 44.
104. DAKO, p-1/3/285, fols. 61, 62.
105. DAKO, p-1/3/291, fol. 51.
106. DAKO, p-1/3/290, fol. 6.
107. DAKO, p-1/3/290, fol. 8.
108. DAKO, p-1/3/330, fol. 159.

Chapter Six

1. TsDAHOU, 1/23/3868, fols. 25, 26.
2. TsDAHOU, 1/23/3868, fol. 30.
3. TsDAHOU, 1/23/3868, fol. 30.
4. Kostyrchenko, *Tainiia politika Stalina*, 242–49.
5. Kostyrchenko, "The Genesis of Establishment Anti-Semitism in the USSR," 182–84.
6. TsDAHOU, 1/23/863, fol. 1.
7. TsDAHOU, 1/23/863, fol. 1.
8. TsDAHOU, 1/23/863, fol. 2.
9. Manley, 230–33.
10. TsDAHOU, 1/23/4913, fol. 3.
11. TsDAHOU, 1/23/1389, fol. 18.
12. TsDAHOU, 1/23/1389, fols. 13–14. Fefer's visit is described in Redlich's introductory essay to his *Evreiskii anti-Fashistskii komitet v SSSR*, 90–101, 184–88.
13. TsDAHOU, 1/23/1389, fol. 7. The "conversation" mentioned here is part of a NKGB UkrSSR document compiled from information garnered by the questioning of Tokar and others in September 1944. For a translation of this document, see Gitelman, ed., *Bitter Legacy*, 300–307.
14. TsDAHOU, 1/23/1363, fol. 2.
15. TsDAHOU, 1/23/1363, fol. 24.
16. TsDAHOU, 1/23/2366, fols. 1, 2, 5–9.
17. TsDAHOU, 1/23/2366, fols. 3, 4, 10, 11.

18. TsDAHOU, 1/23/2366, fol. 7.
19. TsDAHOU, 1/23/2366, fols. 6, 7.
20. TsDAHOU, 1/23/2366, fols. 1, 2.
21. TsDAHOU, 1/23/2366, fols. 7–9.
22. TsDAHOU, 1/23/2366, fols. 3–4.
23. TsDAHOU, 1/23/2366, fol. 4.
24. TsDAHOU, 1/23/2366, fols. 19–22.
25. TsDAHOU, 1/23/2366, fols. 19–22.
26. TsDAHOU, 1/23/2366, fols. 26.
27. For a recent narrative, see Snyder, *Bloodlands*, 339–51.
28. TsDAHOU, 1/41/4, fols. 42–44.
29. TsDAHOU, 1/41/4, fol. 46.
30. TsDAHOU, 1/41/15, fol. 134.
31. TsDAHOU, 1/41/15, fol. 169.
32. TsDAHOU, 1/23/2812, fols. 4v, 5.
33. TsDAHOU, 1/41/15, fol. 172.
34. TsDAHOU, 1/23/2812, fols. 2, 2v, 3, 3v, 4, 4v, 5.
35. TsDAHOU, 1/41/15, fol. 134.
36. TsDAHOU, 1/41/15, fols. 153, 153v. The August 21, 1946, resolution mentioned here, and concerning the journals *Zvezda* and *Leningrad*, condemned these periodicals for publishing the writings of Mikhail Zoshchenko and Anna Akhmatova, which still followed the wartime policy that had allowed writers to make ideological mistakes.
37. TsDAHOU, 1/41/15, fol. 166.
38. DAKO, p-1/3/37, fol. 125.
39. DAKO, p-1/3/37, fol. 128.
40. DAKO, p-1/3/37, fol. 129v.
41. DAKO, p-1/3/37, fols. 127v, 128.
42. DAKO, p-1/3/37, fol. 128.
43. DAKO, p-1/3/153, fol. 5.
44. DAKO, p-1/3/153, fol. 6.
45. *Kyivs'ka Pravda*, November 25, 1944, 4.
46. TsDAHOU, 1/6/748, fols. 89–94.
47. TsDAHOU, 1/6/748, fols. 89–94.
48. TsDAHOU, 1/6/748, fols. 89–94.
49. DAKO, p-5/2/423, fol. 70.
50. DAKO, p-5/2/423, fol. 69.
51. DAKO, p-1/3/155, fol. 35.
52. DAKO, p-1/3/155, fol. 36v.
53. TsDAHOU, 1/70/423, fol. 1.
54. DAKO, p-1/3/190, fol. 138.
55. TsDAHOU, 1/23/2367, fol. 23.
56. TsDAHOU, 1/41/5, fol. 113.
57. TsDAHOU, 1/41/5, fols. 114–15.

58. TsDAHOU, 1/46/804, fols. 17–18.
59. TsDAHOU, 1/46/804, fols. 23–27.
60. DAKO, p-1/3/192, fols. 246–49.
61. DAKO, p-1/3/192, fol. 246.
62. DAKO, p-1/3/192, fol. 248.
63. *Kyivs'ka Pravda*, March 20, 1946, 4.
64. *Kyivs'ka Pravda*, May 25, 1946, 4.
65. TsDAHOU, 1/46/804, fol. 26.
66. TsDAHOU, 1/46/804, fol. 30.
67. TsDAHOU, 1/23/3635, fol. 2.
68. DAKO, p-1/3/311, fols. 10–22.
69. TsDAHOU, 1/41/5, fols. 78–80.
70. TsDAHOU, 1/41/5, fols. 78–80.
71. TsDAHOU, 1/41/5, fols. 78–80.
72. TsDAHOU, 1/41/5, fols. 85, 88, 89.
73. For example, the paper did note the sentencing of the head of a militia station passport table to ten years of corrective labor for illegally registering large numbers of people in the city in return for bribes ranging from 2,000 to 5,600 rubles. *Kyivs'ka Pravda*, November 22, 1944, 4.
74. TsDAHOU, 1/23/2362, fol. 63.
75. TsDAHOU, 1/23/2362, fols. 65–67.
76. TsDAHOU, 1/23/2362, fols. 71–72.
77. TsDAHOU, 1/23/2362, fol. 74.
78. TsDAHOU, 1/23/2364, fols. 1–4.
79. TsDAHOU, 1/23/2364, fol. 3.
80. TsDAHOU, 1/23/2362 fol. 63. Such a stereotype would become more prominent in the city's life in later years.
81. DAKO, p-5/3/18, fol. 16.
82. DAKO, p-1/3/347, fols. 35–36.
83. DAKO, p-1/3/285, fols. 63–65.
84. DAKO, p-1/3/311, fol. 24.
85. DAKO, p-1/3/285, fol. 7.
86. TsDAHOU, 1/41/15, fol. 53.
87. TsDAHOU, 1/41/15, fols. 51–52.
88. TsDAHOU, 1/41/15, fols. 62–63.
89. TsDAHOU, 1/23/3190, fols. 1–2.
90. TsDAHOU, 1/23/3190, fol. 14.
91. TsDAHOU, 1/41/8, fols. 104–6.
92. TsDAHOU, 1/41/8, fols. 113, 114, 116.
93. DAKO, p-1/3/276, fols. 17–19.
94. TsDAHOU, 1/41/7, fol. 192.

Bibliography

Archives

Archive of the Ministry of Internal Affairs of Ukraine—Arkhiv Ministerstva Vnutrishnykh Sprav Ukrainy (AMVSU)

f. 1. Ministry of the Internal Affairs of Ukrainian SSR
op. 3. (Title Remains Classified)

Central State Archive of Civic Organizations of Ukraine—Tsentral'nyi Derzhavnyi Arkhiv Hromads'kykh Obied'nan Ukrainy (TsDAHOU)

f. 1. Central Committee of the Communist Party of Ukraine (TsK KP(b)U)
op. 6. Protocols of the Meetings of the Politbiuro TsK (KP(b)U), 1919–67
op. 16. Protocols of the Meetings of the Politbiuro, Orgbiuro, and Secretariat of the TsK (KP(b)U) (Secret File), 1923–90
op. 23. Documents of the General Department (Special Sector) of the TsK KP(b)U (Secret Part), 1941–59
op. 30. Documents of the General Department of the TsK KP(b)U (Non-Secret Part)
op. 41. Documents of the General Department of the TsK KP(b)U (Letters and Declarations Sent by Workers), 1944–87
op. 46. Documents of the Department of Organizational-Party Work of the TsK KP(b)U, 1940–67
op. 70. Documents of the Department of Agitation and Propaganda of the TsK KP(b)U, 1941–67
f. 70. Central Committee of the Komsomol of Ukraine (TsK LKSMU)
op. 3. Documents of the Departments of the TsK LKSMU, protocols of meetings, conferences, plenums of oblast committee biuros, city committees, and raion committees, 1942–47

f. 166. Commission for the Study of the History of the Great Patriotic War with the Academy of Sciences of the URSR, 1941–50

Central State Archive of the Higher Organs of Power of Ukraine— Tsentral'nyi Derzhavnyi Arkhiv Vyshchykh Orhaniv Vlady Ukrainy (TsDAVOVU)

f. 2. Soviet of Ministers of the Ukrainian SSR
op. 7. Resolutions of the Soviet of Ministers of the Ukrainian SSR

Russian State Archive of Socio-Political History—Rossiskii Gosudarstvennyi Arkhiv Sotsial'no-Politicheskoi Istorii (RGASPI)

f. 17. Central Committee of the Communist Party of the Soviet Union (TsK CPSU)
op. 88. Organization and Instruction Directorate of the TsK CPSU
op. 125. Propaganda and Agitation Directorate of the TsK CPSU

State Archive of Kyiv Oblast—Derzhavnyi Arkhiv Kyivs'koi Oblasti (DAKO)

f. p-1. Kyiv City Committee KP(b)U
op. 3. Documents and Materials of the Kyiv Oblast Committee, 1943–48
f. p-5. Kyiv Oblast Committee KP(b)U
op. 2. Documents and Materials of the Kyiv Oblast Committee, 1943–45
op. 3. Documents and Materials of the Kyiv Oblast Committee, 1945–48

State Archive of the City of Kyiv—Derzhavnyi Arkhiv misto Kyieva (DAmK)

f. r-1. Kyiv City Soviet

State Archive of the Russian Federation—Gosudarstvennyi Arkhiv Rossisskoi Federatsii (GARF)

f. 9401 op. 1a. Collection of Top Secret Orders of the NKVD SSSR
f. 9415 op. 3. Main Directorate of the Militia (GUM) NKVD SSSR

Published Sources

Abramenko, L. M. *Kyivs'kyi protses: Dokumenty ta materialy.* Kyiv: Lybid', 1995.

Altshuler, Mordechai. *Soviet Jewry on the Eve of the Holocaust: A Social and Demographic Profile.* Jerusalem: Hebrew University Press, 1998.

Anatoli, A. [Anatolii Kuznetsov]. *Babi Iar: A Document in the Form of a Novel.* London: J. Cape, 1970.

Armstrong, John. *Ukrainian Nationalism.* Englewood, CO: Ukrainian Academic Press, 1990.

Arzamaskin, Iurii. *Zalozhniki vtoroi mirovoi voiny: Repatriatsii sovetskikh grazhdan v 1944–1953 gg.* Moscow: Iurii Arzamaskin, 2001.

Barber, John, and Mark Harrison. *The Soviet Home Front, 1941–1945: A Social and Economic History of the USSR in World War II.* London: Longman, 1991.

Berkhoff, Karel. "Dina Pronicheva's Story of Surviving the Babi Yar Massacre: German, Jewish, Soviet, Russian, and Ukrainian Records." In *The Shoah in Ukraine: History, Testimony, Memorialization*, edited by Ray Brandon and Wendy Lower, 219–317. Bloomington: Indiana University Press, 2008.

———. *Harvest of Despair: Ukraine under Nazi Rule, 1941–1944.* Cambridge, MA: Harvard University Press, 2004.

———. "Hitler's Clean Slate: Ukraine under Nazi Rule, 1941–1944." PhD diss., University of Toronto, 1998.

———. *Motherland in Danger: Soviet Propaganda during World War II.* Cambridge, MA: Harvard University Press, 2012.

———. "'Total Annihilation of the Jewish Population': The Holocaust in the Soviet Media, 1941–45." In *The Holocaust in the East: Local Perpetrators and Soviet Responses*, edited by Michael David-Fox, Peter Holquist, and Alexander Martin, 83–117. Pittsburgh: University of Pittsburgh Press, 2014.

———. "Ukraine under Nazi Rule, 1941–1944: Sources and Finding Aids, Part I." *Jahrbücher für Geschichte Osteuropas* 45 (1997): 85–103.

Bordiugov, Gennadi. "The Popular Mood in the Unoccupied Soviet Union: Continuity and Change during the War." In *The People's War: Responses to World War II in the Soviet Union*, edited by Bernd Bonwetsch and Robert Thurston, 54–70. Urbana: University of Illinois Press, 2000.

Brandenberger, David. *Propaganda State in Crisis: Soviet Ideology and Indoctrination, and Terror under Stalin, 1927–1941.* New Haven, CT: Yale University Press, 2011.

Brooks, Jeffrey. *Thank You Comrade Stalin!: Soviet Public Culture from Revolution to the Cold War.* Princeton, NJ: Princeton University Press, 2000.

Brown, Kate. *A Biography of No Place: From Ethnic Borderland to Soviet Heartland.* Cambridge, MA: Harvard University Press, 2004.

Budnik, David, and Iakov Kaper. *Nichego ne zabyto: Evreiskie sud'by v Kieve.* Konstanz: Hartung-Gorre, 1993.

Buts'ko, Nikolai. *Kommunisticheskaia partiia: Organizator vsenarodnoi pomoshchi Sovetskoi Ukraine v vostanovlenii narodnogo khoziastva v gody Velikoi Otechestvennou voini*. Kiev: Izdatel'stvo Kievskogo Universiteta, 1962.

Danilov, A. A., and A. V. Pyzhikov. *Rozhdenie sverkhderzhavy: SSSR v pervye poslevoennye gody*. Moscow: Rospenn, 2001.

Danilov, V. N. *Sovetskoe gosudarstvo v Velikoi Otechestvennoi voine: Fenomen chrezvychainykh organov vlasti 1941–1945 gg*. Saratov: Izdatel'stvo Saratovskogo Universiteta, 2002.

Davies, Sarah. *Popular Opinion in Stalin's Russia: Terror, Propaganda, and Dissent, 1934–1941*. New York: Cambridge University Press, 1997.

Denysenko, P. I. *Komunistichna partiia Ukrainy: Orhanizator bidbudovy narodnoho hospodarstva respubliky, 1943–1945*. Kyiv: Politvydav Ukrainy, 1968.

Dmytruk, V. M., ed. *Narysy istorii Kyivs'koi oblasnoi partiinoi orhanizatsii*. Kyiv: Politvydav Ukrainy, 1967.

Dobroszycki, Lucjan, and Jeffrey Gurock, eds. *The Holocaust in the Soviet Union: Studies and Sources on the Destruction of the Jews in the Nazi-Occupied Territories of the USSR, 1941–1945*. Armonk, NY: M. E. Sharpe, 1993.

Dubyna, Kuz'ma. *778 trahichnykh dniv Kyieva*. Kyiv: Derzhvydav, 1945.

Edele, Mark. "Soviet Veterans as an Entitlement Group, 1945–1955," *Slavic Review* 65 (Spring 2006): 111–37.

Filtzer, Donald. *Soviet Workers and Late Stalinism: Labor and the Restoration of the Stalinist System after World War II*. Cambridge: Cambridge University Press, 2002.

———. *Soviet Workers and Stalinist Industrialization: The Formation of Modern Soviet Production Relations, 1928–1941*. Armonk, NY: M. E. Sharpe, 1986.

Fitzpatrick, Sheila. *The Russian Revolution*. New York: Oxford University Press, 1984.

Forostivs'ky, Leontii. *Kyiv pid vorozhymy okupatsiiamy*. Buenos Aires: M. Denysiuk, 1952.

Getty, J. Arch. *Origins of the Great Purges: The Soviet Communist Party Reconsidered*. New York: Cambridge University Press, 1985.

Gilboa, Yehoshua. *The Black Years of the Soviet Jewry, 1938–1953*. Boston: Little, Brown, 1971.

Gitelman, Zvi, ed. *Bitter Legacy: The Holocaust in the Soviet Union*. Bloomington: Indiana University Press, 1997.

Glagolev, A. "Za drugi svoia: O zverstvakh fashistov protiv evreiskogo naseleniia Ukrainy, 1941 g.: Vospominaniia." *Novyi Mir* 10 (1991): 130–39.

Goncharov, G. A. "Voina i trud: stereotipy grazhdanskoi voiny v organizatsii trudovykh otnoshenii v USSR, v 1941–45 gg." In *Chelovek i voina: Voina kak iavlenie kul'tury*, edited by I. V. Narvskii, and O. Iu. Nikonova, 433–34. Moscow: Airo-XX, 2001.

Gorlizki, Yoram, and Oleg Khlevniuk. *Cold Peace: Stalin and the Soviet Ruling Circle, 1945–1953*. New York: Oxford University Press, 2004.

Grigorovich, D. F. *Kiev: Gorod geroi*. Moscow: Voenizdat, 1962.

Hagenloh, Paul. "'Socially Harmful Elements' and the Great Terror." In *Stalinism: New Directions*, edited by Sheila Fitzpatrick, 286–307. London: Routledge, 2000.

———. *Stalin's Police: Public Order and Mass Repression in the USSR, 1926–1941*. Washington D.C.: Woodrow Wilson Center Press, 2009.

Hahn, Werner. *Postwar Soviet Politics: The Fall of Zhdanov and the Defeat of Moderation, 1946–1953*. Ithaca, NY: Cornell University Press, 1982.

Hamm, Michael. *Kiev: A Portrait*. Princeton, NJ: Princeton University Press, 1993.

Hillis, Faith. *Children of Rus': Right-Bank Ukraine and the Invention of a Russian Nation*. Ithaca, NY: Cornell University Press, 2013.

Ignatkin, I. A. *Kyiv*. Moscow: Izdatel'stvo Akademii Arkhitektury SSSR, 1948.

Institut Istorii Akademii Nauk UkrSSR. *Istoriia gorodov i sel Ukrainskoi SSR v dvadtsati shesti tomakh: Kiev*. Kiev: Glavnaia Redaktsiia Ukrainskoi Entsiklopedii, 1979.

———. *Istoriia Kieva v dvukh tomakh*. 2 vols. Kiev: Izdatel'stvo Akademii Nauk UkrSSR, 1963–64.

———. *Istoriia Kieva v trekh tomakh, chetyrekh knigakh*. Kiev: Naukova Dumka, 1982.

Ivanov, A. F. "Ukreplenie riadov Kompartii Ukrainy v 1945–1952 gg. v krivom zerkale burzhuaznogo 'Ukrainovedeniia'." *Nauchnye Trudy po Istorii KPSS* 5 (1988): 145–55.

Ivanova, G. M. *Labor Camp Socialism: The Gulag in the Soviet Totalitarian System*. Armonk, NY: M. E. Sharpe, 2000.

Iurchuk, Vasilii. *Kommunisticheskaia partiia vo glave vse narodnoi bor'by za vosstanovlenie i razvitie narodnogo khoziaistva Sovetskoi Ukrainy, 1946–1950 gg*. Kiev: Politizdat, Ukrainy, 1986.

Iurchuk, Vasyl'. *Borot'ba Kommunistychnoi partii Ukrainy za vidbudovi i rozvitok narodnoho hospodarstva, 1945–1952 rr*. Kiev: Politizdat Ukrainy, 1965.

Iushenko, Mikhail. *Deiatelnost' Kompartii Ukraini po mobilizatsii trudiashchikhsia respubliki na razgrom fashizma v 1943–1945 gg*. Kyiv: Vyshcha Shkola, 1977.

Jones, Jeffrey. *Everyday Life and the "Reconstruction" of Soviet Russia during and after the Great Patriotic War, 1943–1948*. Bloomington, IN: Slavica, 2008.

Kaplan, Cynthia. "The Impact of World War II on the Party," in *The Impact of World War II on the Soviet People*, edited by Susan Linz, 157–87. Totowa, NJ: Rowman and Allenheld, 1985.

Khlevnuik, Oleg. "The Reasons for the 'Great Terror': The Foreign-Political Aspect." In *Russia in the Age of Wars*, edited by Silvio Pons and Andrea Romano, 160–69. Milan: Feltrinelli, 1998.

Kievshchina v gody Velikoi Otechestvennoi voiny, 1941–1945: Sbornik dokumentov. Kiev: Oblastnoe Knizhnoe Izdatel'stvo, 1963.

Kostyrchenko, Gennadi. "The Genesis of Establishment Anti-Semitism in the USSR: The Black Years, 1948–1953." In *Revolution, Repression, and Revival: The Soviet Jewish Experience*, edited by Zvi Gitelman and Yaacov Ro'i, 179–92. Lanham, MD: Rowman and Littlefield, 2007.

———. *Tainiia politika Stalina: Vlast' i anti-Semitism*. Moscow: Mezhdunarodnye Otnosheniia, 2001.
Kotkin, Stephen. *Magnetic Mountain: Stalinism as a Civilization*. Berkeley: University of California Press, 1995.
Koval', Mykhailo. "Pid 'kovpakom' beriis'koi derzhbezpeki (Ukrains'ka nauchno-tvorches'ka intelihentsiia)." *Ukrains'kyi Istorychnyi Zhurnal* nos. 10–11 (1992): 111–22.
———. *Ukraina, 1939–1945: Malovidomi i neprochytani storinky istorii*. Kyiv: Vyshcha Shkola, 1995.
———. *Ukraina v Druhii Svitovyi i Velykii Vitchyznianii viinakh, 1939–1945 rr.* Kyiv: Al'ternatyvy, 1999.
Koval', Mykhailo, and P. I. Mel'nyk. "Trudiashchi Kyieva v borot'ba za vidbudovu mista, 1943–1945 rr." *Ukrains'kyi Istorychnyi Zhurnal* no. 2 (1982): 61–73.
Kozhukalo, I. P. "Diial'nist' partiinykh komitetiv Ukrainy po zmitsneniu pervinnykh orhanizatsii, 1945–1961 rr." *Ukrains'kyi Istorychnyi Zhurnal* no. 7 (1988): 67–78.
Khrushchev, Nikita. *Khrushchev Remembers*. Boston: Little, Brown, 1970.
Kommunistychna partiia Ukrainy v rezoliutsiiakh i rishenniakh z'izdiv, konferentsii i plenumiv TsK. V dvukh tomakh. 2 vols. Kyiv: Politvydav Ukrainy, 1977.
Kudlai, Oleksandr. *Robitnychyi klas Ukrains'koi RSR u borot'bi za vidbudovu i rozvytok promyslovosti v pisliavoiennyi period*. Kyiv: Naukova Dumka, 1965.
Kul'chyts'kyi, Stanislav, and Tamara Vron'ska. "Malovidomi storinky istorii: Radians'ka pasportna systema." *Ukrains'kyi Istorychnyi Zhurnal* no. 3 (1999): 33–43; 4 (1999): 3–14.
———. "Z istorii trudovykh pochyniv robitnykiv promyslovykh pidpryemstv m. Kyieva: Do 1500 richchia Kyieva." *Arkhivy Ukrainy* no. 1 (1981): 64–68.
Kuromiya, Hiroaki. *Stalin's Industrial Revolution: Politics and Workers, 1928–1932*. Cambridge: Cambridge University Press, 1988.
———. *Voices of the Dead: Stalin's Great Terror of the 1930s*. New Haven, CT: Yale University Press, 2007.
Lewin, Moshe. *The Making of the Soviet System: Essays in the Social History of Interwar Russia*. New York: Pantheon Books, 1985.
———. "Rebuilding the Soviet Nomenclatura, 1945–1948." *Cahiers du Monde Russe* 44, nos. 2–3 (2003): 219–51.
Liber, George. *Soviet Nationality Policy, Urban Growth, and Identity Change in the Ukrainian SSR, 1923–1934*. Cambridge: Cambridge University Press, 1992.
Linz, Susan, ed. *The Impact of World War II on the Soviet People*. Totowa, NJ: Rowman and Allenheld, 1985.
Luk'ianova, H. "Litopys. Uryvky zi shchedennyka viiny: 22 chervnia. 1941 r.—28 sichnia 1944 r., m. Kyiv." *Suchasnist'* no. 5 (1995): 148–67.
Malakov, Dmytro. *Kyiv. 1941–1943. Fotoal'bom. Za materialamy fotodukumental'noi vystavky, shcho vidbulasia voseny 1998 r. v Muzei istorii mista Kyieva*. Kyiv: Kii, 2000.

———. *Kyiany, viina, nimtsi*. Kyiv: Amadei, 2008.
Manley, Rebecca. *To the Tashkent Station: Evacuation and Survival in the Soviet Union at War*. Ithaca, NY: Cornell University Press, 2009.
Marples, David. *Heroes and Villains: Creating National History in Contemporary Ukraine*. New York: Central European University Press, 2007.
Martin, Terry. *The Affirmative Action Empire: Nations and Nationalism in the Soviet Union, 1923–1939*. Ithaca, NY: Cornell University Press, 2001.
Matushevych, A. O. *Khreshchatyk*. Kyiv: Vydavnytsvo Akademii Arkhitektury Ukrains'koi RSR, 1950.
McLoughlin, Barry, "Mass Operations of the NKVD, 1937–8." In *Stalin's Terror: High Politics and Mass Repression in the Soviet Union*, edited by Kevin McDermott and Barry McLoughlin, 118–52. New York: Palgrave, 2003.
Meir, Natan. *Kiev: Jewish Metropolis, A History, 1859–1914*. Bloomington: Indiana University Press, 2009.
Merridale, Catherrine. *Ivan's War: Life and Death in the Red Army, 1939–1945*. New York: Picador, 2006.
Mitsel', Mikhail. *Evrei Ukrainy v 1943–1953 gg.: Ocherki dokumentirovannoi istorii*. Kyiv: Dukh i Litera, 2004.
Moskoff, William. *The Bread of Affliction: The Food Supply in the USSR during World War II*. Cambridge: Cambridge University Press, 1990.
Mukhovs'kyi, I., and O. Lysenko. "Z istorii mobilizatsii liudskykh rezerviv Ukrainy do chervonoi armi v 1941–1945 pp." *Rozbudova Derzhavy* no. 4 (1995): 40–45.
Osokina, Elena. *Our Daily Bread: Socialist Distribution and the Art of Survival in Stalinist Russia, 1927–1941*. Armonk, NY: M. E. Sharpe, 2001.
Overy, Richard. *Russia's War: A History of the Soviet War Effort, 1941–1945*. New York: Penguin, 1998.
Pastushenko, Tetiana. *V'izd repatriantiv do Kyieva zaboronennyi: Povoienne zhyttia kolyshnikh ostarbaiteriv ta viis'kovopolonenykh v Ukrainy*. Kiev: Institut Istorii Ukrainy NAN Ukrainy, 2011.
Pauly, Matthew. "Tending to the 'Native Word': Teachers and the Soviet Campaign for Ukrainian-Language Schooling, 1923–1930." *Nationalities Papers* no. 3 (2009): 251–72.
Pavlenko, Iuryi. *Narys istorii Kyieva*. Kyiv: Feniks, 2004.
Pershina, Tamara. *Hospodars'ka nomenklatura v Ukrainy, 1943–1945*. Kyiv: NAN Ukrainy, Institut Istorii Ukrainy, 1997.
Petliak, Feliks. *Partiinoe rukovodstvo Sovetami na Ukraine v gody Velikoi Otechestvennoi voiny, 1941–1945*. Kiev: Vyshcha Shkola, 1986.
Pinkus, Benjamin. *The Soviet Government and the Jews, 1948–1967: A Documented Study*. Cambridge: Cambridge University Press, 1984.
Pons, Silvio, and Andrea Romano, eds. *Russia in the Age of Wars*. Milan: Feltrinelli, 1998.
Qualls, Karl, *From Ruins to Reconstruction: Urban Identity in Soviet Sevastopol after World War II*. Ithaca, NY: Cornell University Press, 2009.

Raleigh, Donald, ed. *Provincial Landscapes: Local Dimensions of Soviet Power, 1917–1953.* Pittsburgh: University of Pittsburgh Press, 2001.

Redlich, Shimon. *Evreiskii anti-Fashistskii komitet v SSSR, 1941–48: Dokumentirovannaia istoriia.* Moscow: Mezhdunarodnye Otnoshennie, 1996.

Rees, E. A. "The Great Purges and the XVIII Party Congress of 1939." In *Center-Local Relations in the Stalinist State, 1928–1941,* 208. New York: Palgrave, 2002.

Resheniia partii i pravitel'stva po khoziaistvennym voprosam: Sbornik dokumentov za 50 let. V 5-ti tomakh. 5 vols. Moscow: Politizdat, 1968.

Rigby, T. H. *Communist Party Membership in the U.S.S.R., 1917–1967.* Princeton, NJ: Princeton University Press, 1968.

Rubenstein, Joshua. *Stalin's Secret Pogrom: The Postwar Inquisition of the Jewish Anti-Fascist Committee.* New Haven, CT: Yale University Press, 2005.

Sharandachenko, Aleksandra F. *Registrator zagsa: iz dnevnika Kievlianki.* Moscow: Sovetskii Pisatel', 1964.

Shearer, David. "Social Disorder, Mass Repression, and the NKVD during the 1930s," In *Stalin's Terror: High Politics and Mass Repression in the Soviet Union,* edited by Kevin McDermott and Barry McLoughlin, 85–117. New York: Palgrave, 2003.

———. *Policing Stalin's Socialism: Repression and Social Order in the Soviet Union.* New Haven, CT: Yale University Press, 2009.

Shephard, Ben. *The Long Road Home: The Aftermath of the Second World War.* New York: Knopf, 2011.

Simon, Gerhard. *Nationalism and Policy towards the Nationalities in the Soviet Union: From Totalitarian Dictatorship to Post-Stalinist Society.* Boulder, CO: Westview, 1991.

Smishko, Victor. "Vklad trudiashchykh Radians'kykh respublik u vidbudovi i dal'neishi rozvitok stolytsi Radians'koi Ukrainy—Kyieva, 1945–1950 rr." *Ukrains'kyi Istorychnyi Zhurnal'* no. 8 (1983): 101–8.

———. *Vozrozhdennyi Kiev: Trudovoe sodruzhestvo narodov SSSR v vosstanovlennii stolitsi Ukrainy, 1943–1950 gg.* Kiev: Vyshcha Shkola, 1990.

Snyder, Timothy. *Bloodlands: Europe Between Hitler and Stalin.* New York: Basic Books, 2010.

Somov, A. *Po zakonam voennogo vremeni: ocherki istorii trudovoi politiki SSSR v gody Velikoi Otechestvennoi voiny (1941–1945 gg.)* Nizhnyi Novgorod: NGU, 2001.

Sovietskaia Ukraina v gody Velikoi Otechestvennoi voiny, 1941–1945: Dokumenty i materialy v trekh tomakh. 3 vols. Kiev: Naukova Dumka, 1980.

Subtelny, Orest. *Ukraine: A History.* Toronto: University of Toronto Press, 1994.

Tarakhovskii, Mark. *Vospominnaiia ochevidtsa.* Kiev: Astarta, 1994.

Timchenko, A. P. "Deiatel'nost' organov militsii SSSR po ukrepleniiu sotsialisticheskoi zakonnosti i pravoporiadoka na territorii, osvobozhdennoi ot nemetsko-fashistskikh zakhvatchikov, 1943–1945 gg." *Nauchnye Trudy po Istorii KPSS* no. 167 (1990): 55–61.

Ukrainskaia SSR v gody Velikoi Otechestvennoi voiny Sovetskogo Soiuza: khronika sobytii. Kiev: Politizdat Ukrainy, 1985.

Ukrains'ka RSR u Velykii Vitchyznianii viiny Radians'koho Soiuzu 1941–1945 rr. Kyiv Politvydav Ukrainy, 1969.

Veidlinger, Jeffrey. *The Moscow State Yiddish Theatre: Jewish Culture on the Soviet Stage.* Bloomington: Indiana University Press, 2001.

———. "Soviet Jewry as a Diaspora Nationality: The Black Years Reconsidered." *East European Jewish Affairs* no. 33 (2003): 1, 4–29.

Vrons'ka, Tamara. *V umovakh viiny: Zhyttia ta pobut naseleniia mist Ukrainy, 1943–1945 rr.* Kyiv: NAN Ukrainy, Institut Istorii Ukrainy, 1995.

Weiner, Amir. *Making Sense of War: The Second World War and the Fate of the Bolshevik Revolution.* Princeton, NJ: Princeton University Press, 2001.

Werth, Alexander. *Russia at War, 1941–1945.* New York: Carroll and Graf, 1992.

Yekelchyk, Serhy. "The Civic Duty to Hate: Stalinist Citizenship as Political Practice and Civic Emotion (Kiev, 1943–53)." *Kritika: Explorations in Russian and Eurasian History* 7, no. 3 (Summer 2006): 529–56.

———. "The Making of a 'Proletarian Capital': Patterns of Stalinist Social Policy in Kiev in the mid-1930s." *Europe Asia Studies* 50, no. 7 (1998): 1229–44.

———. *Stalin's Empire of Memory: Russian-Ukrainian Relations in the Historical Imagination.* Toronto: University of Toronto Press, 2004.

———. *Ukraine: Birth of a Modern Nation.* New York: Oxford University Press, 2007.

Zima, V. F. "Poslevoennoe sovetskoe obshchestvo: golod i prestupnost', 1946–1947 gg." *Otechestvennaia Istoriia* no. 5 (1995): 45–59.

Zinchenko, Iuri. "Razom z narodom: Kompartiia Ukrainy u pershi misiatsi viiny." *Polityka i Chas* no. 7 (1991): 64–68.

———. *Sovety deputatov trudiashchikhsia Ukrainskoi SSR v gody Velikoi Otechestvennoi voiny, 1941–1945.* Kiev: Naukova Dumka, 1989.

Zubkova, Elena. *Obshchestvo i reformy, 1945–1964.* Moscow: Rossiia Molodaia, 1993.

———. *Poslevoennoe sovetskoe obshchestvo: Politika i povsednevnost', 1945–1953.* Moscow: Rosspen, 2000.

Index

Please note: Page numbers in italics refer to illustrations; "Party" in subentries refers to the Communist Party. Please see the glossary and abbreviations (pp. xiii–xiv) for abbreviations used in entries and subentries.

agricultural oblasts: *orgnabor* deserters in, 47–48, 49, 50; *orgnabor* exemption of, 43–44, 45, 187
agriculture: collectivization of, 5, 7–8; and drought (1946), 85, 127, 153–54; and food supply, 7–8, 43, 111–12; and harvest labor, 104, 105, 112; machinery/vehicles for, 3, 26, 65, 114; and support of Red Army, 26, 83, 111
Akhmatova, Anna, 149
Alabian, Karo, 137
Aleksandrov, Georgii, 160, 178
Alekseenko, Hnat I., 91
Alekseeva, M. Kh., 110
Alidin (Ukrainian TsK official), 162
All-Union Academy of Architects, 137
All-Union Communist Party Central Committee (TsK), 74, 108, 160, 167, 178
All-Union Ministry of Food Processing, 66, 182
All-Union Ministry of Internal Affairs (MVD), 65, 67, 185
All-Union Ministry of State Security (MGB), 163
All-Union NKVD Directorate of Camp no. 62, 56–59, 66, 117–19
All-Union People's Commissariat of Defense, 34, 42, 76, 183
All-Union People's Commissariat of Internal Affairs (NKVD; later All-Union MVD), 1, 22–23, 27–28, 30, 36, 42, 46, 47, 53, 141; corrective labor camps of, 5, 6, 47; and German POWs, 54–60, 66, 67, 79, 117–20; and Party reacceptance, 90–91
All-Union People's Commissariat of the Aviation Industry, 26, 55–56, 75, 118
All-Union Supreme Soviet, 47–50, 121–22, 144–46; elections for (1946), 145–49, 176, 190. See also *ukazi* (decrees) of All-Union Supreme Soviet
Andreev Railway Depot, 98, 149
anti-Semitism, 1–2, 10, 11–15, 159–67, 178, 179, 186; in evacuation policies, 159–60; and housing scarcity/disputes, 9, 158–59, 160, 162, 164–66, 167, 188, 190; as hushed up, 132–33, 165; and "Soviet Patriotism," 12–14, 190–91; and Ukrainian nationalism, 13–15, 132–33, 148, 163–67, 186, 190–91; against unorganized returnees, 11, 158–59, 161–63, 165–66, 167, 168, 190
Antonov (aircraft firm), 26, 118. See also aviation factories

apartment buildings, 31, *58*, 104, 144–45; and crime, 170, 174, 176; repair/occupation of, 108–9
apartments: battles over, 9, 102, 106–10, 113, 158–67, 186, 188; "compressions" of, 81, 82, 109–10; eviction from, 35, 37–38, 61, 73, 81–83, 102, 104–5, 107–8, 110, 113, 158, 166; illegal occupation of, 82–83, 106–8; leaders' meeting on "question" of, 30–36; Party members/workers and, 33, 35, 80–83, 110; of servicemen/families, 34–39, 52, 60–61, 63, 73, 81–82, 102, 108, 113, 125–26, 148, 166, 188. *See also* housing
architecture/city planning projects, 133–40, 189–90
Armored Tank Repair Factory no. 7, 76
Arsenal Factory, 55, 57–58, 75–76, 78, 142
Artificial Fibers Factory no. 512 (Darnytsa), 8, 56, 64–65, 77–78, 120, 152
artists, 4, 34, 83–85, 156. *See also* intelligentsia
Artobol'skii, Vladimir M., 19–20
Auto-Repair Factory no. 1, 183–84
aviation factories: (no. 473; now Antonov), 26, 58, 79, 118–19; (no. 485), 58, 79, 145
aviation industry, 26, 55–56, 75, 118–19, 145

Babchenko (commissar of justice), 52, 171
Babenko (engineer), 166
Babyn Iar massacre, 4, 21–22, 131, 132
Banderites, 51, 121, 148
Baranovskii, Anatolii, 52, *86*
Bashkulat, Aleksei, 140
bazaars, 32, 84, 127, 145, 162, 168. *See also* markets

Beregovenko (Kyiv Obkom employee), 73, 74, 101
Beriia, Lavrenty, 163
Bessarabs'kyi Market, 127, 137, 142
Bila Tserkva Gorkom, 94
Bitniia-Shliakhta (aggrieved resident), 73
Blomberg, Sara, 160–61
Bohdan Khmel'nyts'kyi Square, *143*
Bol'shevik (Party propaganda journal), 150
Bol'shevik chemical/electrical equipment factory (Zhovtnevyi Raion), 8, 56, 66, 77–78, 80, 139
Bolshevism, 139, 152, 153
"bourgeois nationalism," 5, 6–7, 10, 25, 155–56
Bozhenko Furniture Factory, 156
Brand, Genia, 158–59, 160
Brezhnev, Leonid, 94
Brodskii, Ivan, 24
Bronshtein, Kalman, 159–60
"building Communism." *See* Communism, building of
Burdeniuk, F., 140–41, 144–45
bureaucracy, 3, 7; and Party membership, 92, 95; postoccupation return of, 33, 122
Buriak (worker), 154
Burmenko (engineer), 166
Bystrov, V. V., 24

cadres, 127, 149; of demobilized servicemen, 121, 144–45; failings/corruption of those responsible for, 36, 51, 87, 114, 182–85; and Party confirmation/acceptance process, 74–75, 88, 90; preparation/education of, 114, 151–55
camps: of corrective labor, 5, 6, 47; for German POWs, 56–60, 66, 67, 79, 117–19
Chebotarev, Fedor, 63–64, 69, 80, 89–90

Cheliabinsk (RSFSR), 4, 90
Chernenikii, D., 179–81
children, 27, 33–34, 140; as conscripted laborers, 6, 42–43, 114–17; of servicemen, 102, 111, 123–24, *124*; in Victory Day parade, *143*
Chornovol, V. O., 61–64, 69, 81, 107
cinemas, hooliganism/crime at, 146, 168–69, 170
City Construction trust (*Gorstroi*), 166
City Party Committee of Kyiv. *See* Kyiv Gorkom
City Trade Department (*Gortorgotdel*), 179–81
coal industry, 44–45, 47–49, 51, 54, 67–69, 187
Cocktail-Hall (restaurant), 85
collective farms, 145; and food supply/prices, 112, 126–27, 180; and *orgnabor* desertion, 47–48, 49, 50
collectives, factory: evacuation of, 46, 55–56; and Party acceptance, 95; and repair/occupation of apartment buildings, 108–9
collectivization, 5, 6–8, 32
Commission on the History of the Patriotic War in Ukraine, 19–20, 33–34, 140–41
Communism, building of, 12, 13, 54, 133, 189; as briefly superseded by war effort, 10–11, 23, 133, 163, 187, 189; *Zhdanovshchina* and, 11, 150–53, 155, 157, 189
Communist Party. *See* All-Union Communist Party Central Committee (TsK); Ukrainian Communist Party; Ukrainian Communist Party Central Committee (TsK)
concentration camps, 89, 93; Syrets, 21–22, 24
conscripted laborers: desertion by, 40, 47–50, 115, 116–17, 187; German POWs as, 6, 54–60, 66–67, 70, 79–80, 117–20, *118*, 187; and resettlement (1943–44), 6, 39–45, *41*, 134; and resettlement (1944–46), 6, 47–54, 64–70, 115–17, 176; and work on Khreshchatyk, 24–25, 40, *41*, 50–51, *118*, *135*, 134–36; youth/children as, 6, 40, 42–43, 44–45, 114–19, 187. *See also orgnabor*; temporary labor mobilization of Kyivans
Construction Details Factory (*Buddetal'*), 105
consumer goods: access to, 7, 8, 77, 110–11, 112–13, 126–27; production of, 77–78, 79, 112–13, 189; regulation of trade in, 78, 126–27, 179–81
corruption, 11–12, 159, 177–85; and consumer goods trade, 179–81; in factories, 155, 181–84; and food trade/processing, 155, 180, 181–83; in ministries, 184–85; voter dissatisfaction with, 147, 148
crimes: as committed during occupation, 37–38; of Party members/aspirants, 80–81, 89, 155, 179, 181–83, 185; servicemen as victims of, 121–22. *See also entry below*; Nazi war crimes
crimes committed by Red Army enlistees/deserters, 11, 159, 167–77, 186; as blamed on unorganized return, 168, 177, 186, 190; hooliganism and, 110, 146, 161, 165, 168–76, 178; at markets, 168, 170, 172; officials' "battle" against, 170–71, 174–77; passport regime and, 170, 174–77; punishments for, 169–70, 172, 173

Darnytsa Wagon Repair Factory, 40, 42
Davydov, Aleksei, 75, 76–77, 96–97, 126
Davydov, Vasilii, 160–61, 162

Davydov, Vladimir, 21–22
"defense-related" industries, 105–6; access to food at, 105; deserters from, 47–49, 187; as exempt from mobilization, 24; as prioritized over reconstruction, 55–56, 75–76, 137, 187
Degtiarev (Ukrainian TsK official), 54, 122
demobilized servicemen, 2, 8–9, 47, 113, 120–27, 144–45; and anti-Semitism, 163, 165, 167; complaints by, 1, 108, 121, 122, 125–26; and crime/hooliganism, 173, 177; as crime victims, 121–22; families/children of, 102–3, 120, 123–24; food/consumer goods for, 126–27; homelessness of, 69; housing/residency of, 34–35, 52–53, 60–61, 63, 66, 69, 123, 125–26, 190; Party reacceptance of, 91–92, 165; privileged position of, 120–21, 123–25, 190; work for, 53–55, 122–23. *See also* families of servicemen; Red Army
deserters: from defense industry, 47–49, 187; from *orgnabor*, 40, 47–50, 115, 116–17, 187; from Red Army, 23, 25, 28, 29, 30, 42, 168, 169–70
Diatlov (Ukrainian NKVD/All-Union MVD), 65, 175
Dirin (acting procurator), 174–75
Dirin (Kyiv Obkom instructor), 102
dissolute behavior, 177–79, 183, 184–85, 190
Dnipro (restaurant), 84
Dnipro River, 3, 4, 43, 117, 133, 181; industries on/near, 8, 75–76, 115, 139; new railroad bridge over, 24–25, 26, 75
Dobrovol'skii (Kyiv Cinema Directorate head), 168–69
Donbas Anthracite Trust, 54, 67

Donbas region, 90; coal industry of, 44–45, 47–49, 51, 54, 67–69, 187
Drozdetskii (Ukrainian NKGB official), 115
Dzerzhinsky Tram Factory, 79, 105–6

economy, 6–7, 8, 27, 74–77, 101, 167, 188
Efimenko, V. S., 51
elections, to All-Union Supreme Soviet (1946), 145–49, 176, 190; and ballot box notes, 147–49
electrical infrastructure, 26, 104–5
elite, Communist Party. *See* reassembled elite; Ukrainian Communist Party
Elizarov (Ukrainian MVD official), 185
Enakiev, P., 184
Epishev, A. A., 184, 185
evacuation of Kyiv, wartime, 1, 3–4, 19, 93; health as issue in, 46; and housing for returnees, 52, 80, 108, 162, 166, 180; and illegal sale of personal items, 180; industrial/academic, 4, 46, 55–56, 97, 105, 159–60; and Party acceptance, 87, 90–91, 93, 95, 97; unorganized returnees from, 2, 5–6, 11, 33–39, 47, 60–70, 132, 161, 165–66. *See also* German evacuation of Kyiv; unorganized returnees
evictions, from housing, 81–83, 104–5, 158; servicemen/families and, 35, 61, 73, 102, 107–8, 110, 113, 166; *ukaz* on (1937), 81–82; *ukaz* on (1944), 37–38
evictions, from Kyiv/Kyiv Oblast, 27–32, 35–39; and Kyiv's status as "regime city," 5, 28, 30, 69
Evstigneev (*okruzhenets*), 87–88, 89

factories, 7–8, 9; evacuation of, 4, 46, 55–56, 95, 97; housing of workers at, 54, 56–59, 64–65; *nomenklatura* in, 74–75, 183–84, 189; nonreevacuation of, 46, 55–56, 105; rebuilding of, 46, 56–59, 65, 75–78, 120; and repair/occupation of apartment buildings, 108–9; training facilities for, 42–43, 44, 59, 105–6, 114–17, 120; and unmandated returnees, 36; wartime production by, 25–26, 40, 42. *See also specific factories and industries*

factory training schools (FZO), 43, 44, 59, 114, 116, 120

families of servicemen: delayed reevacuation of, 1, 108, 121; after demobilization, 102–3, 120, 123–24; as homeless, 69; housing for, 34–39, 52–53, 55, 60–61, 63–64, 73, 81–82, 102, 107–10, 113, 125–26, 148, 166, 188; insults against, 148; ration cards for, 111; subsidies/pensions for, 112. *See also* demobilized servicemen; Red Army

Fefer, Itzik, 161

Fel'dman (engineer), 166

firewood, 110, 120; Kyivans' collection of, 40–41, 43, 104, 105, 135–36

First and Second Five-Year Plans, 6, 7–8

First Ukrainian Front (Red Army), 20, *21*, 27; and rebuilding of Kyiv, 25–26, 75

Fleish (construction directorate head), 152–53

food: for factory workers, 105, 112; for *orgnabor* workers, 115–16, 120; Party members' access to, 7, 8, 83–85, 126, 152; Party members' corruption and, 155, 180, 181–83; prices of, 83–84, 85, 112, 126–27, 149, 153–54, 180; proposed vegetable gardens for, 48, 55, 113; rationing of/ration card system for, 5, 7, 8, 103, 111–12, 126, 142, 149, 153, 155, 168; for Red Army, 26, 83, 111; scarcity of, 103, 110–13; speculation in, 126, 147, 168, 180

food processing, 3, 182; Kyiv technical institute of, 66–67, 119

Food Store (*Gastronom*) no. 1, 84

formerly occupied citizens of Kyiv, 8–9; as able to secure better housing, 87, 93, 113, 114, 141, 158–59; and battles for apartments, 9, 102, 106–10, 113, 158–67, 186, 188; leniency toward, 38–39; after liberation (1945), 103–9; and Nazi collaborators, 29, 147; *okruzhentsy* as, 8, 87–93, 189; Party acceptance of, 95, 97; during resettlement, 20–32

Fourth Five-Year Plan, 54, 61, 120, 177, 183; and closing of Kyiv, 6, 47, 64–70, 187, 190; and Party revival, 74, 149–57

Fourth State Shoe Factory, 118

frontoviki (frontline fighters), 121–22, 123, 145, 166, 190

Galitskii Market, 127, 168

gardens, vegetable, 48, 55, 113

Gerasimenko, V. F., 37, 170, *171*

German evacuation of Kyiv (1943), 4, 29, 140; citizens' experiences of, 19–20; and destruction of utilities grid, 26; as followed by looting/ stealing, 20, 80–81, 106–7

German occupation of Kyiv (1941–43), 4, 20–32; Communists living under, 8, 87–93, 189; corruption/ profiteering during, 180–81; Jewish casualties of, 4, 10, 21–22, 131, 132; Kyivan casualties of, 81; Kyivan labor conscripts of, 4, 22, 53, 132; last days of, 19–20, 140; and Nazi war crimes/criminals, 4, 21–22, 131–33, 140–41, 146–47; nonresidents living under, 27–32; *politzai* under, 28–29; resistance movement against, 97–101;

German occupation of Kyiv (1941–43)—*(cont'd)*
  search for traitors/collaborators during, 22–24, 29–30, 31, 35, 37–38; societal effects of, 5–6, 10, 13; women and, 37, 38. *See also* formerly occupied citizens of Kyiv; Nazi collaborators
German POWs, 47, 113, 146; camps for, 56–60, 66, 67, 79, 117–19; as conscripted laborers, 6, 54–60, 66–67, 70, 79–80, 117–20, *118*, 187; as paraded through Kyiv, 56, *57*, 117, 141
Germany, Nazi regime of. *See entries immediately above;* Nazi collaborators, *and entries following*
GKO. *See* State Committee of Defense
Goebbels, Joseph, 27, 95, 142
Golovko, Grigorii, 138
Gorban, Boris, 80, 83, 95, *96*, 113, 162; on Party corruption, 154–56; on people's mood, 146–49, 171; and resettlement issues, 52, 60–61, 69–70
gorkoms (city Party committees). *See* Bila Tserkva Gorkom; Kyiv Gorkom
Gorky Machine Tool/Textile Factory (Protiasiv Iar), 8, 43, 46, 77, 95
Gorshnov, M. N., 122
"Government Square" project, 133–34
Grabar, Ivan, 161–63
"Great Breakthrough," of 1930s, 6, 8, 9–10, 101, 188
"Great Terror," 5, 6, 7, 9–10, 103, 188
Gritsiuk (KTIPP director), 66–67
Grobchak (Kyiv train station head), 66
Gumo-Generator light factory, 56

harvest: of 1946, as poor, 85, 127, 153–54; mobilization of labor for, 104, 105, 112
Hitler, Adolf, 23, 29, 87, 133, 141, 148

Hoikhberh-Tul'chins'kyi, D. A., 90
hooliganism, 110, 146, 161, 165, 168–76, 178
housing, 104–10; "compression" of, 81, 82, 109–10; of factory workers, 54, 56–59, 64–65, 108–9; of German POWs, 56–60, 66, 67, 79, 117–19; of mobilized laborers, 104–5; repair of, 106, 108–9, 115, 120; scarcity of, and anti-Semitism, 9, 158–59, 160, 162, 164–66, 167, 188, 190; as secured by formerly occupied, 87, 93, 109, 113, 114, 141, 158–59; of servicemen/families, 34–39, 52–53, 55, 60–61, 63–64, 73, 81–82, 102, 107–10, 113, 125–26, 148, 166, 188. *See also* apartment buildings; apartments
Hrushevs'kyi, Mykhailo, 155, 156

Iahnyn, A. D., 99
Iakubovich (yeast factory director), 155, 182
industry/manufacturing, 3, 6, 7–8; evacuation of, 4, 46, 55–56, 97, 105; German POWs in, 54–60, 117–20, 187; *orgnabor* workers in, 39–45, 47–54, 64–70, 115–17; Party members in, 74–80, 156–57; postoccupation war effort of, 25–26. *See also* factories; *specific factories and industries*
intelligentsia, 4, 52, 83, 149; and anti-Semitism, 161, 163–67; Party acceptance of, 95–96, 97; and Party revival, 150, 155–56, 165, 190
invalid servicemen, 123–24, 125, 141, 160, 165; crime by, 176, 177; housing/residency rights of, 34, 36, 63; Kyiv Circus brawl involving, 172; unemployment among, 122
Istomin (Podil' Raikom member), 154

Iuryshev (Ukrainian Oil Construction official), 56–57
Ivanov, G. M., 88–89

Jewish Anti-Fascist Committee (JAFC), 14, 163
Jews: evacuation of, 4, 22; as Nazi casualties, 4, 10, 21–22, 131, 132, 188; and Ukrainians, 1, 2–3, 4, 9, 10, 15, 113, 122–23, 132–33, 147–48, 187–91; unorganized return of, 11, 159, 161–63, 165–66, 167, 168, 190. *See also* anti-Semitism

Kabalkin, Anatoli, 160
Kaganovich Raion, 97, 147, 161–62
Kalinin, Mikhail, 29, 55
Kalinin Square (now Independence Square), 136, 146–47
Karl Marx Confectionery Factory, 97
Karpman, Rakhil', 160
Kharkiv, 3, 33, 36, 39, 22, 75, 83, 87
Khmel', M., 95
Khmel'nitskii, R., 138
Khrapunov (Ukrainian TsK instructor), 103
Khreshchatyk (Kyiv's main street), 4, 21, 78, 84, 181; conscripted labor's work on, 24–25, 40, *41*, 50–51, *118*, 134; factory collective's work on, 108–9; German POWs paraded on, 56, *57*, 117, 141; Kyivan civilians' work on, 134–35, *135*; planned rebuilding of, 133–40, 189–90; Red Army on, *21*; sewer construction on, 104, 137
Khreshchatyk Construction Trust, 50, 95
Khrushchev, Nikita, 25, 33, 47, 79–80, *86*, *96*, 99, 132, 141, *164*, *171*; and anti-Semitism, 160–61, 165; citizens'/workers' letters to, 46, 55–56, 122, 147, 170–71, 174, 182, 184; and crime/hooliganism, 170–71, 174–75; on housing for workers/

German POWs, 59, 79; leadership of, 14, 20–21, 26; on liberation day, 20–21; and Party corruption, 182–84; and proposed exhibitions/monuments, 137–39; and rebuilding/modernization, 104, 108, 133–34, 139, 189
Khvoinskii, Kuzma, 144–45
Kinkalo (Ukrainian TsK member), 110
Kirichenko, Aleksei, 56
Kolos, V. S., 109
Komarov, V. M., 24, 27–29, 30, 35, 64, 69, 167–68
Konik, Mrs. (serviceman's wife), 111
Korniets, Leonid, 30, 31–32, 33, 35–36, *86*, 160
Korotchenko, Demian, 48, 54, 56, 69, *86*, 113, 115, 126, 162, *171*, 183
Kostenko (Red Army officer), 1, 108, 121
Kostiuk (Lenin Raion worker), 95–96
Krivoshein (Kyiv Oblast Militia chief), 69
Krizhanovskii (Kyiv procurator), 81–82, 107–8
Kruglov, S., 117
kulaks, 5, 6
Kuroid, O., 142
Kuznetsov (*Gortorgotdel* director), 180, 181–82
Kyiv, 2–15; as capital, 3, 33; conscripted labor in, 6, 39–45, 47–54, 64–70, 114–20; evacuation of, 3–4; evictions from, 5, 27–32, 35–39, 69; German occupation of, 4, 20–32, 131–33; industrial development in, 3, 6, 7–8; Party revival campaign in, 150–57, 165, 167, 184, 188–91; passport regime of, 27–32, 60–64, 69–70; postwar city planning/modernization of, 133–40, 189–90; postwar closing of, 6, 47, 64–70, 187, 190; prewar history of, 2–3, 5; reassembled elite

Kyiv—*(cont'd)*
of, 2, 6–7, 8, 73–101; reassembled masses of, 2, 7–9, 102–27; reconstruction of, 24–27, 39–45; as "regime city," 1, 5, 15, 28, 30, 69; relationships with Soviet power in, 2, 11–12, 158–86; relegitimization of Soviet power in, 1–2, 9–11, 131–57; resettlement of, 2, 5–6, 19–70; return of citizens to, 20, 23, *107*; as shielded from *orgnabor*, 2, 9, 39–45, 57, 79, 101, 104, 116, 135–36, 187; and "Soviet Patriotism," 11, 12–15, 153, 157, 190–91. *See also specific topics*
Kyiv Beer Factory, 182–83
Kyiv Circus, 172
Kyiv City Directorate of Catering (*Obshchepit*), 155
Kyiv Committee of Soviet Youth (*Komsomol*), 40, 116–17
Kyiv Consumer Goods Trade (*Kievpromtorg*), 78, 91, 179–81
Kyiv Department Store, 181
Kyiv Garrison, 55, 168–69, *171*
Kyiv Gorkom, 24, 26, 31, 73–101, 112–13, 121, 140, 162, 189; and crime/hooliganism, 167–77; and factories, 42, 56–58, 64–65, 104–5, 109, 114, 189; and markets, 126–27; and *orgnabor*, 114–20; and Party corruption, 181, 184–85; and people's mood, 145–50, 189–90; and resettlement issues, 27, 29, 35, 39, 52–53, 69, 104–5, 109; and resistance movement, 98–101; and temporary labor mobilization, 40–41, 104–5, 134–35; and *Zhdanovshchina*, 150–57
Kyiv Industrial Construction (*Kievpromstroi*), 64–65, 66, 120
Kyiv Locomotive Repair Factory, 26
Kyiv Military Region Construction Directorate, 26, 79

Kyiv Obkom, 25–27, 30, 40, 41–43, 73, 85, 102, 106, 109, 111, 189; and corruption, 81, 179–81; and crime/hooliganism, 170–71, 176–77; and German POWs, 57–58, 66; and Nazi occupation/war crimes, 22, 23, 26–27, 131–32, 140–42; new Party members in, 75; and *orgnabor*, 42–43, 49, 116; and Party reacceptance, 88–94; and people's mood, 144–50, 189–90; and unemployed servicemen, 53–54, 122
Kyiv Oblast, 23, 81, 84, 109, 116, 121, 123, 144; and crime/hooliganism, 171, 177; food supplies from, 43, 111, 112, 120; housing conditions in, 126; mobilized labor in, 41, 43–44, 53, 59; *orgnabor* exemption of, 43–44, 45, 187; Party membership in, 97; and Party reacceptance, 88–94; and passport regime/evictions, 30, 36, 37–38, 69
Kyiv Regenerated Resin Factory, 75, 77
Kyiv State University, 156
Kyiv Steam Engine Repair Factory, 7
Kyiv Technological Institute of the Food Industry (KTIPP), 66–67, 119
Kyiv Wagon Repair Factory, 40, 127
Kyiv Yeast Factory, 155, 181–82, 183
Kyivs'ka Pravda (*Kyiv Truth*) (newspaper), 136, 139, 150–53, 169–70, 176, 179

labor. *See* conscripted laborers; German POWs; *orgnabor*; *Ostarbeitery*; temporary labor mobilization of Kyivans
Ladyr, Mikhail, 139
Langunovskii (Kyiv City procurator), 102
Lebed', Luka, 29, 34, 56, 106
Lenin, Vladimir, 137, 139
Lenin Raion, 34, 90, 95–96, 100, 117, 169

Lenin's Forge (*Leninskaia Kuznitsa*) (shipbuilding factory), 7, 25–26, 116, 140
Leont'ev, Georgii, 80–81
Lepse Tractor Factory, 26, 58–59, 105, 114, 115, 147
Lesi Ukrainky State Russian Drama Theatre, 83
Lev, L., 167
Likholat (Ukrainian TsK official), 26–27
living permits, 91, 146, 174–75; as given to unemployed, 32; irregularities in issuance of, 60–64, 69–70, 174–75; for *Ostarbeitery*, 65–66; refusals of, 30; sale of, 35; for servicemen/families, 34, 52, 61. *See also* passport regime
Lombard (prewar pawn shop), 117, 180
looting: by Kyivans, 106–7, 183; by Nazis, 4, 20, 80. *See also* stealing

Mahaziner, Abram, 89
Makeev (Kyiv Obkom Military Department head) 122, 123
Makhinia (Food Processing Ministry official), 182–83
Malenkov, Georgii, 48, 59, 160
Malevynchuk, M. U., 99
markets, 8, 32, 84, 137, 142, 145, 162, 164; and crime/hooliganism, 168, 170, 172; disorder at, 111–12, 127; prices/speculation at, 126–27, 180
Marx, Karl, 12, 150, 189
Marxism-Leninism, 11, 95, 150–51, 153, 156, 178
massoperatsii ("mass operations"): against criminals/"enemy elements," 5, 22–25, 177; for Red Army mobilization, 24–25, 31, 42, 61, 141, 168, 177, 187
Mazanov (auto repair factory director), 183–84
Mazur, Sophiia, 158

Medvedev (Ukrainian MGB employee), 184–85
Mekhed, Andrii H., 92–93
Mel'nikov, Nikolai, 161–63
Metro Construction Trust (*Metrostroi*), 139
Mikhailovsky Monastery, 133
Mikhoels, Solomon, 14, 161, 163
Minin (Automobile Transport Minister), 184
Mironov, G., 169–70
Mironov, Ivan, 21, 134
Miroshnichenko, I. D., 115
Mitsman, R. E., 62–63
Mokienko, Fedor, 26, *96*, 113, 134, *164*, 170; and Nazi war crimes/collaborators, 29, 31; and resettlement/housing issues, 26, 29, 35–36, 52, 60–61, 63, 81–83, 107–8
Molotov Raion, 95, 96, 97, 100, 125–26, 145, 155, 182
Moskalets (Kyiv Gorkom secretary), 162
Mukhomorov (Markets Directorate employee), 127
museums, 19–20, 136, 137, 138–39

Natiaga, K. O., 116
nationalism: "bourgeois," 5, 6–7, 10, 25, 155–56; Russian (Imperial), 2–3; Russian (Soviet), 9, 12–13; Ukrainian-German, 51, 121, 148, 162. *See also entry below*
nationalism, Ukrainian, 6–7, 42, 155–56, 159–67, 185–86, 187, 189–90; and anti-Semitism, 13–15, 132–33, 148, 163–67, 186, 190–91
nationalities policy, 10, 160
Nazi collaborators: Kyivans' attitude toward, 29, 147; in Party, 87, 163; postoccupation search for, 22–24, 29–30, 31, 35, 37–38; punishment of, 24, 31

Nazi occupation. *See* German evacuation of Kyiv; German occupation of Kyiv
Nazi regime, defeat of: vs. "building Communism," 10–11, 23, 133, 163, 187, 189
Nazi war crimes: executions for, 146–47; investigation of, 131–33; against Jews, 4, 10, 21–22, 131, 132, 188; and postoccupation tension, 140–41
Neliubin (Molotov Raion secretary), 95
Nelli, V. A., 83
Nesterenko, Grigorii, 145
Nezhinskii (Lenin Raikom secretary), 34–35, 140
NKZhGS UkrSSR. *See* Ukrainian People's Commissariat of Housing and Civilian Construction
nomenklatura, 74, 154–55; in factories, 74–75, 183–84, 189
Noshchenko, P., 68, 125
Nosov (Ukrainian NKGB official), 37–38
Novichenko (OSMCh no. 305 director), 67
Novosibirsk (RSFSR), 58, 138

obkoms (oblast Party committees). *See* Kyiv Obkom; Voroshilovgrad Obkom
oblasts: Dnipropetrovs'k, 49, 125; Kamianets'-Podil's'k, 67–69; Kirovohrad, 45, 116; Rivne, 44, 121; Stalin, 83, 90; Ternopil', 42, 44, 50–51; Vinnytsa, 13, 45; Voronezh, 22–23. *See also* agricultural oblasts; Kyiv Oblast
October theater (cinema), 168–69
Odinokov (Podil' Raikom secretary), 91–92
okruzhentsy (Communists living under German occupation), 8, 87–93, 189
Ol'shanetsk (demobilized serviceman), 122

Organization of Ukrainian Nationalists, 14
orgnabor: (1943–44), 6, 39–45, *41*, 134; (1944–46), 6, 47–54, 64–70, 114–17, 176; desertion from, 40, 47–50, 115, 116–17, 187; in Donbas coal industry, 44–45, 47–49, 51, 54, 67–69, 187; under Fourth Five-Year Plan, 64–70, 120; German POWs used in, 54–60, 117–20, *118*, 187; housing for, 117–20; origins of, 6; poor living conditions/food in, 114–17; shielding of Kyiv/Kyiv Oblast from, 2, 9, 39–45, 57, 79, 101, 104, 116, 135–36, 187; youth/children used in, 6, 40, 42–43, 44–45, 114–17, 187
OSMCh (Special Construction and Assembly Unit) No. 305, 40, 51, 67, 79, 95, 119, 134
Ostarbeitery ("East Workers"), 4, 22, 43, 47, 50, 132; diligence of, 15, 53, 65–66
Ostromogil'skii family, 102
Ovchar, V., 145
Ovcharenko (Kyiv Obkom official), 142, 145–46

Paliev (serviceman), 173
"partyness" of *okruzhentsy*, 88–93
passport regime: abuses discovered in, 62–63; creation of (1933), 5, 8, 10, 32, 188; and crime, 170, 174–77; and demobilized servicemen, 53–54; and issuance of living permits, 62–64, 69–70, 174–75; and *orgnabor* workers, 65, 176; reregistration/enforcement process of (1944), 27–32, 60–64, 65, 69–70, 163; statute of (1940), 27, 28, 30, 37, 170
Pavlovich (Pechersk Raikom worker), 94
Pechersk Raion, 76, 93, 98–99

Peremolotova (shipbuilding factory worker), 114–15
Petlichenko, L., 138
Petrushko, B. I., 99–101
Pirkin (OSMCh no. 305 official), 51
Pirohivs'kyi, Oleksandr Sydorovych, 98–99
Platonov (Dzerzhinsky Factory director), 105
Pochenkov, Kondrat, 47
Podil' Raion, 92, 99, 100, 116, 122, 134, 148, 154–55, 172
Podol'skii (demobilized serviceman), 125
politzai, 28–29
Porokhova, V. I., 68–69
Pospelov, Petr, 163
Postnov (shipbuilding factory instructor), 114–15
Pravda (*Truth*) (newspaper), 151, 163, 165–66, 167
prisoners of war (POWs): civilian, 90; Red Army, 4, 22, 23, 140, 141. *See also* German POWs
Progrebniuk, G. B., 109
Pronicheva, Dina and Lydochka, 33–34
propagandists, school of, 178–79

Radians'ka Ukraina (*Soviet Ukraine*) (newspaper), 155, 165, 167
Raevskii (Museum of Russian Art director), 138
raikoms (district Party committees), 79, 88, 94, 121–22, 154, 177; Darnytsa, 75, 78, 173; Lenin, 34–35, 91, 140; Molotov, 149, 155, 182; Pechersk, 94, 98–99, 147; Petriv (later Podil'), 21, 91–92, 100, 134, 154, 183; Zaliznychnyi, 76, 90, 98–99, 149
railroad vocational schools (ZhU), 42–43
railroad workers, 59, 173; as formerly occupied/POWs, 25, 90, 158; Party and, 90, 149
railway stations: greetings of *frontoviki* at, 121–22; hooliganism at, 173
railways/railway industry, 3, 7, 26, 39, 42, 53, 59, 106, 149; and bridge building, 3, 24–25, 26, 40, 103; and mobilized labor, 26, 43, 44, 51, 59, 103; and resistance movement, 98, 99
raions (administrative districts): and All-Union elections (1946), 145–49; anti-Semitism in, 161–62, 164; civilian labor mobilization in, 104–5, 134–35; corruption in, 155, 180–84; crime/hooliganism in, 155, 161–62, 169–72, 175, 176–77; and demobilized servicemen, 53–54, 121–22; German POWs in, 117, 119; and housing of servicemen/ families, 53, 73, 82, 110, 125–26; *orgnabor* difficulties in, 50–51, 54; Party reacceptance decisions in, 88–97; resistance committees in, 98–100; social assistance in, 112. *See also specific raions*
Rapoport, Semen L., 93
Ratkin (Kyiv Gorkom secretary), 145–46
reassembled elite, 6–7, 8, 73–101; acccss to ranks of, 73–74, 85–101; and commandeering of others' housing, 35, 73, 74; living conditions of, 80–85; and reconstruction, 74–80, 101. *See also* Ukrainian Communist Party
reassembled masses, 7–9, 102–27; demobilized servicemen, 120–27; formerly occupied, 103–13; German POWs, 117–20; *orgnabor* workers, 114–20; returnees, 107–10, 113
reconstruction of Kyiv, 24–27; conscription of labor for, 39–45, 47–60, 66–67; factors hindering, 5–6, 9, 15, 26–27; and Khreshchatyk, 133–40, 189–90; as low priority for Moscow, 15, 39–42, 54, 56–57,

reconstruction of Kyiv—*(cont'd)* 59–60, 75–76, 78–80, 114, 187; vs. military/defense priorities, 41–42, 55–56, 75–76, 137, 187; Party elite and, 74–80, 101; Party in-fighting over, 75–76; and rebuilding of factories, 46, 56–59, 65, 75–78, 120; and Soviet power, 133–40

Red Army, 3–4, 8, 31, 59, 66, 77, 123, 138, 140, 147; complaints by members of, 1, 108, 121, 122; and crime, 11, 146, 159, 161, 167–77, 186; deserters from, 23, 25, 28, 29, 30, 42, 168, 169–70; draft dodgers from, 22, 23, 25, 30, 41–42, 51, 103; *frontoviki* of, 121–22, 123, 145, 166, 190; Jews in, 22; liberation of Kyiv by, 33, 75, 90–91, 92, 100, 132, 182; and mobilization of workers, 104, 106; need to find men for, 5, 24–25, 31, 39, 41–42, 61, 141, 168, 177, 187; and Party membership, 74, 75, 88–89, 91, 93–97, 100–101; *politzai* conscripted into, 28–29; POWs from, 4, 22, 23, 140, 141; and ration cards, 111; and resettlement/housing, 34–39, 52–55, 60–61, 63–64, 73, 81–82, 102, 107–10, 113, 125–26, 148, 166, 188; rural grain for, 26, 83, 111; victories by, 87, 142; wartime advances of, 19, 33, 37, 83, 142, 189. *See also* crimes committed by Red Army enlistees/deserters; demobilized servicemen; families of servicemen; invalid servicemen

Red Excavator (*Krasnyi Ekskavator*) (tractor parts factory), 7

reevacuation: factories not undergoing, 46, 55–56, 105; Kharkiv welcome venue for, 36, 39; Red Army officer's complaint about, 1, 108, 121

"regime city," Kyiv as: and eviction/banishment of "socially dangerous," 5, 28, 30, 69; postwar reshaping of, 1, 15, 39, 45, 47, 103, 157, 186, 190–91

relationships with Soviet power, issues of, 2, 11–12, 158–86; anti-Semitism, 159–67; crime/hooliganism, 167–77; dissolute behaviour/corruption of Party members, 177–85

relegitimization of Soviet power, 1–2, 9–11, 131–57; and anti-Semitism vs. Ukrainian nationalism, 13–15, 132–33, 148, 163–67, 186, 190–91; and monitoring of people's mood, 140–50, 189–90; and Party revival campaign, 149–57; through postwar city planning/cultural monuments, 133–40, 189–90; and postwar dissatisfaction/division, 141–48; and "Soviet Patriotism," 11, 12–15, 153, 157, 190–91

resettlement (1943–1944), 19–45; and access to housing, 30, 33–36; and army mobilization, 22–25, 31, 39, 41–42; attempts to control, 27–32; and formerly occupied, 20–32; and *orgnabor* workers, 6, 39–45; and reconstruction, 24–27, 39–45; and search for "enemy elements," 22–24; of servicemen's dependents, 34–37, 38; and social dislocation, 30–31, 32, 36; and "socially dangerous" people, 2, 5–6, 28–31, 37; and unorganized returnees, 2, 5–6, 15, 33–39

resettlement (1944–1946), 46–70; attempts to control, 51–54, 60–64; and Fourth Five-Year Plan/closing of Kyiv, 6, 47, 54, 61, 64–70; and German POWs, 54–60; and *orgnabor* workers, 6, 47–54, 64–70; and reconstruction, 47–60, 66–67; and unorganized returnees, 6, 47, 60–70

resistance, Ukrainian, in occupied Kyiv, 97–101

Riasnoi, Vasilii, 19, 37, 104, 141, 162, 174–77
Rostov Coal Trust, 68
Rostov-on-Don (RSFSR), 13, 22
Roza Luxemburg Textile Factory, 43
Rozenshtein, Iosif, 161–63
Rozhdestvenskaia, Anna, 158–59
Rudin (Communal Services official), 52
Rudnenko, Roman, 37, 48, 110
Russian Soviet Federated Socialist Republic (RSFSR), 22–23, 68, 138, 159, 160, 185; evacuation of Kyivans/factories to, 1, 4, 34, 46, 55, 58, 90
Ryzhkov (Kyiv procurator), 37–38

Saranch, M. L., 172
Savchenko, Sergei, 19, 37, 161, 165, 185
Savkov (Kyiv Political Directorate head), 54
schools: Party-run, 178–79; vocational/industrial, 42–43, 44, 59, 66–67, 105–6, 114–17
Senin, Ivan, 65
Serdiuk, Zinovii, 22, 25–27, 32, 109, 111, 132, 133–36, 141, 147, 171
servicemen. *See* crimes committed by Red Army enlistees/deserters; demobilized servicemen; families of servicemen; invalid servicemen; Red Army
Shamaev (Kyiv Obkom Military Department director), 53, 121–22
Shamberg, Mikhail, 144, 145
Shcherba, M. G., 116
Shcherbakov (Ukrainian TsK employee), 160–61
Sherbakov, Pavel Il'ych, 98–99
Shevchenko Opera House, 3, 140, 156
Shishkin, Ivan, 139
Shumeikov (Ukrainian TsK employee), 160

Shutenko (Repatriation Department head), 65–66
Shuturov, S., 125
Shvartsman, Keli V., 90–91
Skrypnyk, Mykola, 3
Smirnov-Lastochkina Textile Factory, 43
Smyhyn (resistance group member), 99
SNK. *See* Soviet Union Council of People's Commissars; Ukrainian Council of People's Commissars
social dislocation, 5–6, 15, 30–31, 32, 36, 47, 60–61, 64–70, 188
"socialist property," stealing of, 38, 152, 168, 179
"socially dangerous" people, 5–6; as evicted/banished from Kyiv, 5, 28, 30, 69; postwar issues in handling of, 2, 28–31, 37, 60, 187; postwar legitimization of behavior by, 11–12, 158–86, 190. *See also* anti-Semitism; corruption; crimes; hooliganism
"socially useful" labor, 28, 53, 70, 168
Southern Energy Construction Trust (*Iuzhenergostroi*), 104
Southwestern Railroad, 26, 90, 173, 175
"Soviet Patriotism," 11, 12–15, 153, 157, 190–91
Soviet Union Council of People's Commissars (SNK SSSR), 48, 76; and German POWs, 56, 58, 118; and labor mobilization, 25, 49; and Museum of Russian Art, 138–39; and passport regime, 28, 30; and reconstruction of light industry, 77; and *ukaz* on housing of servicemen/families, 34, 52, 83
Special Construction and Assembly Directorates: (no. 11), 64–65, 120; (no. 26), 119, 152
Special Construction and Assembly Unit (OSMCh) no. 305, 40, 51, 67, 79, 95, 119, 134

Spektor (friend of Jewish NKGB officer), 162
Stalin, Joseph, 1, 3, 21, 29, 55; and All-Union elections (1946), 145–47; anniversary speech by, 140; and anti-Semitism, 159–60, 161, 163; and "bourgeois nationalists," 5, 6–7, 10, 25, 155–56; on criminality, 10; "Great Breakthrough" of, 6, 8, 9–10, 101, 188; and "laws of wartime," 28; and "otherness" of Soviet governance, 9, 10–11; and Party members' education/experience, 150, 153; Party official's complaint to, 185; proposed art/architecture celebrating, 136–39; and rule by terror, 5, 6, 7, 9–10, 103, 188; and "socially dangerous" people, 5–6
Stalin Raion, 94, 97, 98, 100, *143*, 180
Stalin Ship-Building Factory, 25–26, 79, 97, 114–15, 154
Starchenko, Vasilii, 58–59, 65
State Committee of Defense (GKO), 3–4, 38, 103, 138; and factory rebuilding/production, 59, 75–76, 78, 105–6; and reconstruction/*orgnabor*, 14, 26, 39, 42, 45, 187; and resettlement, 31, 36, 39, 51, 161
statism, 1–2, 9, 11, 12–15, 190–91. *See also* "Soviet Patriotism"
stealing, 38, 106–7, 115, 168; from demobilized servicemen, 121; by Nazis, 4, 20, 80; by Party members/aspirants, 80–81, 89, 155, 179, 181–83, 185
subway system, 139, 189
Surikov, Vasily, 139
Synehubov (Podil' Raion resistance leader), 99
Syrets: concentration camp at, 21–22, 24; firing range at, 113

Tabulevich, I., 32, 35, 85
Tashkent (Uzbek SSR), 36, 89–90; and Jewish evacuees/anti-Semitism, 4, 132, 161, 165–66
Tatsiia, O., 137
Teatral'nyi (restaurant), 84
Temporary Commission for the Regulation of the Entrance of Citizens into the City of Kyiv, 31, 35–36, 39, 51–52, 61–63
temporary labor mobilization of Kyivans, 25, 26, 103–4; for firewood collection, 40–41, 43, 104, 105, 135–36; housing for, 104–5
Tepliakov (Kyiv draft board official), 39
Teplitskii (Kyiv Komsomol official), 116–17
Terekhova (Ukrainian MVD official), 185
textile industry, 3, 8, 43, 46, 56, 64, 77–78, 120, 152
Tkachenko (Kyiv Gorkom official), 181
Tokar, Khaim, 161
Tolstoy Square, 58
trade vocational schools (RU), 42–43, 114, 116, 120
Trainin, Aron N., 131–32, 133, 138
Transportation Signal Factory (*Transsignal*), 36, 146
Trud na Kreshchatike (*Labor on the Kreshchatyk*) (newspaper), 136
TsK. *See* All-Union Communist Party Central Committee; Ukrainian Communist Party Central Committee
Tsykovskii, I., 139
Tverskii, Viktor, 19
Tychyna, Pavlo, 148, *164*

Ufa (RSFSR), 4, 138, 159
ukazi (decrees) of All-Union Supreme Soviet: on day of Nazi invasion (1941), 38; on defense industry deserters (1941), 47–48; on eviction

(1937), 81–82; on eviction (1944), 37–38; on housing of servicemen/families (1941), 34, 35, 37, 61, 81–82, 108, 188; on Nazi collaborators (1943), 24; as read on May Day (1945), *171*; on vocational schools (1944), 114; on work week (1940), 48

Ukrainian Academy of Sciences, 33, 34; evacuation/return of, 159–60; interviews conducted by, 19–20, 33–34, 140–41

Ukrainian Communist Party: dissolute behavior/corruption within, 11–12, 152–53, 155, 159, 177–85, 190; as elite/privileged group, 6–7, 8, 73–101, 189; first-time civilian applicants to, 95–101; first-time military applicants to, 93–94; and Moscow's "best people" policy, 7, 95–97, 101; Nazi collaborators in, 87, 163; *nomenklatura* of, 74–75, 154–55, 183–84, 189; *okruzhentsy* and, 88–93; postwar access to ranks of, 73–74, 85–101; postwar numbers of, in Kyiv, 26–27, 74–75; resistance members and, 97–101; revival campaign of, 7, 11–12, 15, 74, 149–57, 165, 167, 184, 188–91; self-criticism of, 151–52, 155; self-education/improvement within, 150–57; and Soviet power/relegitimization, 1–2, 9–11, 131–57. *See also entry below*

Ukrainian Communist Party Central Committee (TsK), 11; and anti-Semitism, 159–67; and arts/culture, 138–39, 156; cadres department of, 36, 51, 88, 183, 184; and crime, 170–72, 174–75; and demobilized servicemen, 121–23, 125–27; and food/consumer goods supply, 77, 83–84, 110–13, 126–27;

headquarters of, 3, 117, 133; and *orgnabor*/labor mobilization, 42–44, 47–50, 54–56, 59, 66, 68–69, 103–5, 114–16, 119–20, 135; and Party corruption, 154–55, 178–79, 182–85; and Party membership, 87–90, 97; propaganda/agitation department of, 138–39, 142, 145; and reconstruction, 26–27, 49, 66, 75–80; and repair/occupation of apartment buildings, 108–9; and resettlement, 31, 33, 36–37, 39, 53, 60–64, 69, 102, 110, 125–26

Ukrainian Council of Invalids' Cooperatives (*Ukoopinsovet*), 160

Ukrainian Council of People's Commissars (SNK UkrSSR), 3, 20, 26, 163; and city planning projects, 133–38; and control of entry into Kyiv, 31–32, 60–61, 65; and demobilized servicemen, 121, 123, 125–26, 170; and food/consumer goods, 83–84, 110–13, 126–27; and German POWs, 58–59, 119; and labor mobilization/*orgnabor*, 40, 42–44, 49–54, 59, 65, 104, 114; and reconstruction/factory production, 40, 43, 58–59, 65, 75–80, 103–6; and resettlement/housing issues, 30–36, 39, 81–83, 106–10

Ukrainian Insurgent Army, 14

Ukrainian Ministry of Housing and Civilian Construction (MKZhGS UkrSSR), 80

Ukrainian Ministry of Internal Affairs (MVD), 64, 65, 66, 67, 69, 177, 185

Ukrainian Ministry of State Control, 61, 181

Ukrainian Ministry of State Security (MGB), 184–85

Ukrainian nationalism. *See* nationalism, Ukrainian

Ukrainian Oil Construction, 56, 78

Ukrainian People's Commissariat of Housing and Civilian Construction (NKZhGS UkrSSR; later MKZhGS UkrSSR), 40, 42, 50–51, 66, 78–80, 119

Ukrainian People's Commissariat of Internal Affairs (NKVD; later Ukrainian MVD), 19, 29, 30, 36, 37, 53, 84, 111, 117, 162; and crime, 170–77; *massoperatsii* by, 22–25, 42, 61, 141, 177, 187; Military Tribunal of, 47–48, 49, 158–59, 161; POW camps of, 119–20; as required to finish sewer digging, 104; stealing by workers of, 80–81

Ukrainian People's Commissariat of State Security (NKGB; later Ukrainian MGB), 19, 81, 84, 109, 115; and anti-Semitism, 160–65; and Nazi war crimes/collaborators, 21–22, 24, 37–39

Ukrainian Union of Soviet Writers, 155–56

unemployment, 40, 106, 122; of demobilized servicemen, 53–54, 122–23

unorganized returnees, 2, 15; arrival of (1943–44) 5–6, 33–39; arrival of (1944–46) 6, 47, 60–70, 163, 187–88; as blamed for ethnic hatred/crime, 158–59, 161, 167, 168, 177, 186, 190; Jews as, 11, 159, 161–63, 165–66, 167, 168, 190; numbers of, 6, 15, 34, 42, 47, 60; and *ukaz* on housing for servicemen/families, 35, 37, 61, 81–82, 108, 188

Ural Mountains, factory evacuation to, 46

Urbanskii (Kyiv Gorkom official), 140

Uzbek Soviet Socialist Republic, 4, 166

Vaisberg (Kyiv returnee), 102

Vasiutinskii, Lt. (military tribunal chairman), 47–48

Vaslits, M., 165–66

Vesennyi (Donbas Anthracite Trust *orgnabor* official), 54, 67–69

Victory Day (May 9, 1945): images of, 86, *124*, *143–44*

Vinnitskii, Isai, 140

Vinogradov (military procurator), 181–82

Vishnia, Ostap: "Allow Me to Make a Mistake" (newspaper article), 165–67

Vlasov, Aleksandr, 136–37

vocational schools, 42–43, 44, 59, 114, 116, 120

Voiko, V. U., 50–51

Volchkov, V., 139

Volgozhanin (Ukrainian MVD employee), 185

Voronov, N. I., 61–62

Voroshilovgrad Coal Trust, 47

Voroshilovgrad Obkom, 87

Wehrmacht, 3–4, 87

women: and ethnic hatred, 158–59, 162; on German POWs/Nazis, 141, 142; as intimate with German occupiers, 37, 38; and Party corruption/dissolute behavior, 178–79, 183, 184–85, 190; as unskilled laborers, 42, 105–6; as victims of harassment/crime, 148, 162, 171–72, 175, 176, 178; as young *orgnabor* workers, 115–16

Yalta Conference, 142

"Yeast Affair," 155, 181–82, 183

youth, as *orgnabor* workers, 42–43, 114–17

Zaitsev, Vasilii, and Zinaida Zaitseva, 166–67

Zaliznychnyi Raikom, 76, 90, 98–99, 149
Zaliznychnyi Raion, 170–71, 175
Zelenskii (military captain of justice), 49
Zhdanov, Andrei, Party revival campaign of (*Zhdanovshchina*), 7, 11–12, 15, 74, 149–50; in Kyiv, 150–57, 165, 167, 184, 188–91; and return to "building Communism," 11, 150–53, 155, 157, 189

Zheliak (Zaliznychnyi Raikom secretary), 76
Zhila (SNK UkrSSR official), 33
Zhovtnevyi Raion, 77, 96, 98, 100, 119, 122
Zhuzhelytsi, Ivan I., 55
Zhylyns'kyi (serviceman), 171–72
Zlenko, A. N., 88, 103, 145
Zoshchenko, Mikhail, 149
Zozulenko (Repatriation Affairs head), 53, 66

www.ingramcontent.com/pod-product-compliance
Lightning Source LLC
Chambersburg PA
CBHW070759230426
43665CB00017B/2417